Freedom of Expression
in El Salvador

Freedom of Expression in El Salvador

The Struggle for Human Rights and Democracy

LAWRENCE MICHAEL LADUTKE

McFarland & Company, Inc., Publishers
Jefferson, North Carolina, and London

Library of Congress Cataloguing-in-Publication Data

Ladutke, Lawrence Michael, 1969–
    Freedom of expression in El Salvador : the struggle for human
rights and democracy / Lawrence Michael Ladutke.
      p.   cm.
    Includes bibliographical references and index.

    ISBN 0-7864-1825-7 (softcover : 50# alkaline paper) ∞

    1. Political participation—El Salvador. 2. Political culture—
El Salvador. 3. El Salvador—Politics and government—1992—
Public opinion. 4. Democracy—El Salvador. 5. Human
rights—El Salvador. 6. Civil rights—El Salvador. I. Title.
JL1576.L33   2004
323.44'097284—dc22   2004005812

British Library cataloguing data are available

Manufactured in the United States of America

On the cover: The outdoor Mass on March 24, 2000 at El Salvador del
Mundo in San Salvador on the 20th anniversary of the assassination of
Archbishop Romero *(Photograph by the author)*

McFarland & Company, Inc., Publishers
  Box 611, Jefferson, North Carolina 28640
    www.mcfarlandpub.com

To my wife, Rachel,
and our son, Aidan Joshua

Acknowledgments

This project would not have been possible without the cooperation of many Salvadoran institutions and individuals. Human rights nongovernmental organizations (NGOs) were particularly receptive to my requests for interviews. The Human Rights Institute of the Central American University (IDHUCA) deserves special mention because of the wealth of archival material it has available, especially its collection of newspaper articles on human rights issues since 1995. I also obtained many documents at the Peace Center (CEPAZ).

I am also grateful to the Central American University (UCA) and the University of El Salvador. Scholars from both schools granted interviews and provided useful advice. I obtained a substantial number of documents from the UCA's library and its Center for Information, Documentation, and Research Support.

Various government institutions were also very helpful. Current and former members of the Office of the Human Rights Counsel (PDDH) deserve particular recognition for the insights they provided during interviews. Former human rights counsels Carlos Molina Fonseca and Victoria Velásquez de Avilés were particularly helpful. The PDDH also published many of the reports I have cited in this project.

Naturally, the cooperation of the Salvadoran media was especially important for this project. I interviewed journalists from *El Diario de Hoy, El Mundo,* and *CoLatino.* Interviews with television and radio journalists were particularly important because I could not find tapes or transcripts of news programs broadcast after early 1995. I am particularly grateful to the former business manager of the defunct alternative newspaper *Primera Plana* for allowing me to borrow his collection of every edition published. He also gave me important insight into the obstacles confronting attempts to create new voices in the concentrated media industry. Media organizations including the Journalists' Association of El Salvador (APES), the Union of Journalists and Related Fields in El Salvador (SINPESS), and the Association of Participatory Radio and Programs of El Salvador (ARPAS) also granted interviews.

I also owe a great deal of gratitude to those who helped me find my way around El Salvador. Professors Tommie Sue Montgomery and John L. Hammond gave me useful information for getting started. I received further aid from fellow graduate students who had begun their fieldwork before my arrival, including Ellen Moodie and Adam Flint. CEPAZ director Henrietta Shannon was also able to provide me with lots of nuts and bolts information.

I am grateful for the support I have received over the years from faculty members of the Political Science Program at the Graduate Center of the City University of New York (CUNY). I am especially thankful for the support and constructive criticism from my sponsor and readers, Professors Kenneth Erickson, Adamantia Pollis, and I. Leonard Markovitz. I am particularly appreciative of Professor Pollis's interest and support, because she has devoted an important share of her time to me and others at the CUNY Graduate Center while also carrying out her duties at the New School University. I am also grateful for the careful reading and constructive criticism of the other two members of my defense committee, Professors Sherrie Baver and John L. Hammond.

The process of researching and writing has been very expensive. I owe special gratitude to my wife, Rachel Rubin Ladutke, for her willingness to work as a legal secretary throughout this difficult period. The Institute for the Study of World Politics provided funding for my fieldwork in El Salvador. I am also grateful for additional support from the CUNY Graduate Center, including the Kenneth B. and Mamie Phipps Clark Fellowship for Doctoral Research with Potential for Social Action, the Styskal Dissertation Award, and the American Conscience Award. The Athena Pollis Human Rights Dissertation Award was especially helpful because it enabled me to devote myself to dissertation writing during the 2001–2002 academic year.[1] I am also grateful to the executive officer of my program, Professor W. Ofuatey-Kodjoe, who allowed me to defer some of my work as his research assistant while I conducted fieldwork in El Salvador.

While financial assistance has been crucial, my family has given me other forms of support which have been equally important. My wife has given me wonderful companionship and support, especially during the period of my absences in the field and the intense focus on write-up. My parents, Lawrence and Jean Ladutke, have also shown patience and support despite my overly optimistic predictions that I would earn my Ph.D. in only four or five years.

Contents

Contents

Preface

Both academics and diplomats have frequently cited the case of postwar El Salvador as an example of successful conflict resolution and democratization. My research, however, places serious qualifications upon this optimistic assessment of the postwar transition. While Salvadorans have had unprecedented opportunities to express themselves about human rights issues, authoritarian forces have continued to threaten and attack human rights advocates on a selective basis. Despite substantial professionalization of the Salvadoran media, the dominant news organizations have continued to censor themselves and have supported editorially many of the government's violations of the 1992 peace accords. As a result, freedom of expression has remained a privilege rather than a universal right in postwar El Salvador.

On the positive side, my research has illustrated how pro-human rights forces in El Salvador have managed to overcome these barriers in some cases. Nongovernmental organizations and victims' relatives have been willing to face serious risks to express themselves and demand justice. Opposition groups have had the most success getting their messages out when the dominant media owners and news directors understood that authoritarian groups such as the military security forces were a threat to their own institutional and elite interests.

Some observers—both foreign and Salvadorans—have argued that domestic pressure was not a significant factor in the implementation of the 1992 peace accords. They claim that the progress that has been achieved resulted from international pressure. The international community certainly did play an important role. My research clearly demonstrates, however, that Salvadorans helped bring about gains such as the removal of human rights abusers from the Salvadoran military and the

1

dissolution of the military's abusive internal security forces by expressing themselves on these issues.

This book addresses two key debates in the literature on democratization. Some scholars have approached democratization as a process of pact-making among elites. These authors argue that widespread citizen participation undermines the new democracies by threatening these agreements. Other scholars have responded by highlighting the limited nature of democracy that results from such pacts and by claiming popular participation is necessary for moving toward genuine democracy. In the case of El Salvador, my research demonstrates that citizens can indeed play an important role in bringing about greater levels of democracy by publicly expressing themselves on issues such as demilitarization and police reform. Without such participation, authoritarian institutions such as the military would have remained strong—stronger than they are today—while democratic institutions such as the new National Civilian Police would be much weaker and more compromised by military influence. Salvadoran human rights advocates also contributed to stability by publicly demanding the investigation of postwar human rights abuses and by contributing to such investigations.

The second debate concerns the question of how to deal with the legacy of human rights abuses committed under the authoritarian regime. Some scholars advocate accommodating the authoritarian elites by granting them impunity for the crimes they committed while in power. Doing so, these authors argue, will protect the elite pacts which they believe are crucial to the stability of the new democratic governments. Those on the other side of the debate argue that failure to punish human rights abusers and remove their influence from state structures limits the quality of democracy and contributes to political instability by allowing authoritarian elites to retain significant resources that can be used to challenge the elected government. My research demonstrates that unpunished human rights abusers continued to use resources such as military structures and death squads to threaten the continuation of the peace process by blocking the implementation of key elements of the 1992 accords, attacking opposition figures, undermining the rule of law, and engaging in organized criminal activity.

These findings are the result of extensive empirical research in El Salvador and the United States. I interviewed over ninety respondents, including key Salvadoran and international figures involved in the implementation of the peace accords, public officials, opposition leaders, human rights advocates, media professionals, human rights victims, and relatives of victims. The majority of these interviews were conducted in Spanish. I have also drawn upon a wealth of written material, including coverage in the Salvadoran media.

Two categories of news deserve special mention. I managed to track down television and radio transcripts from the early years of the peace process—sources that most Salvadoran respondents believed no longer existed. I also had access to the complete run of *Primera Plana*, a promising new newspaper that perished in the oligopolistic media market. Many of the remaining primary materials, such as government and non-governmental organization (NGO) reports, are available only in Spanish.

While cases such as the police murder of medical student Adriano Vilanova have received wide coverage in El Salvador, this project is the first scholarly work in English that provides in-depth analysis of such cases.

1

Introduction

Scholars and diplomats have pointed to the case of El Salvador as a model of conflict resolution and democratization that should be emulated by other nations emerging from war and authoritarianism (as discussed in Chapter Three). While the Salvadoran transition has certainly been more successful than those in nations such as Guatemala and Nicaragua, we must not overestimate what has been accomplished. The postwar governments in El Salvador have only partially implemented the human rights provisions of the 1992 peace accords. This study finds substantial empirical evidence that these omissions—as well as state acts of commission which violate the accords—have facilitated further human rights violations and undermined the nation's transition to democracy. Within this context, Salvadoran citizens and social organizations have continued to face serious risks when they have expressed themselves against human rights abuses and violations of the peace accords. Their difficulty has been compounded by the dominant media's bias in favor of the government and its allies.

Given that observers have identified the case of El Salvador as a model transition, it is important to identify the factors that have contributed to the achievements that have been made. Most observers have explained the advances made in El Salvador following the 1992 peace accords by focusing on the international factors—particularly the role of the United Nations and the U.S. government—or the actions of the state and guerrilla elites who signed the agreements and thus assumed responsibility for implementing them. These accounts therefore leave out an important factor which has gained attention in the democratization literature in recent years, namely citizen participation. This study, in contrast, examines how Salvadorans have used one form of participation—freedom of expression—to pressure the Salvadoran government to fulfill its promises under the accords and to take other actions necessary to protect human rights. It finds that Salvadoran human rights advocates have indeed had an important positive impact on this aspect of democratization.

We must also understand why the postwar transition has fallen short of the democratic nation envisioned in the peace accords, in which all citizens can freely exercise and enjoy their civil and political rights. Part of the answer obviously lies in the government's lack of political will to implement the accords. The government's attitude, in turn, depends upon the costs and benefits associated with noncompliance. This study finds that authoritarian forces inside and outside of the Salvadoran state were able to decrease pressure on the government to comply by silencing or marginalizing those calling for it to fulfill its promises and obligations regarding human rights.

The current prevalence of democracies in Latin America contrasts sharply with the situation during the 1960s and 1970s. During those decades, most nations in the region were ruled by authoritarian regimes that were often dominated by the military. Many of these governments committed widespread and systematic human rights violations—including murder and torture—against their own citizens. In the case of El Salvador, military hard-liners and their allies continued to commit grave human rights violations until the end of the civil war in 1992. By then, roughly seventy-five thousand Salvadorans—mostly civilians—had been killed. The military and its powerful economic allies were responsible for the vast majority of these deaths (Commission on the Truth for El Salvador 1995, p. 311).

While such widespread killing is certainly cause enough for serious concern, these figures do not represent a complete picture of human rights violations during this period. Authoritarian governments and their allies violated a wide range of rights during this period, including (but not limited to) the rights to due process, freedom of association, freedom of religion, and freedom of expression. When a death squad killed a journalist, it not only violated his or her right to life, but also permanently silenced the victim. Furthermore, death squads used such murders to intimidate other journalists and thus violate their right to express themselves. There were, of course, many other human rights violations which did not involve murder. Governments could also limit the right to expression, for example, through censorship, the forced closure of independent media, or the arbitrary arrest of dissidents. As discussed in Chapter Two, the Salvadoran government used all of these methods to violate human rights during the war.

By the mid 1990s, almost all of these Latin American regimes had been replaced by elected civilian governments. In countries such as Argentina, Chile, and Brazil, citizens and their newly elected governments began rebuilding—and perhaps improving—democracies which had been destroyed by military takeovers. In nations such as El Salvador, however, the citizens have found themselves in an entirely new environment. While the nation had passed through repeated cycles of liberalization and repression, Salvadorans had never had a truly democratic form of government prior to the 1992 peace accords. Now that they had greater freedom—including freedom of expression—than ever before, it remained to be seen to what degree Salvadoran citizens would exercise their rights, and what effects such participation would have on the consolidation or breakdown of democracy.

Some scholars have argued that widespread political participation is a threat to democratic transitions. Authors from this perspective view democratization as a matter of pact-making among elites. Samuel Huntington, for example, argues that "the exchange of guarantees" among elites is of "central importance" to almost all transitions. He further suggests that elites should be "willing to betray their followers" for the sake of establishing a stable democracy (Huntington 1993, pp. 161, 169).

Other authors make a similar argument which focuses on the issue of the legitimacy of a transitional regime. Carlos Nino, for example, chastises human rights organizations for undermining Argentine President Alfonsín's credibility by criticizing him in public. By doing so, he argues, they weakened the democratic regime while strengthening the position of the military. Nino even goes so far as to criticize the legislative and judicial branches for interfering with the president's wise decision to make a deal with the military (Nino 1995, pp. 425, 429). Such advice favors the creation of an oxymoronic form of democracy, one without any kind of accountability other than elections. Furthermore, it is hard to imagine how voters can make informed choices without access to such criticism.

Alfred Stepan has put forward a participatory model of democratization. He argues that democratic transitions involve "a complex dialectic of regime concessions and societal conquests." Stepan emphasizes the importance of the "societal conquests" side of the dialectic for two particularly important reasons. One part of his argument relates back to the issue of the definition of democracy. The authoritarian forces in the state will likely attempt to limit the transition to *liberalization* rather than *democratization* (Stepan 1988, p. 45). Military hardliners would, for example, refuse to submit to civilian authority. As a result, democratic forces within society have to press the regime to establish civilian control over the armed forces. If they are successful, they will have transformed civilian control over the military into societal conquest by forcing the regime to make this additional concession.

Stepan further explains that regimes may eventually take back the concessions they have made unless democratic forces in society can defend their previous gains (Stepan 1988, p. 45). Using the example above, authoritarian forces may not be willing to keep their promise to establish civilian control over the military. Democratic forces in society therefore have to create pressure on the regime so that it will actually carry out the concessions that it has made. They must also be vigilant in order to prevent hard-liners from undermining civilian control over the Armed Forces once it has been established.

While Stepan's model is certainly an interesting point of departure, it can not be applied to the case of El Salvador without some important modifications. In the case of Brazil, Stepan and Linz argue that the moderate sector of the military began the process of liberalization when General Ernesto Geisel became president in 1974. This faction of the armed forces did not do so with the goal of creating a genuine democracy, however. Instead, opposition forces in civil and political society took advantage of the limited opening and pushed the regime to make concessions in favor of democratization (Linz and Stepan 1996, pp. 168–9).

In El Salvador, the regime—under pressure from the United States government—began a period of liberalization in the mid 1980s, especially during the early years of José Napoleon Duarte's term as president. By the end of the decade, however, military hard-liners and their allies—including the new president, Alfredo Cristiani—took back these limited concessions and restricted the political space available to nonviolent opposition forces. It was not civil society that succeeded in pressuring hard-liners in the Salvadoran government and military to make the substantial concessions found in the 1992 peace accords. Rather, the powerful guerrilla forces of the Farabundo Martí National Liberation Front (FMLN) forced the National Republican Alliance (ARENA) government and its allies to do so. International diplomats—especially those from the U.S. government—also put pressure on both sides to negotiate an end to the conflict.

The transition in El Salvador is very different from the pattern in countries such as Brazil and Argentina, where transitional governments came to power during the move from liberalization to democratization. In El Salvador, the very government which presided over the resurgence of human rights violations in 1989 remained firmly in power after the signing of the 1992 peace accords. As the FMLN demobilized its troops and thus relinquished an important component of its leverage against the government, it remained to be seen whether or not democratic forces within Salvadoran society could use nonviolent mechanisms such as freedom of expression to press for implementation of the peace accords. The Cristiani Administration showed little political will with regard to implementing these agreements. In this manner, it increased the ability of authoritarian forces within both state and society to take back the concessions which the government had made at the negotiating table. Using Stepan's terminology, democratic forces in El Salvador faced the daunting challenge of claiming ownership of the Cristiani government's concessions and thus transforming the peace accords into societal conquests.

J. Patrice McSherry has also emphasized the role of popular participation during democratization. She explains, for example, that pressure from society prevented the Argentine government from making the types of elite pacts and concessions to the military advocated by Huntington and Przeworski. In more general terms, McSherry argues that pressure from below pushed the democratic transition forward (McSherry 1997, pp. 113, 270, 290).

The fact the Salvadoran transition to democracy began upon the basis of a written agreement between the government and its main rival, the FMLN, might lead the reader to mistakenly assume that this process has proceeded along the lines of the pacted transitions favored by Huntington and Przeworski. As discussed above, however, the inter-elite pacts advocated by these authors involve important concessions to the authoritarian elites and significant restrictions upon the quality of the new democracies. Such agreements also generally protect those individuals and institutions responsible for widespread human rights violations. In contrast, the Salvadoran accords contain many important provisions designed to reduce the power of these authoritarian forces. As a result, Susanne Jonas has argued, "There is a world of difference between a true negotiation ... as in El Salvador ... and a more limited 'pact' simply between civilian and military elites, as in Chile" (Jonas 1997, p. 9). The question remained, however, of whether or not hard-liners within the Salvadoran government could negotiate new pacts with elites from important opposition groups in order to undermine key provisions of the peace accords, such as the agreement to remove human rights violators from the armed forces (as discussed in Chapter Five). Or could democratic opposition groups use public expression to prevent such deals, as McSherry's findings suggest?

Scholars who focus on the human rights component of democratization also argue in favor of participation. These authors claim that people need to participate in order to protect their rights. According to Ignacio Ellacuría, for example, "Rights are the result of a struggle, which the dominant sector wishes to use in its favor, but which the dominated sector should put in its service" (Ellacuría 1990, p. 593). Philosopher Henry Shue puts forward the concept of "basic rights," which he defines as that set of rights which are necessary for the enjoyment of all other rights. He offers physical security as an example; without this right, an individual's enjoyment of any other right, including the right to life, would be reduced to a mere contingency. As a result, he argues that basic rights must not be derogated under any circumstances. He specifically identifies the right to participation as a basic right (Shue 1980, pp. 18, 21, 71). In the same vein of Ellacuría and Shue, this project examines how Salvadorans have used their right to freedom of expression in order to protect other human rights.

Common citizens cannot participate, however, without adequate mechanisms to facilitate their participation. In the case of freedom of expression, citizens depend on the press to provide information and to help them disseminate their own views. Freedom of expression therefore rests upon the foundation of media which are independent from the government. Unfortunately, the situation is more complicated than it may appear. In his study of Mexico, for example, Fromson claims, "official censorship is unnecessary" because the media owners censor themselves without overt pressure from the government (Fromson 1996, p. 127). Given the dominant media organizations' historically close ties to hardliners within the Salvadoran state, it is important for us to examine whether they have continued to censor themselves after the government eliminated formal censorship at the end of the war.

Media access is also limited by economic inequality. Authors such as Huntington, Berger, and Friedman have argued that capitalism—and its unrestrained neoliberal variant—create the necessary conditions for democratization, such as a growing middle class and private financial resources which can be used by opposition groups (Huntington 1993, pp. 66–7; Berger 1991, p. xii. xv; Friedman 1982, p. 17). Authors such as Paulo Sérgio Pinheiro, however, have found that growing inequality has led Latin American nations to become "democracies without citizenship" (Pinheiro 1996, p. 17). Belejack has argued that "the increasing concentration of the media in the hands of a few powerful conglomerates" has been one of the greatest threats to freedom of the press throughout Latin America in the 1990s (Belejack 1998, p. 9). It is therefore crucial to evaluate the degree to which the established media organizations in El Salvador have opened themselves to previously excluded voices and viewpoints. We must also determine whether or not some new, independent media have been able to emerge and to consolidate themselves in the postwar era.

This project also addresses the scholarly debate over how governments should treat those individuals and institutions responsible for widespread and systematic human rights violations under the previous regime. During the authoritarian period, human rights violators committed these actions with impunity, that is, with guarantees that they would not be held accountable for their crimes. Authors on one side of this debate argue that it is necessary for new democracies to accommodate human rights abusers by providing them with impunity for their actions prior to the onset of democratization. In essence, this approach is a variation of the argument in favor of pacts between elites. It is therefore associated with anti-participatory arguments.

The scholars on this side of the debate argue that it is better to maintain a limited democracy than to risk a coup by authoritarian figures in response to attempts to hold them accountable for their past crimes. According to Carlos Nino, for example, "the preservation of the democratic system is a prerequisite of those very prosecutions and the loss of it is a necessary antecedent to massive violations of human rights" (Nino 1995, p. 418). Similarly, Huntington blames the trials of military figures following the collapse of the authoritarian regime in Argentina for three attempted coups. Huntington further advises leaders in democratizing nations to compromise on every issue—including impunity—with the sole exception of free and fair elections (Huntington 1993, pp. 162–3, 220–1).

Some authors on the other side of this debate dispute the contention that impunity for human rights violators encourages stability. McSherry, for example, goes beyond the simple contention that Argentine military hard-liners revolted because the government provoked them through its efforts to establish justice. She does so by studying the hard-liners' actual behavior, as well as the dominant ideology within the military. She places particular emphasis on the National Security Doctrine. Subscribers to this ideology narrowly identify the nation's interests with those of the armed forces. Many military figures therefore believed that they must destroy any attempts to limit their power, or even to express disagreement with them. Another important factor was the military leadership's attitude toward compromise. Rather than viewing concessions as evidence of goodwill that invites reciprocation, most officers saw them as examples of weakness to be exploited. As a result, Alfonsín actually encouraged further revolts by conceding to military hard-liners on issues such as limiting the trials to those at the very top of the command structure (McSherry 1997, pp. 227–8, 286).

In his study of Argentina, Greece, and South Korea, Terence Roehrig argues that the question of whether or not the prosecution of human rights violators will create instability depends on how such prosecutions are integrated into a new government's overall strategy of (re)establishing civilian control over the military. He finds that the Greek and South Korean governments were more successful at preventing unrest while prosecuting military officers than the Alfonsín government in Argentina because they did a much better job of reducing military prerogatives prior to the start of human rights trials. Like McSherry, he finds that Alfonsín's concessions to the military encouraged further insubordination. In contrast, Greek President Karamanlis responded to an attempted coup by prosecuting the rebellious soldiers. This precedent helped prevent further unrest. Roehrig therefore suggests that we should ask *how* to successfully prosecute human rights violators *rather than whether* or not to prosecute them. (Roehrig 2002, pp. 2, 186–90)

The postwar governments in El Salvador have made important concessions to human rights abusers, from the passage of amnesty laws covering wartime violations, to the use of military forces for public security purposes. According to the theories of Huntington and Nino, human rights violators such as the death squads should have been satisfied that they would not be prosecuted for past crimes. Since the amnesty laws did not cover postwar human rights abuses, this argument suggests these clandestine groups had a significant disincentive against committing further political murders for which they could be prosecuted. The fact that the death squads continued killing and threatening opposition figures in El Salvador well after the passage of the 1992 amnesty law supports the argument that impunity actually encourages such forces to continue to violate human rights and to promote political instability.

The authors who oppose elite pacts that give impunity to wartime violations also question the claim that these agreements lead to democracy. J. Samuel Valenzuela, for example, has identified a pattern that he refers to as "perverse institutionalization," in which "reserved domains of authority and policy-making" take away the authority of elected officials and allow undue influence from non-elected state actors, such as the military hard-liners (Valenzuela 1992, pp. 62, 64). Stepan similarly argues that making excessive concessions to authoritarian actors cannot protect democracy because it results in a "white coup" in which the military has de facto control (Stepan 1988, p. 101).

Taking Valenzuela's and Stepan's theories into account, we must recognize that the concept of impunity must include two dimensions: individual and institutional. That is, it consists not only of a government choosing not to punish the individuals who committed human rights abuses under the authoritarian regime. It must also include structural impunity, which describes cases where governments foster impunity by failing to or refusing to dismantle the institutions that facilitate further violations. While the Cristiani government agreed to establish a new civilian police force, for example, it transferred the military Commission for the Investigation of Criminal Acts (CIHD), which was known for protecting human rights violators, into the new organization. This unit was then able to protect postwar human rights abusers, such as the death squad that executed FMLN leader Francisco Velis (as discussed in Chapter Seven).

Democratic forces in Salvadoran society have used the unprecedented political opening in postwar El Salvador to denounce their government's failure to fulfill its obligations under the accords. Human rights victims and their supporters have also been able to use their right to expression to pressure the government to punish violators and to dismantle dangerous structures in some prominent postwar cases.

The study also finds, however, that not all Salvadorans have had equal opportunity to exercise their right to freedom of expression. Through the passage of two amnesty laws, the Salvadoran government has given wartime human rights violators impunity for their past actions. The three postwar administrations have provided these criminals—and many new ones—with additional impunity by placing them in key state positions and by preserving (or failing to dismantle) the structures which facilitated human rights abuses during the war. As a result, human rights abusers have been able to protect themselves by silencing their opponents. The dominant, pro-government sector of the Salvadoran media has also restricted the opposition's ability to use freedom of expression to challenge human rights violations and policies of impunity.

Research Objectives and Data Collection

The data for this study was gathered through interviews and archival research, including the analysis of Salvadoran media's coverage of human rights issues.

It would be impossible to evaluate the impact of freedom of expression without establishing how free Salvadorans have actually been to exercise this right. The first step is to examine the evolution of the right to freedom of expression in Salvadoran history prior to the 1992 peace accords. How has the security of this right varied throughout the nation's history? Was this right ever secure enough so that all (or even most) Salvadorans could express themselves about human rights issues without fear? What factors have traditionally hindered freedom of expression in El Salvador? More specifically, which institutions and actors have prevented Salvadorans from exercising their right to freedom of expression? Which institutions and actors have helped Salvadorans express themselves?

The next step is to examine the extent to which these factors have continued to restrict free expression in El Salvador. Does accommodating those responsible for widespread and systematic human rights abuses prior to the start of democratization encourage stability and thus protect human rights, as authors such as Nino suggest? Or does such a policy encourage and facilitate further political violence, as scholars such as McSherry suggest? What, if anything, is there to prevent past violators from committing further abuses if they are not punished? How does structural impunity—the failure to remove or dismantle institutions which facilitated human rights abuses in the past—affect the right to freedom of expression? The fact that human rights violations were widespread and systematic under the elected governments of the 1980s and early 1990s undermines the claim that elections in and of themselves discourage human rights abuses. What happens if a party tied to past abuses continues to win elections in the democratic era? Have elites accepted that all citizens have the right to participate in public affairs by exercising their right to freedom of expression? Have new media outlets been able to establish themselves and compete with those that dominated the industry during the 1980s? Do the dominant media outlets distort and misrepresent human rights issues? Have they justified human rights abuses and attacked the character of human rights victims and advocates? Has the removal of direct state censorship been sufficient to guarantee freedom of expression? Or have most media organizations continued to censor themselves? Do all Salvadorans have equal access to the media? Have professional ethics had an impact on the media's coverage of human rights issues? Or have factors such as profit and political bias overshadowed ethical concerns? When are the media more likely to support pro-rights forces and oppose the government's moves to maintain impunity?

The main objective of this project is to evaluate the hypothesis that fundamental human rights are likely to be better protected when citizens and civil society institutions can and do exercise their right to freedom of expression in support of human rights. If human rights violators are not punished by the state, society must develop other mechanisms to prevent them from engaging in future violations. Freedom of expression has the potential to play a central role here. While elections are very important in and of themselves, freedom of expression is a crucial supplement because it provides a mechanism for citizens to communicate problems to state actors outside of the ballot box. Public expression also allows citizens to discuss and evaluate the performance of their elected representatives in regard to important issues, such as protecting their rights. This, in turn, increases their ability to hold representatives accountable for their actions. Public communication also helps individuals to form organizations and mobilize others. Furthermore, freedom of expression provides an important link to the international community, which can then intervene in order to prevent further violations.

In this hypothesis, the independent variable is the degree to which pro-human rights forces in Salvadoran society are able to reach important audiences when they denounce threats to human rights and express themselves in favor of actions to protect human rights. The dependent variable is the degree to which state officials and other relevant actors— such as intergovernmental organizations, for example—will either take actions to protect human rights or substantially decrease their activities which threaten human rights. If authoritarian forces are able to intimidate democratic forces into silence on an issue, the likelihood of positive action decreases. The dominant media can also decrease the possibility of a positive outcome by preventing human rights advocates from getting their message out to the general population. Pro-rights forces in Salvadoran society do not need to rely upon the media, however, to express themselves to foreign governments, intergovernmental organizations, international nongovernmental organizations (NGOs), and democratic sectors within the Salvadoran state. Even if they cannot reach the general population, human rights advocates can increase pressure on human rights violators by communicating with these institutions.

I focus on Salvadorans' attempts to protect four human rights in particular: the right to life, the right to integrity of the person, the right to association, and the right to due process. This project examines the ability of pro-human rights groups and individuals to use freedom of expression to influence the actions of those institutions and officials who are responsible for protecting human rights. Have the ARENA governments been willing to follow through on their commitments in the peace accords, or have they attempted to take back their concessions as Stepan warned? If the latter, Stepan's dialectic suggests that pressure from pro-rights forces would be necessary to protect these agreements. Have Salvadoran groups and individuals been able to force the government to keep its promises? Which factors make it easier for state actors to take back concessions? Which factors prevent them from doing so? Have Salvadorans been able to use freedom of expression to bring international pressure in favor of human rights and the peace accords on their government? Have civil society groups been able to use such expression to stop the creation of new pacts which contain major concessions to authoritarian forces and human rights abusers? Have democratic forces been able to use public expression to reduce structural impunity? Have Salvadoran groups and individuals had an impact on the investigation and resolution of postwar human rights violations by expressing themselves as victims, advocates, journalists, and witnesses?

It is important to point out that I did not simply focus on cases where I expected to find positive outcomes resulting from the use of freedom of expression. I have examined the debate over the 1992 and 1993 amnesty laws, for example, in order to identify why NGOs, religious organizations, and opposition parties were unable to prevent the ARENA government from passing them. I also analyze cases relating to the rights of a very unpopular segment of society, those accused of criminal activity.

The Material Covered in This Project

Chapter Two contains a review of the history of freedom of expression in El Salvador prior to the signing of the 1992 peace accords. It demonstrates that freedom of expression remained a privilege of the powerful rather than right of all citizens throughout this period. This chapter also briefly reviews the human rights provisions of the peace accords.

Chapter Three examines the status of freedom of expression in the postwar era. Salvadorans have enjoyed greater freedom of expression during this period than ever before. Nonetheless, the Salvadoran government has implemented policies of individual and structural impunity which have allowed human rights abusers use violence against human rights advocates.

Chapter Four describes a significant improvement in the media's coverage of human rights issues. It shows, however, that social and economic inequality associated with unrestrained capitalism has limited citizen participation in postwar El Salvador. The media industry has remained highly concentrated. Journalists have continued practices of self-censorship and misrepresentation.

Chapter Five focuses on Salvadorans' attempts to deal with the legacy of wartime human rights violations. Human rights advocates were unable to prevent the government from passing amnesty laws in 1992 and 1993. The denunciations from human rights organizations and other opposition groups failed to prevent the passage of a limited amnesty law in early 1992. Democratic forces did, however, assist two key investigative bodies established by the peace accords—the Ad Hoc Commission and the Truth Commission—by testifying, providing documentation, and using other forms of expression. This chapter also examines why human rights advocates were more successful in using public expression to pressure the government into implementing the Ad Hoc Commission's recommendations than those of the Truth Commission.

Chapter Six examines how the Salvadoran opposition used freedom of expression in its efforts to force the government into compliance with one of the central elements of the 1992 accords: the demilitarization of public security. The dominant media supported most of the government's efforts to avoid eliminating the military security forces, as well as its attempts to remilitarize the new National Civilian Police (PNC). The media changed their position dramatically, however, when key events such as an armored car robbery by active National Police troops demonstrated that the government's policies of individual and structural impunity threatened elite interests. The resulting pressure led to important achievements, such as the demobilization of the National Police.

Chapter Seven demonstrates that the Salvadoran opposition was eventually able to use public denunciations to force the Cristiani administration to establish an independent commission to investigate politically motivated death squad activity despite the dominant media's repeated denials that such groups continued to attack government opponents. This commission, in turn, relied upon information provided by Salvadorans exercising their right to express themselves. This information enabled it to establish that many of these murders were indeed politically motivated. This chapter also examines how the FMLN, NGOs, and family members used public expression to keep open the investigation of the murder of one high-ranking FMLN leader, Francisco Velis. In sharp contrast to similar cases, several individuals were eventually convicted of killing Velis.

Chapter Eight examines the role of freedom of expression in the case of Adriano Vilanova, a young medical student murdered by PNC agents. Freedom of expression played a central role in this case through investigative journalism, the family's calls for justice, and the testimony of a whistleblower inside the police. Despite numerous attempts to intimidate the family and the witnesses, their testimony—along with the journalistic investigation—led to the conviction of the five police agents who killed Vilanova. Nonetheless, those individuals who used their right to expression to help bring about this conviction continued to suffer threats and attacks.

Chapter Nine provides a striking contrast to the Vilanova case. It focuses on the investigation of twenty-one murders committed by the vigilante death squad known as "Sombra Negra." As a result of widespread anxiety over crime, few Salvadorans were inclined to speak out against these killings. The media contributed to this climate through its sensationalistic coverage of crime. There was therefore very little public pressure to move this case forward. No one has been convicted of committing these crimes.

Chapter Ten discusses the implications of my findings for theories of democratization. This chapter also presents some suggestions for increasing freedom of expression in transitional societies such as El Salvador. These include measures aimed at democratizing the media, reducing impunity, and increasing citizen participation.

2

Powerful Obstacles to Expression in Salvadoran History

In order to evaluate freedom of expression in postwar El Salvador, we must first understand the history of this right prior to the signing of the peace accords in 1992. We must also place it within the broader context of the nation's history of human rights violations, especially because this study focuses on a specific category of expression—denunciations of human rights violations and of the impunity enjoyed by human rights violators. This will help us to evaluate the extent to which freedom of expression has increased since the end of the war.

Simply put, there is no history of the right to freedom of expression in El Salvador. While some Salvadorans were able to express themselves freely prior to 1992, they did so by exercising a privilege they enjoyed due to their social and political positions. The widespread impunity for human rights violators meant that most Salvadorans risked arrest, torture, or death if they spoke out about violations. As conflict escalated, even some of those individuals whose position had traditionally protected them came under attack when they dared to denounce human rights abuses. The majority of the Salvadoran media also played an important role in limiting expression, through self-censorship, disinformation, and justification of attacks on dissidents.

We must also place this history within the broader framework of the literature on democratization. Numerous scholars have suggested that transitions to democracy are much more likely to achieve consolidation in *redemocratizing* nations, those nations which have previous experience as democracies (see Huntington 1993, p. 270, for example). El Salvador, however, is a first-time democratizing nation. As Philip J. Williams and Knut Walter argue, "there was no significant breakthrough toward a democratic transition [in El Salvador] until the peace accords were signed in January 1992" (Williams and Walter 1997, p. 115). Elections did take place prior to this date, but they were marred by factors such as fraud, vote buying, voter intimidation, attacks on opposition candidates, outright bans on some parties, and media restrictions. As a result, El Salvador did not even meet Huntington's single criterion for democracy, holding free and fair elections (Huntington 1993, pp. 162–3). Furthermore, the military often exercised its prerogative to overturn elections through coups. Even when civilian presidents such as José Napoleon Duarte were tolerated by the military, they proved incapable of establishing control over the Armed Forces.

A Nation Built on Exclusion

During the second half of the nineteenth century, the government of the newly independent nation used a combination of discriminatory laws and brute force to transfer the indigenous (mostly Pipil) and mestizo populations' communal lands into the private hands of what was to become known as the "oligarchy" or the "fourteen families" (Montgomery 1995, p. 30). This, in turn, facilitated the rise of haciendas that grew cash crops—especially coffee—using the cheap labor of the dispossessed campesinos.

In order to promote and protect its new interests, the oligarchy developed a mindset that Montgomery has called "Thomas Hobbes with a vengeance: classical liberalism that assigned to government the sole responsibility of maintaining order so that the economic elite could pursue laissez-faire economic policies" (Montgomery 1984, p. 69). As this metaphor suggests, this system of exclusion required a powerful and autonomous state apparatus capable of repressing any challenges to the status quo. Indeed, the state structures which would later play a major role in human rights violations during the civil war began to emerge. The government of Manuel Enrique Araujo (1911 to 1913) established the National Guard, for example. This institution functioned as a rural police force, giving the military control of public security.

The Manuel Enrique Araujo presidency also saw the creation of the paramilitary network of rural patrols (*patrullas cantonales*). The military organized these patrols out of the ranks of campesino conscripts who had finished their regular military service. Both the National Guard and the rural patrols provided the intelligence that allowed the state to monitor rural life (Williams and Walter 1997, pp. 14–7). The military used this information, in turn, to target campesinos who expressed criticism of the state or the economic system.

This system faced increasing challenges during the next decades. Wages for coffee workers in western El Salvador fell sharply during the 1920s. By 1931, the population of this small nation (roughly the size of Massachusetts) had grown to nearly 1.5 million—roughly three times its size in 1879 (Pearce 1986, pp. 21–2). The onset of the Great Depression caused further problems for the nation's economy. The landowners decided not to harvest the coffee crops in 1931, thus creating further hardship for the campesinos who relied on this seasonal employment for their livelihood.

These factors contributed to growing labor unrest during the presidency of Arturo Araujo in 1931. Despite Araujo's progressive electoral promises to distribute land and elevate employment, government forces brutally repressed the opposition. The financial crisis also contributed to friction between the president and the Armed Forces. By November 1931, the government had failed to pay both officers and enlisted men for nine consecutive months (Lentner 1993, p. 109). Military hard–liners overthrew Araujo in December, bringing his vice-president, General Maximiliano Hernández Martínez, to power.

La Matanza and Its Aftermath

Following the fraudulent legislative and municipal elections in January 1932, campesinos in the western region of the country became increasingly militant and pushed the Salvadoran Communist Party to revolt. Aware of their own organizational and logistical constraints, the leadership of the party reluctantly agreed to organize an uprising. The government learned of the plot and captured several of its leaders, including Communist Party founder Farabundo Martí. The remaining leaders were unable to call off the revolt. It turned out to be very poorly organized, with campesinos using machetes to attack soldiers with rifles.

The military and the oligarchy, however, were not satisfied with simply putting down this revolt. Instead, they carried out collective punishment by executing somewhere between eight thousand and thirty thousand campesinos without discriminating between those who took part in the rebellion and those who did not.[1] According to most scholars, such as Tommie Sue Montgomery, the military specifically targeted the indigenous communities (Montgomery 1995, p. 37). The soldiers continued killing "until there were no more targets (or until coffee growers became concerned that there would be no one to harvest the crop)" (Stanley

1996a, p. 53). This bloodbath is often referred to simply as *La Matanza*—"The Massacre."[2]

Despite its failure, the uprising itself reinforced the right's deepest fears. This led to increasing anti-communism and further justification for the military's growing role.

The events of 1932 also had a profound impact on freedom of expression and other forms of social mobilization. The massacre instilled terror in potential opponents by providing a dramatic example of the cost of opposing the regime. This created a society in which "there was no room for major discussion or debate" (Williams and Walter 1997, p. 23). The western part of the country, where most the killing took place, developed a reputation as a more cautious and conservative area in which the population could not be mobilized.

Many scholars have argued that the military's strategy of targeting indigenous communities while putting down the rebellion resulted in a cultural genocide. While the military and its allies did not kill the entire indigenous population, the equating of "Indian" with "Communist" terrorized the indigenous population to such an extent that almost all indigenous Salvadorans chose to assimilate (for example, see Stanley 1996a, p. 42). Following such a massacre, publicly identifying oneself as an Indian would have implicitly stated that indigenous people have the right to freedom of association. It also would have asserted that Indians have the right to life. By giving up their languages and traditional dress, these Salvadorans also surrendered important tools for expression against the repression.

This does not mean, of course, that the traumatic memory of 1932 was the only reason why Salvadorans were unable to safely exercise the right to freedom of expression during the decades that followed. Rather, the military leadership used the power it had gained by putting down the rebellion to further develop its repressive apparatus. General Hernández Martínez's regime expanded existing paramilitary structures, such as the rural patrols, and created new ones, such as the Civic Guard and the Salvadoran Civic Association (ASC). It thus created "an impressive system of incorporation and oversight of the population that left hardly any room for the exercise of civil and political rights." The government even issued a decree outlawing criticism of the ASC or any of its members. It also banned all political organizations other than the official National Party (Williams and Walter 1997, pp. 23–9).[3]

One might imagine that the Journalists' Association of El Salvador (APES), which was founded in 1936, would provide an important challenge to such restrictions. As APES President David Rivas explains, however, "it was a very closed club" where journalists who criticized the government "could not enter" (Rivas 2000).

Indeed, the majority of the Salvadoran media have had a reputation of being biased in favor of the government, the military, and powerful economic figures throughout most of the twentieth century. As the current director of *CoLatino* explained, "95% [of the media] were at the service of the system. They participated in disinformation. They participated in manipulation" (Valencia 2000).

Following the overthrow of General Hernández Martínez himself in 1944, reformist military officers led several attempts to increase political space—within limits, of course. In the 1950s, the government allowed factory workers to organize unions, but limited their activities to strictly economic issues. At the same time, it forbade rural and domestic workers from forming unions. Even this "space could be closed as easily as it was opened," however, as military hard-liners overthrew a series of governments in the cyclical pattern mentioned above (Williams and Walter 1997, pp. 32, 41)

The Political Opening of the 1960s

The cycle of liberalization followed by a resurgence of repression repeated itself once again during the 1960s. The Christian Democratic Party emerged as a centrist force which could seriously challenge the military's new official party, the National Conciliation Party. It did particularly well in urban areas, and founding member José Napoleon Duarte became mayor of San Salvador. In this manner, the Christian Democrats helped to increase room for public expression in the municipalities under opposition control (see Williams and Walter 1997, pp. 69–75).

Also during the 1960s, the United States government became interested in promoting reform through President John F. Kennedy's Alliance for Progress in an effort to prevent further revolutions like the one in Cuba in 1959. There was indeed cause for concern, as the creation of cotton and sugar haciendas increased social pressure by driving even more campesinos off their land (Newfarmer 1986, p. 212). In 1962, the U.S. government worked with the American Institute for Free Labor Development (AIFLD) to set up and support unions and campesino associations affiliated with the Christian Democrats. According to Pearce, these organizations operated in a top-down, corporatist manner that attempted to control the campesinos rather than to empower them. Therefore, they did not create genuine vehicles for expression. Salvadoran military leaders and the oligarchy, however, accused even these modest attempts at reform of being Communist subversion (see Pearce 1986, pp. 94–101).

Promoting limited reform was only part of the U.S. government's strategy, however. During this same period, the United States sent Green Berets to help establish the Nationalist Democratic Organization (ORDEN). This paramilitary organization used a combination of threats and patronage to organize as many as one hundred thousand campesinos into a system of espionage in the countryside (Williams and Walter 1997, p. 77). ORDEN would later become the foundation for the death squads organized by Roberto D'Aubuisson.

The liberation theology movement emerged following the second Vatican Council of 1964 and Medellín conference of 1968. While the Salvadoran Church remained deeply divided over its position regarding social problems, Archbishop Chávez was receptive to many of the new ideas. Salvadoran priests who followed the new doctrine with its preferential option for the poor began helping campesinos to organize Christian Base Communities (CEBs). These organizations encouraged and empowered poor Salvadorans to express themselves through literacy classes, Bible readings, and critical discussions about social issues and everyday life.

These activities helped CEB members to begin to overcome some important obstacles which had hindered their use of the right to expression. In the context of widespread illiteracy, the groups facilitated communication by helping the campesinos learn to read and to write. The organizations also helped Salvadoran campesinos to overcome their belief that they did not have a right to express themselves. The experience that CEB members gained from expressing themselves to each other helped them to learn to value what they themselves had to say, thus helping them to develop leadership skills (Hammond 1998, pp. 7, 21; see also Pearce 1986; Montgomery 1995, 81–99).

Many poor Salvadorans were continuing to cross the border into Honduras and settling vacant land without legal permission during this period, as they had done for several decades. This safety valve for the problems of population growth, landlessness, and unemployment helped to prevent unrest. In 1969, however, the Honduran government sought to deal with its own land problems by expelling these Salvadorans from its territory. The two nations were also at odds over their roles in the Central American Common Market, an arrangement which benefited El Salvador at the expense of Honduras. In July 1969, El Salvador invaded its neighbor, leading to a five-day war. Over one hundred thousand Salvadorans were forced to return home, creating further pressures on the already strained social and economic systems. The Salvadoran campesinos who were drafted to fight this war also contributed to pressure for land reform (Pearce 1986, p. 32; Williams and Walter 1997, pp. 78–9; Montgomery 1995, pp. 59–60).

Increasing Repression and Moves Toward War

During the 1970s, the government closed the political space that had been opened in the 1960s. In the midst of increasing repression, the Christian Democrats formed the National Opposition Unity coalition with two leftist parties for the 1972 elections. Duarte received enough votes to win the Presidency, but the ruling party stole the election through fraud. Although Duarte supported a coup attempt that followed, there is evidence that the rebellious officers did not have any intention of making him president (Williams and Walter 1997, pp. 81–2, 85–6). Duarte was captured by the military, beaten, and sent into exile.

The CEBs played an important role in the attempts to reopen room for expression during the next several years. According to CEB organizer Father José Alas, the progressive sector of the church had been willing to support Duarte's moderate reformism because of the belief that elections could bring about change (quoted in Pearce 1986, p. 121). The disillusionment with electoral politics was compounded by the campesinos' unfavorable experiences with the Christian Democrats' attempts to mobilize them. As one member of a base community explained, "They just talked to us nicely, but in practice they did nothing" (quoted in Pearce 1986, p. 123). Clergy members such as Alas believed that their role was to provide support so that poor Salvadorans could organize themselves and make their own decisions. As a result, they came to support new, more confrontational organizations that were willing to fight for their members' rights, such as the Union of Rural Workers. The CEBs had also created the social networks which facilitated the growth of these new vehicles for public expression.

These campesino-led organizations also began receiving support from the newly emerging guerrilla organizations, particularly the Popular Forces of Liberation (FPL). Like the liberation theology priests, FPL leaders believed that the poor must organize themselves and make their own decisions. As a result, the FPL required its members to respect the autonomy of the campesinos' organizations, including the popular church (Pearce 1986, p. 139).

This does not mean, however, that the newly emerging guerrilla forces had a perfect record of respecting and promoting freedom of expression. In particular, the People's Revolution Army (ERP) came to prioritize the military struggle over political development. Some guerrilla leaders also had serious problems respecting opposing views within their own organizations. ERP founder Roque Dalton, for example, argued that his group needed to place greater emphasis on political work. Members of his own organization responded by assassinating him (Montgomery 1995, pp. 104–5). The guerrilla organizations also committed abuses which were not directly linked to freedom of expression issues, such as kidnapping wealthy individuals for ransom.

The Salvadoran government responded to growing unrest with increasing repression designed expressly for the purpose of silencing political expression. One important landmark occurred when the National Guard opened fire on University of El Salvador students protesting against government spending on the 1975 Miss Universe pageant. At least thirty-seven students were killed, with dozens left unaccounted for (Montgomery 1995, p. 67; Williams and Walter 1997, p. 91). In another major case, government forces killed at least forty-eight people protesting the fraudulent election of General Romero in February 1977 (Montgomery 1995, p. 72).

The military government and its allies were committing these atrocities within the context of growing international concern about human rights issues in the late 1970s. In an effort to deflect criticism from the international community, the Salvadoran government ratified several important human rights treaties, including the American Convention on Human Rights in June 1978 (Popkin 2000, p. 14). Given the fact that human rights violations continued to increase after El Salvador approved these agreements, it is clear that they were mere paper commitments. General Romero's government attempted to put a legal face on the increasing repression by issuing the "Law for the Defense and Guarantee of Public Order." Through this legislation, it entirely removed due process protection from those accused of political crimes. It went so far as to allow courts to use any news account as evidence, without any verification (Popkin 2000, p. 36). This perverted the right to freedom of expression by converting it into a privilege that pro-government media owners could—and did—use to convict people through public slander.

The government specifically targeted freedom of expression in this law by making it illegal to attempt to "disturb the constitutional or legal order, the tranquility or security of the country, the economic and monetary system, or the stability of public values" through communication with the international community. Amnesty International reported that these provisions were aimed at organizations involved in the denunciation of human rights violations (Popkin 2000, p. 36).

This period also saw the emergence of the right-wing death squads that would play a very prominent role in during the coming war. The state sought to conceal its responsibility for murders and abductions through the use of groups such as the White Warriors' Union. Nonetheless, these paramilitary organizations maintained clandestine links to official security forces (Arnson 2000, p. 87). The death squads also spread terror by placing newspaper ads threatening those whom they deemed subversive. The papers published thirty-two such threats against the church between November 29, 1976 and May 31, 1977 alone (Pearce 1986, p. 168).

These attacks on the church were clearly intended to silence the progressive sector's expression on behalf of the rights of the poor. In February of 1977, Father Rutilio Grande claimed that the message of the Bible itself had become "subversive" in the context of increasing injustice. He went so far as to claim "if Jesus were to cross the border" into El Salvador, the authorities "would arrest him…. They would crucify him again." Less than a month later, assassins killed Grande.

In the midst of these attacks, the Catholic Church faced an important decision: whom to choose as the replacement for retiring Archbishop Chávez? As mentioned earlier, the Catholic hierarchy in El Salvador had become divided over the emergence of liberation theology. While many clergy members were working with CEBs and popular organizations, others—including powerful bishops—saw such actions as an improper politicization of the church. The Vatican, of course, ultimately made the decision. The papal nuncio selected Oscar Arnulfo Romero, who was viewed as "the one most able to neutralize the 'Marxist priests' and the CEBs and improve relations between the Church and the military government" (Löwy 1996, p. 105).

Romero would not play this role, however. Over the next three years, he became one of the most prominent Salvadoran figures to denounce human rights violations. His weekly homilies condemning recent abuses were broadcast on church radio (YSAX) and soon achieved the largest audience in the country. While Romero criticized violations by both the right and the left, his accounts reflected the reality that the state and its allies committed the majority of the abuses (Montgomery 1995, pp. 95–6). The Archbishop also encouraged family members of victims to organize and demand justice, by supporting the Committee of Mothers and Family Members of Prisoners, the Disappeared and the Politically Assassinated (COMADRES). Perhaps most importantly, Romero used his privileged position to express the needs and concerns of those who were otherwise excluded from the media. As one member of a CEB later explained, "campesinos are never listened to … [but] Monseñor Romero made himself their voice" (quoted in Peterson 1997, p. 102).

The context of growing unrest and persecution, however, had already begun to undermine the Church's privileged position in Salvadoran society. Nine priests were killed and sixty others were forced to leave El Salvador between March 1977 and June 1981 (Montgomery 1995, p. 97). YSAX became the target of ten bombings during Romero's tenure as Archbishop. Many of those who listened eagerly to Romero's radio broadcasts used headphones, fearing repressive consequences if their interest in this program became known (Pearce 1986, p. 170).

Eventually, even Romero's position as head of the Catholic Church in El Salvador could not guarantee his privilege to speak out against injustice. On March 23, 1980, Romero gave one of his most powerful sermons on YSAX, in which he called upon soldiers to disobey orders to kill civilians. He justified this command by arguing that such orders conflicted with God's law and were therefore illegitimate. Naturally, this speech outraged those who wished to continue using the state apparatus to eliminate and silence opponents. In retaliation, forces organized by Roberto D'Aubuisson—one of the main figures behind the death squads—assassinated Romero while he was saying mass the following day (Commission on the Truth for El Salvador 1995, pp. 354–7). For the remainder of the war, it would be dangerous for Salvadorans to possess a picture of Archbishop Romero or even to mention his name in a positive context.

It is also important to point out that Archbishop Romero's denunciations over YSAX contrasted sharply with the mainstream media's performance during this period. The dominant media did not just shrink from their responsibility to report truthfully about human rights violations, however. Rather, they took part in the persecution by justifying the repression. One glaring example of the Salvadoran media's misuse of its privilege to express itself was its smear campaign directed against Archbishop Romero. The Truth Commission, for example, quoted two *El Diario de Hoy* articles that refer to him as "a demagogic and violent Archbishop ... (who) preached terrorism from his cathedral" and suggest that "the armed forces should begin to oil their weapons" for use against him (Commission on the Truth for El Salvador 1995, pp. 355, 407).

The Failure of the Reformist Coup

Shortly before Monseñor Romero's death, there appeared to be a chance to prevent a full-blown civil war. In October 1979, a group of young reformist officers overthrew General Romero and installed a combined military-civilian junta. Human rights issues played a major role in the proclamation issued to justify the coup. The document promised that the new government would guarantee human rights such as freedom of association and due process of law. The coup leaders further pledged to combat "extremist organizations that violate Human Rights" and to dismantle the paramilitary organization known as the Democratic National Organization (ORDEN). The document also contained several provisions related to the right to freedom of expression (Proclamation of the Armed Forces ... 1996, p. 268).

Popular movement organizations attempted to use the political space that the coup leaders had proclaimed. Events quickly demonstrated, however, that the reformist officers' promises were not backed by the power needed to actually carry them out. On October 16, the military killed ten protesters and arrested many others during its assault on six factories that were being occupied during a strike. Another one of many attacks on freedom of expression took place on January 22, 1980, as a quarter of a million Salvadorans marched in the capital to protest the weakness of the civilian members of the junta. State forces responded by shooting into the crowd and killing forty-nine people (Pearce 1986, pp. 187, 190). Roughly fifty thousand mourners attended Archbishop Romero's funeral in March 1980. Machine-gun fire killed somewhere between twenty-seven and forty individuals in the crowd and wounded over two hundred others (Commission on the Truth for El Salvador 1995, p. 302).

While specific incidents such as these provided sufficient cause for doubting the state's intentions, the failure to dismantle the repressive apparatus had an even more significant impact on freedom of expression and other human rights. Despite the coup leaders' promise to dissolve ORDEN, its structures remained intact under a new name—the Broad National Front (FAN). D'Aubuisson then used the FAN to build a new political party, the National Republican Alliance (ARENA). Furthermore, many of ORDEN's members became involved in other institutions, such as the civil patrols. These sectors would help create one of the most terrifying categories of human rights violators, the death squads (see Americas Watch 1991, p. 8; Arnson 2000, p. 93; Pearce 1986, p. 190). Furthermore, the reformist officers had not even directly mentioned repressive institutions such as the National Guard, the National Police, the Treasury Police, and the civil patrols in their proclamation. In addition to committing human rights violations while acting in their official capacity, these institutions also organized their own death squads (Arnson 2000, pp. 97–100; Commission on the Truth for El Salvador 1995, pp. 357–60).

The October 15th proclamation remained nothing more than paper because the overthrow of General Romero was quickly followed by a struggle within the Armed Forces themselves. While the officers behind the coup had hoped that limited reform would prevent a revolution like the one that had just taken place in Nicaragua, more conservative officers feared that such an opening would actually facilitate a rebel victory. Within ten weeks, the conservative forces had regained the upper hand within the military (Williams and Walter 1997, pp. 96, 101–2).

The civilian junta members found themselves unable to stop the Armed Forces' assault on civil society. They therefore resigned in protest in early January 1980. A few days later, the Christian Democrats agreed to form a second junta with the military. In February, a death squad assassinated Mario Zamora, a Christian Democrat leader whom D'Aubuisson had just denounced on television. A week later, the head of the second junta, Hector Dada, resigned and fled into exile. Duarte, who had returned from exile, also threatened to leave the government. Despite his inability to impose civilian control over the military, however, Duarte came to lead the third junta and never carried through on his threat to resign.

Many others had lost hope, however. Some Christian Democrats, including Mario Zamora's brother Rubén, left the party and became part of the Democratic Revolutionary Front, a social democratic coalition allied with the guerrillas. In May, the five separate guerrilla organizations finally came together to form the Farabundo Martí National Liberation Front (FMLN) and began preparing for what they believed would be the "final offensive" in January of 1981.

In reality, however, the war would not end until 1992. At least 75,000 Salvadorans were killed during this time—the majority of them civilians.[4] It is important to remember that this figure represents roughly 1.5% of the nation's population of approximately five million people. As Stanley argues, "Salvadoran state terror was among the most severe in the hemisphere.... The only Latin American nation that may have matched El Salvador in the number of state murders per capita is Guatemala" (Stanley 1996a, p. 3).

FMLN Violations During the War

It is important to point out, of course, that this death toll does not provide us with a complete picture of human rights violations during the war. Both sides of the conflict committed many more violations which did not result in the victims' deaths, such as arbitrary arrests and death threats. The Truth Commission created to investigate wartime human rights violations found the FMLN responsible for approximately 5% of the abuses that took place between January 1980 and July of 1991. In contrast, the commission blamed the state forces and their allies for the overwhelming majority of the human rights violations that took place during the war—roughly 85% (Commission on the Truth for El Salvador 1995, p. 311).[5]

While the human rights violations committed by the guerrillas cannot be justified under any circumstances, the majority of their abuses were not aimed at freedom of expression. These crimes included forced recruitment, the use of minors as combatants, kidnapping for ransom, the indiscriminate use of land mines, the summary execution of presumed spies, and the assassination of mayors in areas under guerrilla control (Commission on the Truth for El Salvador 1995, pp. 365–8).

Nonetheless, the FMLN did directly violate the right to freedom of expression through some of its actions. Rival guerrillas sometimes used violence to resolve ideological disputes. The most famous incident of this type was the 1984 murder of Mélida Anaya Montes, a Popular Forces of Liberation (FPL) leader who had advocated negotiations with the state and greater unity with other guerrilla factions. The FMLN determined that FPL founder Salvador Cayetano Carpio was responsible and forced him to commit suicide (Montgomery 1995, p. 195).

On the basis of his conversations with Salvadoran journalists working with foreign reporters during the war, anthropologist Mark Pedelty claims that "intimidation of the press was never part of the FMLN strategy." He does, however, preface this finding by writing that FMLN threats against the media "occasionally occurred" (Pedelty 1995, p. 53). The Truth Commission blamed the guerrillas for the assassination of at least one *El Diario de Hoy* columnist, Francisco Peccorini Lettona (Commission on the Truth for El Salvador 1995, p. 302).

As mentioned above, however, the Truth Commission found the Salvadoran state and its allies to be responsible for at least 85% of human rights abuses during the war. As a result, the remainder of this chapter will focus on the violations committed by that side of the conflict.

The Height of Repression: 1980 to 1983

The height of repression occurred during the early part of the war, from 1980 until 1983. Salvadorans reported 12,501 deaths to Christian Legal Aid (*Socorro Jurídico Cristiano*) in 1981 alone. According to the Truth Commission, "the main characteristics of this period were that violence became systematic and terror and distrust reigned ... arbitrary arrests, murders, and selective and indiscriminate disappearances of leaders became common practice" (Commission on the Truth for El Salvador 1995, pp. 301, 303).

The death squads grew and became increasingly visible during this period. In a declassified report, the U.S. Embassy stated that these groups sought to "terrorize those who are still working for a moderate outcome" (quoted in Arnson 2000, p. 94). The death squads often left mutilated bodies in the street, on public buses, or at the offices of opposition groups, as a warning to terrorize anyone who would even consider speaking out against the regime. In 1983, these clandestine forces killed up to eight hundred victims per month (Burgerman 2001, p. 34).

The death squads also continued to pervert freedom of expression by publishing lists of intended victims. One such ad, specifically targeted COMADRES's right to freedom of expression, ordering the group to cease its press conferences denouncing human rights abuses (Tula 1994, p. 110). Another ad condemned thirty-four individuals—mostly journalists—to death for "discrediting the armed force" (Commission on the Truth for El Salvador 1995, p. 304).

Even non-political forms of expression were extremely dangerous during this period. Salvadorans who simply acknowledged their grief over the fate of disappeared relatives would draw suspicion, for example. The basic desire to claim the body of a loved one also led many Salvadorans into traps, as the military and its allies sought to wipe out the victims' surviving family members (Tula 1994, p. 109).

The legal system did not provide any protection for victims during this period. The security forces used mass arrests combined with prolonged periods of detention to disrupt the activities of opposition groups. The judicial system released most political prisoners only after receiving a bribe or significant international pressure (Popkin 2000, pp. 24, 40–1).

The combination of these repressive strategies had a great impact on the Salvadoran opposition during the 1980s. The government and its allies decapitated the popular movement by arresting or murdering its most experienced leaders. Many members of opposition groups abandoned their political work in San Salvador to join the guerrillas in the countryside (Pearce 1986, pp. 196–7). Naturally, the sharp reduction in the size of the popular movement led to a corresponding decrease in the level of political expression.

Civilians killed by regular military units made up the largest category of victims during this period. This was the result of a state strategy that viewed all those living in conflicted areas as guerrilla supporters and thus legitimate targets. In May 1980, for example, Salvadoran troops killed at least three hundred civilians who were attempting to cross the Sumpul River into Honduras (see Commission on the Truth for El Salvador 1995, pp. 351–3).

In perhaps the most infamous single human rights incident during the war, the Atlacatl Battalion seized control of several villages in the area surrounding El Mozote in the department of Morazán. Many local residents had fled their villages and congregated in El Mozote on the basis of a rumor that the military would not kill anyone in that town. The rumor proved to be false as the soldiers proceeded to kill everyone they encountered in El Mozote proper. A decade later, forensic anthropologists working for the Truth Commission found evidence to establish that well over five hundred civilians had been murdered in cold blood (Commission on the Truth for El Salvador 1995, pp. 347–53; Binford 1996, p. 18). The actual number of people killed may have been as high as one thousand (Americas Watch 1991, p. 109).

The military succeeded in driving large numbers of civilians out of the countryside. By the end of 1983, there were four hundred thousand internally displaced persons. The United Nations High Commission on Refugees reported that roughly seven hundred thousand Salvadorans had fled the country by this time (Commission on the Truth for El Salvador 1995, p. 304). Most of the internally displaced persons headed to the cities, where they continued to be extremely vulnerable to human rights violations. Some refugees went to camps in Honduras. European nations provided asylum for some Salvadorans. Other refugees headed for the United States, where the government denied the majority of them asylum as part of the Reagan Administration's denial that the Salvadoran government violated human rights.

The Salvadoran state and its allies systematically repressed freedom of expression by targeting journalists and media outlets that denounced human rights violations. Over three dozen journalists were killed during the course of the war (Americas Watch 1991, p. 39). David Rivas, the president of the Journalists' Association of El Salvador (APES), recalls, "when a media outlet [that was] different from the majority of the most influential media appeared ... they bombed it, they burned it down, or they closed it" (Rivas 2000). In 1980, for example, the alternative newspaper *El Independiente* suffered several attacks, including bombings, shootings, and three attempts to assassinate the editor. That same year, *La Crónica del Pueblo,* which Americas Watch identified as "the only other paper [besides *El Independiente*] that did not practice self-censorship" was forced to close after the death squads murdered its managing editor and one of its photographers. *El Independiente* finally closed in early 1981 after the army assaulted the paper's offices and arrested eight of its employees (Americas Watch 1991, p. 40).

The right-wing media played an important role in the repression against their fellow journalists. The day after the Treasury Police interrogated Dutch journalist Jacobus Andries Koster in 1982, for example, *El Diario de Hoy* printed a picture of him and three of his colleagues under the headline "Foreign Journalist [is] Contact of Subversives" (Americas Watch 1991, p. 40). Five days later, a Salvadoran colonel staged an ambush designed "deliberately to surprise and kill the [four] journalists and their escort" (Commission on the Truth for El Salvador 1995).

The only news organizations that enjoyed freedom of expression during this period were the privileged media outlets that supported the military and the far right. Furthermore, the dominant media outlets did not practice journalistic ethics such as commitment to truthful reporting. According to the Truth Commission, these media "helped to forge" impunity through silence and disinformation (Comisión de la Verdad para El Salvador 1993, p. 54). In its coverage of the El Mozote massacre, for example, *La Prensa Gráfica* issued a terse report that "at least 175 terrorists and twelve soldiers were killed during the operation" (quoted in Human Rights Watch/Americas 1992a, p. 6). As discussed above, at least five hundred unarmed civilians died in this one-sided assault in which the military forces faced no armed resistance. It is very difficult to understand how twelve soldiers could have perished while carrying out this massacre.

The only other major paper, *El Diario de Hoy*, was well known for its support of death squad organizer Roberto D'Aubuisson and the ARENA party. Channel 12 News Director Mauricio Funes commented, "*El Diario de Hoy* slandered and attacked everything associated with the opposition. It became an accomplice in the repression" (Funes 2000).

The dominant media also restricted expression by their own reporters. As David Rivas recalls, "there was not much space [for journalists] to do different, honest, decent things" (Rivas 2000). Similarly, Pedelty writes, "it would have been professional suicide [for Salvadoran journalists] to contradict their bosses" (Pedelty 1995, p. 205).

The international media became more interested in El Salvador during this period. At the same time, the Cold War mentality in some sectors of the U.S. press, along with disinformation from the Reagan Administration, served to curtail freedom of investigation and expression regarding El Salvador even in some of the leading U.S. media outlets.[6] Despite such limitations, the international media were beginning to make an important contribution to freedom of expression in El Salvador—one that is still developing long after the war ended. According to APES President David Rivas, "Many young people started to go to university to study journalism, motivated by arrival of many foreign war correspondents." "Little by little," he continued, "They began to make their way into the media" (Rivas 2000).

Another category of international actors, solidarity groups, became involved in El Salvador during this period. The Committee in Solidarity with the People of El Salvador (CISPES) was formed in October of 1980. CISPES and other organizations served as an important channel for Salvadoran groups' denunciations of human rights violations. These organizations also raised material aid for nongovernmental organizations (NGOs), unions, religious groups, and other organizations in El Salvador that were denouncing human rights abuses.

Another important development was the arrival of international delegations whose members were able to see the effects of human rights abuses first-hand. Tula recalls that COMADRES "had many visits from international delegations" beginning in the early 1980s. COMADRES helped these observers arrange meetings with students, labor leaders, and human rights organizations (Tula 1994, p. 109).

Testing the Limits on Political Expression During the Mid 1980s

Late 1983 marked the beginning of another cycle of limited political opening, which would be followed by resurgence of repression in 1988. Pope John Paul II helped to open some political space in El Salvador. His position as head of the Catholic Church gave him the privilege to publicly speak out against human rights violations during his March 1983 trip to El Salvador. He also took the opportunity to praise slain Archbishop Romero and to call for dialogue as a means of ending the war.

The overwhelming scale of state-sponsored atrocities during these early years of the war threatened continued support for the Salvadoran military in the U.S. Congress. The Reagan Administration therefore took a series of steps to demonstrate that conditions were improving and that El Salvador was indeed "on the road to democracy." One important piece of the Reagan Administration's argument was the new Salvadoran Constitution of 1983. This document did not, however, offer any real protection for freedom of expression and other civil and political rights. Although Article 6 specifically guarantees the right to freedom of expression, it does so with the vague reservation, "as long as it does not it subvert the public order" (*Constitución de la República de El Salvador de 1983* 1998). Given the right's view that denunciations of human rights violators were subversive, this article effectively continued the ban on this type of expression.

The Reagan Administration also used the 1984 elections in El Salvador as a key component of its efforts to convince Congress and the U.S. public to support continued involvement in the war. The credibility of these elections would be seriously compromised in the United States, however, if the Salvadoran state and its allies continued to commit human rights abuses at the same rate as they had from 1980 to 1983. As a result, the Reagan Administration put pressure on the military and the death squads to restrain themselves. In December 1983, Vice President George Bush traveled to El Salvador, where he warned that U.S. aid would be jeopardized if the murders continued and death squad leaders were not punished. At the same time, he promised the military increased materials support in exchange for cooperation. As Arnson points out, however, this pressure was Machiavellian—"the hierarchy of U.S. security interest remained unchanged: aid would flow and reach unprecedented levels despite the lack of progress on the concrete steps Bush outlined with such clarity" (Arnson 2000, pp. 101–4; Americas Watch 1991, p. 124).

The Reagan Administration also needed someone with a democratic image to become the next president of El Salvador. Continued congressional support would have been seriously undermined if death squad leader and ARENA party founder D'Aubuisson had won the election. As a result, the U.S. government secretly spent eleven million dollars to ensure Duarte's victory. Furthermore, the U.S. even imposed its own balloting plan on the elections and "did nearly everything possible to elect Duarte except cast a majority of the ballots" (Diskin and Sharpe 1986, p. 70; LaFeber 1984, p. 312).

The most important development of this period, however, was the fact that some Salvadorans took advantage of the small spaces that had opened up and began expressing themselves politically. According to Tula, COMADRES "broke the silence that prevailed" by marching "to proclaim that the streets belong to the people." This, in turn, inspired other Salvadorans to follow their example (Tula 1994, p. 119). In 1987, internationally respected opposition leaders Rubén Zamora and Guillermo Ungo arrived back in El Salvador and formed a new political coalition, the Democratic Convergence. They thus helped lay the groundwork for attempts to use electoral campaigns to increase the range of expression in El Salvador.

In 1988, the Catholic and Lutheran churches joined forces with sixty other organizations from civil society to create the Permanent Committee for the National Debate (CPDN). Leaders of these groups discussed issues related to the war and arrived at a general consensus around key issues related to resolving the conflict. This process, along with surveys conducted by the recently created University Institute of Public Opinion (IUDOP), created pressure on both the state and the FMLN to negotiate an end to the conflict (Montgomery 1995, p. 210).

This relative opening was not large enough nor secure enough, however, to ensure that Salvadorans could finally exercise freedom of expression as a right. One important reason for this was a secret pact between Duarte and Defense Minister Eugenio Vides Casanova, which included a promise to not prosecute military figures involved in past abuses. As a result, Duarte did not establish civilian control over the military, but rather reinforced military autonomy (Williams and Walter 1997, 127–9). This outcome supports scholars who argue that such pacts hinder democratization. Indeed, the lack of military subordination to civilian power demonstrated that the authoritarian forces were only willing to concede to liberalization, not democratization.

This meant that those who dared to criticize human rights violations remained vulnerable to reprisals. While sources such as Stanley and the Truth Commission report a decrease in human rights violations during the mid-eighties, they all qualify their findings by pointing out that this decrease was largely due to greater selectivity by the violators. Furthermore, Stanley emphasizes that this period represented an improvement only when compared to the early 1980s—it remained worse than the final months of rule by General Romero, "a period widely perceived at the time as extremely bloody" (Stanley 1996a, pp. 230–1; Commission on the Truth for El Salvador 1995, p. 304).

The political opening in San Salvador must also be viewed in the context of ongoing repression in the countryside. At the same time as the Reagan Administration was putting pressure on the death squads in late 1983, the Salvadoran Air Force increased bombing in conflicted zones. It then stepped up these strikes just prior to the elections in March of 1984, resulting in the death of two hundred and thirty five civilians between March 16th and March 29th. In 1985, Colonel Ochoa justified the military's strategy of indiscriminate attacks in these areas by asserting that there were no civilians in the area—only guerrillas. This was, of course, a gross misrepresentation (Pearce 1986, pp. 227–9). The Air Force carried out this bombing campaign in the larger context of indiscriminate military violence that was intended to drive the civilian population from large areas of the countryside.

Another important limitation of the political opening in the mid 1980s was that the popular movement was unable to create sufficient pressure to force Duarte to keep his reformist promises. One reason for this was simple and obvious—the military continued to hold the real power. The U.S. government and its allies also sought to insulate Duarte from popular pressure. When unionists affiliated with the Christian Democrats began to criticize the president, the American Institute for Free Labor Development (AIFLD) forced them out of the federation it had organized. In 1986, these dissidents helped form the National Unity of Salvadoran Workers (UNTS), a federation of one hundred unions that became "the most powerful center of opposition to the government." The U.S. government moved to divide the new federation through dirty tactics, such as paying off leaders to pull their unions out of it. AIFLD also helped the Christian Democrats form another rival labor federation, National Unity of Workers and Campesinos (Montgomery 1995, pp. 192–5; Sims 1992, p. 89).

The majority of the Salvadoran media remained biased in favor of human rights violators during this period. Powerful media organizations continued to take part in efforts to slander the opposition groups struggling to open more political space. In one particularly heinous strategy, the Salvadoran government organized press conferences in which political prisoners denounced human rights organizations as FMLN fronts. The pro-government news organizations then reported these claims as the truth. Accounts by surviving prisoners such as Tula clearly demonstrate that these "confessions" were coerced through torture (Tula 1994, pp. 145, 156).

There was, however, a very important positive development for freedom of expression during this period. At the beginning of the war, one pro-government company owned by Boris Esersky controlled all three private VHF television stations. In 1985, Jorge Zedan launched Channel 12, along with *Al Día*, a popular news show that boldly proclaimed, "Channel 12 dares" (Herrera Palacios 1998). The new station has been credited with providing "more open, diversified and balanced coverage." Competition from the popular new channel also forced Esersky's stations to cover serious issues related to the war, in contrast to its prior focus on social events (Janus 1998, p. 12).

Channel 12 had to pay a high price for journalistic professionalism, however. In 1987, dominant businesses in the Salvadoran economy launched an advertising boycott against Channel 12 that would last eight years, well beyond the end of the war. Narciso Castillo, a former manager of Channel 12, claims that the station was punished because it "was the first channel that began to speak of peace. It began to speak of negotiation and this nation's business owners did not believe in peace nor in negotiation" (Castillo 2000b).

The international media paid a great deal of attention to El Salvador during the 1984 electoral campaign. They did not maintain this level of coverage once Duarte became president, however, because they were not as interested in the less visible and less spectacular violations that persisted in this period. Despite this decline in attention to El Salvador, international pressure from civil society groups was still important during the Duarte years. Tula has provided an important example of how this pressure worked in her memoirs. After she was abducted, raped, and tortured, President Duarte called a press conference to explain that Tula was being released due to "the democracy and respect we have for human rights in this country." Tula, however, wrote, "the only reason I was set free was because of international pressure and my own innocence. Thanks to the CO-MADRES office in Washington, Amnesty International, and the solidarity efforts of many people who sent cards, letters, and telegrams—thanks to them I was freed" (Tula 1994, pp. 165–6).

The Resurgence of Repression in the Late 1980s

The opening of the mid-eighties proved to be too weak to sustain itself. Americas Watch argues that the decline in human rights violations during the mid-eighties was the result of "an ephemeral shift in policy, whereby the perpetrators apparently decided for a time to kill fewer people, remaining free to reverse that policy whenever they saw fit." It also points to the 1987 amnesty law for human rights violators as a factor that provided a green light for the resurgence of the repression that was soon to follow (Americas Watch 1991, pp. 18, 87). This outcome provides further support for the scholars who argue against accommodating authoritarian elites in this manner. Furthermore, the Reagan Administration's efforts to rein in the violators did not have a long-term impact because they were limited by its overarching goal, the military defeat of the FMLN (Stanley 1996a, p. 230; Arnson 2000, p. 111).

Another reason for the failure of the limited opening was that the Salvadoran and U.S. governments failed to punish corruption and other non-political crimes within the Armed Forces. Corruption—such as salaries drawn for nonexistent troops—reinforced impunity by serving as a patronage network which helped ensure loyalty to one's benefactors. Some officers also took advantage of the climate of impunity to branch out beyond politically motivated human rights violations and into the field of organized crime. For example, one group led by the National Police chief and the head of intelligence abducted five rich Salvadorans—including ARENA supporters—for ransom between 1983 and 1986. Even this clear example of criminal activity went unpunished—despite substantial information yielded by an international investigation involving the FBI and Venezuelan assistants (Montgomery 1995, pp. 65–6, 201–2, 205–6).

The U.S. government was unable to maintain its support for the "center" as the Christian Democrats became racked with internal disputes and Duarte's energies were sapped by liver cancer. ARENA took advantage of the Christian Democrats' weakened position and nominated Alfredo Cristiani as its candidate for president in the 1989 elections. According to Pedelty, the Bush Administration ran "a carefully orchestrated [press] campaign" which changed Cristiani "from 'the standard bearer of the far-right' to a 'moderate'" (Pedelty 1995, p. 181). Cristiani's new image was also intended to show the U.S. public that ARENA was no longer the party of D'Aubuisson and the death squads. The U.S. government has since declassified CIA documents from the time, however, revealing, "D'Aubuisson's public deference to Cristiani [was] largely cosmetic" (Arnson 2000, pp. 122 n. 96).

ARENA's new image contrasted with the rise in human rights violations that preceded the 1989 elections. The death squads sharply increased their killings in 1988, resulting in an average of eight victims a month—for a total of three times as many death squad victims as there had been the previous year. They targeted unions, human rights organizations, and social movements (Commission on the Truth for El Salvador 1995, pp. 307–8).

Regular Armed Forces units also committed an increased number of violations during this period. Colonel Vides Casanova used Duarte's illness as an opportunity to consolidate the High Command in the hands of the infamous *Tandona*, the military school's hard-line class of 1966 that wanted to overcome U.S. pressures for restraint (Williams and Walter 1997, pp. 135–6). The Truth Commission found that "the army reverted to its practice of mass executions" in 1988 (Commission on the Truth for El Salvador 1995, p. 308).

The military also killed three journalists covering the 1989 elections. On March 18th, the night before the elections, soldiers killed a Salvadoran photojournalist working for Reuters and a sound technician from Channel 12. They also wounded, but did not kill, another Salvadoran working for Reuters. A Dutch cameraman was killed the following day when the Air Force strafed the clearly marked press vehicle that was taking him to the hospital after he had been injured during crossfire (Americas Watch 1991, pp. 40–1).

Not surprisingly, relations between the military and the civilian government improved after the election of an ARENA president. This gave the Armed Forces even greater autonomy, and they took advantage of this situation to target freedom of expression (García 1992, p. 100). They arrested over sixty members of opposition groups shortly before Cristiani's inauguration and resumed "more drastic methods of torture" after the elections (Hammond 1998, p. 94; Americas Watch 1991, p. 18).[7]

The government and the FMLN made very little progress in the peace talks taking place during the first several months of the new administration. In June 1989, Cristiani announced that negotiating a political settlement to the war would be among his top priorities (Burgerman 2001, p. 83). Nonetheless, military hard-liners and their allies saw little need to negotiate because they continued to believe that they were close to defeating the guerrillas. While talks were proceeding slowly, bombs exploded in the offices of the National Union Federation of Salvadoran Workers (FENASTRAS) and COMADRES on October 31, 1989.

The FMLN responded by withdrawing from the negotiations on November 2nd. On November 11th, the guerrillas launched one of the largest military actions of the war. They extended this offensive throughout the nation, including parts of the capital that had previously remained relatively untouched by the war. International observers strongly criticized the Salvadoran Armed Forces for ruthlessly bombing poor neighborhoods occupied by the FMLN, especially when they then showed restraint against guerrilla positions in rich neighborhoods (Americas Watch 1991, p. 62).

The Armed Forces and the death squads decided to use the offensive as cover for an assault on leaders of the civilian opposition. The military began by forcing all radio stations to cease independent coverage and to carry the Armed Forces' programming. It went beyond simply restricting freedom of expression, however, and joined with far-right civilians in denouncing "political personalities of the opposition, trade union leaders, members of the clergy, [and] representatives of non-governmental organizations." The broadcasts "generally incited listeners to violence against those persons specified" (International Commission of Jurists 1992, p. 18).

Those making these slanderous attacks paid special attention to one individual, Father Ignacio Ellacuría, the head of the Jesuit Central American University (UCA). They singled out the priest precisely because of his denunciations of human rights violations and his calls for negotiation. One of his admirers had recently remarked, "not since they murdered Archbishop Romero has anyone spoken out so plainly in this country" (quoted in Peterson 1997, p. 104). In contrast, Vice President Francisco Merino took to the airwaves during the offensive to accuse the priest of "'poisoning the minds' of Salvadoran youths" (International Commission of Jurists 1992, p. 18).

These accusations were certainly nothing new, however. The pro-government media had already laid the foundation for Merino's claims by using biased, misrepresentative language which identified the Jesuits with the FMLN. The Truth Commission found that 56% of new stories about Ellacuría and his colleagues prior to November 16, 1989 referred to them as "subversives." The remaining media accounts referred to them as "Communists" (20%), "leftists" (20%), and "extremists" (4%) (Comisión de la Verdad para El Salvador 1993, p.34). In this manner, the dominant media had also helped set the stage for the massacre that would follow.

A few days later, during the early hours of November 16th, members of the Atlacatl battalion murdered Ellacuría, along with five other Jesuits, their cook, and her teenage daughter. The Truth Commission has since established that Colonel René Emilio Ponce, General Juan Rafael Bustillo, Colonel Orlando Zepeda, Colonel Inocente Orlando Montano and Colonel Francisco Elena Fuentes made the decision to kill Ellacuría and to eliminate any witnesses (Commission on the Truth for El Salvador 1995, p. 312).

The Armed Forces, President Cristiani, and the Bush Administration all attempted to blame the FMLN for the massacre. Many members of the international community, including the U.S. media, were highly skeptical. It is very likely that the outrage expressed by citizens and leaders from around the world played an important role in saving other lives in El Salvador. The military broadcasts had been calling for the deaths of many other opposition leaders, including Archbishop Rivera y Damas and Monseñor Rosa Chávez (Stanley 1996a, p. 248). A *Village Voice* reporter later revealed that the military leadership had intended the UCA massacre as the first step in a strategy of mass murder directed against the opposition (Americas Watch 1991, p. 19).

Once again, the Salvadoran government attempted to put a legal face on human rights violations. In 1989, ARENA proposed new "antiterrorist" legislation which would have criminalized fundamental forms of expression, including peaceful protest and human rights monitoring. Criticism from Salvadoran and international human rights groups helped prevent most of these proposals from becoming law (Popkin 2000, p. 75).

A positive development took place in 1989 after the owner of *Diario Latino* abandoned the small afternoon paper, leaving it with substantial debt. The workers assumed ownership and it reemerged as the first opposition newspaper since the early eighties. It should be remembered, of course, that *Diario Latino*'s circulation was dwarfed by that of the two dominant papers, *El Diario de Hoy* and *La Prensa Gráfica*.

That same year, the workers at *Diario Latino* also organized themselves into the new Union of Journalists and Related Fields in El Salvador. This union was also open to journalists working at other Salvadoran media organizations, offering an alternative to APES, which remained corrupt at the time. Many of the union members working outside of *Diario Latino* would have to keep their membership secret, however (Piñeda 2000; Pedelty 1995, pp. 215–6).

The Push for Peace in the Early 1990s

By January of 1990, the guerrilla offensive was over. The Salvadoran government continued to face domestic and international pressure, however, to prosecute those responsible for the massacre at the UCA. The Commission for the Investigation of Criminal Acts (CIHD) quickly proved itself to be incapable of investigating its military masters. According to the International Commission of Jurists, the CIHD's investigation was "marked by limitations, omissions, reticence, and actions that cannot be clearly explained" (International Commission of Jurists 1992, p. 37). As a result of the continuing pressure, the Salvadoran government created an "Honor Commission" to investigate the case. This body quickly identified nine soldiers who would stand trial for the crime. It did so, however, by acting "in an inexplicable manner and using methods that have no basis in judicial procedure" (International Commission of Jurists 1992, p. 34). Nevertheless, this marked the first time that a high-ranking Salvadoran officer had ever stood trial for human rights abuses committed during the war. The courts' inaction against other human rights violators led the Truth Commission to cite "the tremendous responsibility which the judiciary bears for the impunity" in El Salvador (Commission on the Truth for El Salvador 1995, p. 380).

The U.S. Congress also established its own investigative committee, led by Congressman John Joseph Moakley. In August of 1990, Moakley told the media, "the High Command's goal, from the beginning, has been to control the investigation and to limit the number and rank of the officers who will be held responsible for the crimes." In October, Moakley revealed evidence implicating Defense Minister Ponce[8] in the killings—evidence which the U.S. government had possessed and withheld from the Salvadoran investigators (Americas Watch 1991, pp. 104–6).[9]

That same month, growing criticism from U.S. civil society groups, as well as Salvadoran refugees living in the United States, contributed to Congress's decision to withhold half of the military aid that had been allocated to El Salvador for 1991. According to Congressman James McGovern, who served as Moakley's aide during the investigation, the pressure to cut the aid "came in the form of lots of refugees who fled El Salvador during the 1980s who were amongst us here. [They] became activists, who went around and talked to members of Congress. That kind of advocacy helped educate members of Congress" (McGovern 2001). The resulting aid reduction may have had an important impact on the negotiations, as the High Command then became more open to compromise (Williams and Walter 1997, p. 151).

The trial of the nine soldiers selected by the Honor Commission did not begin until April of 1991. The prosecution clearly linked the massacre to freedom of expression by describing the "Jesuits as men crying out for peace and justice, whose 'only crime was that of thinking differently than the military'" (International Commission of Jurists 1992, p. 51). In contrast, the defense fell back upon the Salvadoran right's standard response to accusations of human rights violations—blaming the victim. The defense asserted, for example, "that the Jesuits 'rule the world,' that they 'control congresses,' and that 'they are interested in destabilizing the [Salvadoran] Government.'" (International Commission of Jurists 1992, p. 55).

The International Commission of Jurists has argued that the verdict in the trial "can only be characterized as arbitrary" (International Commission of Jurists 1992, p. 71). The jury convicted Col. Guillermo Benavides of murdering all eight victims. It also convicted Lt. Yusshy Mendoza for killing the cook's daughter, whom the soldiers shot while she was embracing her mother. Yet it exonerated Mendoza in the death of the mother. The jury acquitted all of the remaining defendants, despite having heard transcripts of them confessing to the crime (International Commission of Jurists 1992, pp. 61, 71).

The struggle for freedom of expression suffered an important setback with the firebombing of *Diario Latino* in February 1991. Pedelty visited the paper's offices a few days after the attack and reported, "I was particularly struck by the dead silence of their giant printing press, its huge metal skeleton symbolizing the right's antipathy for press dissent" (Pedelty 1995, p. 48). The employee/owners of the paper eventually rebuilt it. They now publish it under the name *CoLatino*.

On the positive side, a new independent magazine called *Tendencias* published its first issue in 1991. This monthly publication provided a space for both the left and the right to discuss politics, history, and culture. *Tendencias* also provided a forum for journalists to discuss their profession. The magazine's founder and Director, Roberto Turcios, believed that freedom of expression is key to the control of power and the establishment of fundamental human rights. As result, *Tendencias* gave special attention to the issue of freedom of expression (Turcios 2000).

The government and the FMLN resumed serious peace negotiations after the 1989 offensive. The first major breakthrough came in July of 1990 with the signing of the San José Agreement, in which both sides promised to guarantee human rights and agreed to the deployment of a UN mission to monitor human rights prior to any cease-fire (see Government of El Salvador and FMLN 1995b; Burgerman 2001, p. 86). According to the Truth Commission, human rights violations "dropped sharply" after this document was signed—even before the observers were in place (Commission on the Truth for El Salvador 1995, p. 309). The human rights situation improved even further after the arrival of the United Nations Observer Mission in El Salvador (ONUSAL) in July of 1991 (Johnstone 1995, p. 20).

The government and the FMLN reached another important breakthrough in terms of freedom of expression and human rights in general by agreeing to create a truth commission. The FMLN had been willing to limit the investigations to four prominent cases: the assassination of Archbishop Romero, the UCA massacre, the bombing of FENASTRAS and the assassination of Democratic Convergence leader Héctor Oquelí. Salvadoran NGOs criticized this list for its focus on elites. The FMLN responded by amending the list to include the El Mozote and Rio Sumpul massacres. In April of 1991, the two warring sides agreed to allow the Truth Commission itself to determine which incidents it would investigate (Popkin 2000, pp. 89–91).

The death squads continued to operate during this period. Despite the Bush Administration's public commitment to a negotiated solution, the U.S. military continued training forces involved in death squad activities until at least October of 1990 (Arnson 2000, pp. 108–9). This is all the more troubling in light of the emergence of a pattern that would continue well into the postwar period: the death squads began targeting the peace process itself. In July of 1991, death squads issued threats against the UN observer mission and the International Committee of the Red Cross, as well as Salvadorans who worked with or conducted business with these international bodies. There was at least one attempt to kill an ONUSAL observer in December of 1991 (Human Rights Watch/Americas 1992b, p. 9). The ongoing negotiations also led to tensions within the ruling party, as the D'Aubuisson faction of ARENA plotted the assassination of President Cristiani (Arnson 2000, p. 107).

The final elections for the Legislative Assembly and local governments before the cease-fire took place in 1991. Despite the progress that had been in terms of negotiations, the IUDOP's surveys found that 73.9% of Salvadorans were still afraid to express themselves in public. Many of the Salvadorans who wished to vote for the leftist Democratic Convergence coalition could not do so because of the lack of candidates willing to risk their lives (Gibb 1992, pp. 18–9).

Human Rights and Accountability in the 1992 Peace Accords

On January 16, 1992, the government and the FMLN signed the peace accords which officially ended the war. They created the National Commission for Consolidation of Peace (COPAZ), a body composed of representatives of the Salvadoran government, the FMLN, and all of the parties represented in the Legislative Assembly, to oversee implementation of the agreements. Obviously, the cease-fire itself would have an immediate impact on certain categories of human rights violations, such as the massacres and indiscriminate attacks on civilians that had been carried out by the Armed Forces. The gradual dissolution of guerrillas' military structure would prevent the FMLN from committing some categories of human rights violations, such as the use of minors in combat. It would also greatly reduce the FMLN's ability to commit other abuses, such as summary executions.

Given the military's long history of human rights violations, it is not surprising that many of the accords focused on the Armed Forces. The agreement provided for a new military doctrine, subjugating the Armed Forces to civilian control, removing their role in public security, and committing them to respecting human rights. This change was supported by a new Academic Council for the Military College that includes civilian members. This new council, in turn, would help ensure that cadets would indeed receive training in the new pro-rights doctrine. The government agreed to replace the arbitrary system of forced recruitment used during the war with a nondiscriminatory draft and reserve system.

The state also agreed to reduce structural impunity by abolishing several military institutions with the worst human rights records, including the elite counterinsurgency battalions, the National Guard, the Treasury Police, and the civil defense patrols. It also committed itself to disbanding the National Police after the deployment of the new civilian police force. The government promised to reduce the ranks of the Armed Forces and to collect all military weapons in the hands of civilians. The accords also replaced the military's National Intelligence Department (DNI) with the civilian State Intelligence Organization (OIE), which would be subject to legislative oversight (see Government of El Salvador and FMLN 1995c, pp. 194–8). These measures would eliminate many of the state structures that had stifled freedom of expression through their role in monitoring society.

As we have seen, individual human rights violators have used the impunity which they traditionally enjoyed as an effective tool for silencing opponents. The government and the FMLN called for an end to this impunity in peace accords. They established an Ad Hoc Commission comprised of three Salvadoran civilians to identify human rights violators for removal from the Armed Forces. The parties agreed to the creation of an independent Truth Commission composed of international figures, which would have the larger mandate of investigating wartime abuses committed by all sectors. It would then issue a public report of its findings. The accords also empowered the Truth Commission to make binding recommendations designed to prevent further human rights violations.[10]

Another large section of the accords dealt with the creation of the National Civilian Police (PNC) to replace the military's security forces. This change was very important, given the security forces' appalling human rights records, as well as their poor performance in the area of criminal investigations. The accords gave the new force a democratic public security doctrine emphasizing its role in respecting and guaranteeing the rights of all Salvadorans. This was a major change from the old military security forces. The National Guard, Treasury Police, and National Police followed the National Security Doctrine, which emphasized defending the state from subversive forces within the nation. The accords also stipulated that the PNC would emphasize the use of nonviolent means and would use firearms only when necessary to protect human life. The agreement established a new National Public Security Academy (ANSP) to train the PNC. The parties agreed that the majority of new police agents would be drawn from the civilian population. Equal portions of former National Police agents and FMLN troops would also be allowed to join, provided that these individuals met the established criteria for admission to the new academy. Former National Police agents would also be subject to evaluation before being admitted. The accords established that the National Police would continue to function while its duties are gradually taken over by the PNC (see Government of El Salvador and FMLN 1995c, pp. 198–205.).

The peace accords contained one more section that directly addressed civil and political rights, entitled "Political participation by FMLN." There was a provision for all "measures needed to guarantee former FMLN combatants the full exercise of their civil and political rights." The government also promised to free "all political prisoners" and to guarantee the safety of Salvadorans returning from abroad. The accords stipulated that the FMLN has the right to become a political party and guaranteed the right of assembly for all of its members. There was also a provision for "special security measures" for FMLN leaders who needed protection (Government of El Salvador and FMLN 1995c, pp. 209–10).

This section contains the only provisions which deal directly with the media. The government promised to grant licenses for the FMLN's radio stations. It also recognized the FMLN's right to buy advertising space (Government of El Salvador and FMLN 1995c, pp. 209–10). There was no mention of any measure to overcome ARENA's overwhelming resources, such as the provision of free air time for all parties. Nor was there any discussion of the need to promote greater competition and diversity within the media and related industries.

Implications for Freedom of Expression in Postwar El Salvador

The signing of the peace accords and the end to the civil war presented Salvadorans with the opportunity to finally remedy the nation's historic lack of freedom of expression. While there had been periods of liberalization in which some political space opened for expression about human rights issues, there had always been limits to this space. This is best demonstrated by the periods of increased repression that invariably followed. During his speech at the signing of the peace accords in Mexico, even President Cristiani himself recognized, "In the past, the nonexistence or insufficiency of the spaces and mechanisms needed to allow the free play of ideas ... was one of the destructive limits of our national way of life" (Cristiani 1992, p. 165).

El Salvador's history has important implications for the potential development of the right to freedom of expression during the postwar period. The nation entered the new era with the legacy of impunity. The massacre of 1932 had created a polarized society in which the dominant groups' fear of a lower-class rebellion led them to support extreme repression against those who expressed different ideas. The rule of law had never been established because state institutions dominated by a narrow economic elite and the military participated in human rights violations and protected those who committed them. Impunity was also deeply rooted in the structures of the security forces, the death squads, and the courts. While civilians such as President Duarte had nominally ruled El Salvador, they failed to establish control over the Armed Forces and their allies.

The problem was not a lack of state promises to protect freedom of expression and other rights. As we have seen, the Salvadoran government had made many concessions toward liberalization in documents such as the Salvadoran Constitution and the proclamation of the October 1979 coup. Nonetheless, these promises had remained mere pieces of paper. One of the key questions for the postwar transition was therefore whether or not the concessions made by the government in the 1992 peace accords would suffer the same fate.

In nations such as Argentina and Chile, the replacement of the previous authoritarian regime facilitated the transition to democracy. This was not the case in El Salvador, however, as the party that presided over the resurgence of repression in the late 1980s remained firmly in power. This raised serious concerns as to whether or not the government would have the necessary political will to implement the peace accords and to take other measures necessary to protect human rights. As will be discussed in the remainder of this study, the government did indeed resist implementing many of the concessions it made in the peace accords.

Obviously, the international community's involvement in the peace process would have an important role to play in generating the political will needed to make progress on human rights issues during the postwar era. It also became obvious, however, that the world's attention would not last forever. This meant that pressure to implement the accords and to guarantee human rights would also have to come from within El Salvador itself. In Stepan's terms, these groups would have to transform the regime's concessions into societal conquests. The extreme repression of the civil war, however, had taken its toll on civil society organizations that advocated human rights issues, such as NGOs, unions, and the progressive churches. Furthermore, the majority of the population was accustomed to living in a culture of fear and silence.

The historic concentration of the media in the hands of the far right also presented serious implications for freedom of expression during the postwar era. As the war ended, *La Prensa Gráfica* and *El Diario de Hoy* continued to dominate the written news media, and Telecorporación Salvadoreña (TCS) maintained control over three out of four of the nation's private VHF television stations. While new media outlets had emerged during the war, they entered the new period in a tenuous position. *Diario Latino* was still recovering from being firebombed a year earlier, while Channel 12 remained subject to an advertising boycott.

The next two chapters examine the development of freedom of expression during the postwar era and assesses the extent to which impunity and the structure of the media industry have continued to limit this right.

3

Impunity Continues to Constrain Freedom of Expression

Before examining how Salvadorans have used freedom of expression to protect other human rights during the postwar era, we must first explore the degree to which this right has become more secure and accessible in the postwar era. The political opening that followed the end of the civil war has certainly gone far beyond that of any previous liberalization period, such as the 1960s and the mid 1980s. As a result, some international observers have presented the postwar transition as a model to be emulated by nations emerging from long and intense conflicts involving widespread human rights violations. According to David Holiday and William Stanley, for example, "for the United Nations the outcome in El Salvador has been so positive in comparison with other UN interventions that it has become a showcase for what the UN can accomplish" (Holiday and Stanley 2000, p. 38). Alvaro de Soto—the UN official who mediated the peace talks and then made frequent visits to observe the implementation of the agreements—pointed to the creation of the National Civilian Police (PNC) in particular as a "model" for newly emerging democracies (DH, 20 Mar. 1996). U.S. government sources whom I interviewed in 2001 also emphasized the Salvadoran Armed Forces as a model of military reform for countries in the region (Two U.S. Government Sources 2001).

Indeed, the Salvadoran transition does compare favorably to those in nations such Guatemala. The Guatemalan guerrillas did not have the military strength to force the government to make as many concessions as the Salvadoran government had during negotiations (Spence et al. 1998, p. 5). Furthermore, hard-liners in the Salvadoran military such as Colonel Francisco Elena Fuentes advised their Guatemalan counterparts not to follow the Salvadoran model because it would endanger their institutional interests (DH, 13 Feb. 1994; see also Hayner 2001, p. 45). As a result, the human rights situation in postwar Guatemala has been significantly worse than that of El Salvador. This is especially true in terms of political violence directed at journalists (see CPJ 2002).

The Salvadoran government has taken advantage of this praise to create and reinforce the impression that it has faithfully implemented the peace accords. In 1996, for example, President Armando Calderón Sol told the UN General Assembly, "we have complied with and achieved the objectives that we agreed to [and] ... produced deep transformations in Salvadoran society, which have earned universal recognition as one of the broadest peace efforts achieved and the most successful that has been carried out with the help of this organization" (Calderón Sol 1997, p. 928).

This chapter presents substantial empirical evidence, however, that Salvadorans have continued to face serious risks when they have called for compliance with the 1992 peace accords and denounced postwar human rights violations. These risks have continued precisely because the Salvadoran government has not fulfilled its obligations under the peace accords. As representatives of a party with deep historic ties to the death squads, President Cristiani and his successor, Calderón Sol, devised and implemented policies which protected members of their party—as well as other powerful institutions and individuals—from punishment for their previous crimes and from measures aimed at eliminating the impunity they have traditionally enjoyed. The fact that the National Republican Alliance (ARENA) remained firmly in power during this crucial stage created a serious disadvantage for the Salvadoran democratization process in comparison to nations such as Argentina and South Africa, where transitional governments replaced the authoritarian leaders responsible for widespread human rights abuses. While some human rights advocates have been willing to risk their lives by speaking out, many Salvadorans have chosen the safety of silence.

We would be mistaken to simply assume that the political space that has opened up will continue to remain open. As demonstrated in the previous chapter, El Salvador's history has been marked by cycles of political liberalization followed by the resumption of repression. This chapter also examine some troubling indications that this cycle may once again repeat itself, including problems in the Office of the Human Rights Counsel (PDDH), the hostile attitude of current President Francisco Flores, domestic espionage, and a changing international context in the wake of the September 11, 2001, terrorist attacks on the United States.

Impunity Continues to Facilitate Human Rights Abuses

The Salvadoran government has not eliminated impunity during the decade following the end of the war. According to former Human Rights Counsel Dr. Victoria Marina Velásquez de Avilés, El Salvador "would be closer to an authentic peace if the accords had been implemented as they were written" (Velásquez de Avilés 2000). The ARENA administrations, however, have only partially implemented the accords. In areas such the demilitarization of public security, the government has engaged in such direct violations of the accords as assigning military troops to anticrime patrols on an almost permanent basis (see Chapter Six). In 1996, four years after the war ended, the Committee for a Permanent National Debate (CPDN) argued that the accords' objectives of national reconciliation, respect for human rights, and democratization were "growing more distant every day" (CL, 30 Apr. 1996).

Within this context, impunity has continued to impede freedom of expression. Elmer Mendoza Zamora, the president of the Committee of Family Members of Victims of Human Rights Violations in El Salvador (CODEFAM), stated that it would take several generations to eliminate impunity as a barrier to expression (Mendoza Zamora 1999). One young journalist whom I interviewed was even more pessimistic. "Impunity," she said, "is always going to be an obstacle to performing good work" in her field (Female reporter from Canal 33 2000).

One reason for the continuing impunity is that many of the same groups and individuals who violated human rights during the war have continued to hold powerful positions in the postwar era. The Cristiani government and its allies in the Assembly passed the 1992 and 1993 amnesty laws to prevent the prosecution of any wartime violators. Human rights violators such as Colonel Gustavo Perdomo have remained in the military, even after the evaluation by the Ad Hoc Commission.[1] A French judge ordered an arrest warrant against Perdomo after finding sufficient evidence that the colonel was responsible for the 1989 rape, mutilation, and summary execution of nurse Madeleine Lagadec. The Salvadoran government refused to extradite Perdomo on the basis that the military had already been vetted by the Ad Hoc Commission. The French government could not force it to do so without an extradition treaty between the two nations. The government eventually rewarded Perdomo with a promotion to general (Flores 1995; AP 2000).

The Salvadoran government's actions toward Perdomo have several serious consequences in addition to the obvious fact that he remained in a position from which he could potentially commit further human rights abuses. As a high ranking-officer, Perdomo has had an impact on the behavior of the officers and enlisted men serving under his command. Given his past, it is very unlikely that he would fully support the new military doctrine contained in the peace accords. This, in turn, undermines the government's promise to establish civilian control over the military as part of the peace accords. The government further violated the accords by assigning military figures from especially repressive units to important positions in the new supposedly civilian police force, the consequences of which are discussed in Chapters Six, Seven, Eight, and Nine.

The amnesty laws also protected former guerrillas who committed human rights violations during the war. Unlike government soldiers, however, they all left military service as the Farabundo Martí National Liberation Front (FMLN) dismantled its military structures. The world soon discovered, however, that the FMLN had retained some of its best weapons in secret locations throughout El Salvador, Honduras, and Nicaragua (as discussed in Chapter Seven).

Civilian human rights violators have also benefited from impunity. Declassified U.S. documents have clearly identified former Vice President Francisco Merino, for example, as a leader of wartime death squads (Arnson 2000, p. 107). Nonetheless, he has enjoyed special immunity from prosecution as a deputy in the Legislative Assembly, and he continued to enjoy this protection even after he shot a police agent while inebriated (U.S. Department of State 2001).

In this context, it is not surprising that **the majority of Salvadorans do not denounce human rights violations**. Assistant Human Rights Counsel Marcos Valladares Melgar told me that official figures on rights abuses "are only those of which we know, but there are many more violations" (Valladares 2000). Referring to the murders of her own son and Adriano Vilanova, Gloria Giralt de García Prieto has explained, "mistakenly, the people outside [the nation] think that the war ended, there is a genuine democracy, that these things no longer happen here. Our cases are evidence to the contrary. Therefore, they can say, 'there are two cases.' No. We are the two cases who speak out, because there are mountains [of people] who do not talk" (Giralt de García Prieto 2000).

State Officials Continue to Hold Anti-Rights Attitudes

Citizens in any nation must depend upon their government to protect freedom of expression if they are to exercise that right securely. The transition in El Salvador has been very different from the democratization processes in which authoritarian regimes have been replaced by new, democratic governments, for in El Salvador a governing party born out of the death squads signed the peace agreement committing itself to the elimination of impunity. While ARENA has adapted to the new electoral context, it has not outgrown its anti-rights world view. Some military officers have also continued to express attitudes incompatible with democracy and human rights.

It is appropriate to consider the Salvadoran experience in light of the transitions in nations such as Argentina, Chile, and South Africa. The military government of Argentina, for example, fell after being discredited by its defeat in the Falklands/Malvinas war and the manifest failure of its economic policies. While the civilian government that replaced the dictatorship did make some important concessions to the military, it was nonetheless willing to confront the military on certain key issues, including the prosecution of members of the juntas. In Chile, dictator Augusto Pinochet was forced out of political power by a popular referendum. The civilian government of President Patricio Aylwin was unable to eliminate many of the mechanisms of impunity, including General Augusto Pinochet's continuing command of the army. President Aylwin did demonstrate, however, his own democratic beliefs by acknowledging the information contained in the Chilean truth commission's report and apologizing for the crimes carried out by the state (Hayner 2001, pp. 26, 35). In South Africa, a democratically elected government finally replaced a racist regime. The government headed by Nelson Mandela therefore had obvious incentives to eliminate the apartheid system. Rather than passing a blanket amnesty law, the South African government empowered a truth commission to grant pardons to only those human rights abusers who cooperated with its investigation by providing full information about the crimes in which they took part and their knowledge of other human rights violations.

Unlike those nations, however, El Salvador did not benefit from a clean break with the previous authoritarian regime. Instead, President Cristiani, the very leader who served during the resurgence of repression in the late 1980s, remained firmly in power to oversee the crucial first year and a half of implementing the peace accords. Furthermore, his party retained the presidency for at least the next two five-year terms.

I interviewed Renato Antonio Pérez, an ARENA deputy on the Human Rights and Justice Committee of the Legislative Assembly. A poster of death squad founder Major Roberto D'Aubuisson was proudly displayed over his desk. This was not surprising, especially given that similar pictures were placed throughout ARENA's floor of the Assembly building. Rather than responding to my questions, Perez lectured me about how Archbishop Romero was a Communist and the guerrillas killed him because he was worth more to them as a martyr. He blamed the Truth Commission's finding that his hero D'Aubuisson had ordered the priest's death on the nefarious influence of the U.S. Congress, the U.S. State Department, and the United Nations. He then went on to tell me, "over eighty thousand Salvadorans died here. And who created this situation? It was the Jesuits. They were the ones who directed this civil war" (Pérez 2000). These were, of course, the same accusations that the military broadcast just before the 1989 massacre at the Central American University (UCA). Pérez's approval of these past freedom of expression violations has made it hard for me to believe that he would protect this right in the postwar era.

It would be a mistake, however, for the reader to dismiss Pérez's remarks as those of an isolated individual. By appointing someone so overtly hostile to human rights to represent it on such a committee, ARENA has revealed much about its own attitude toward human rights. The mid 1990s saw a shift in the balance of power within the party away from Cristiani's so-called "moderate" wing toward the "old guard, composed of people close to party [founder and] godfather Roberto D'Aubuisson" (Spence et al. 1997, p. 22). One member of the old guard— Armando Calderón Sol—became President of the nation in 1994. He raised serious questions about his willingness to comply with the peace accords when he reportedly stated, "Cristiani signed the accords, I didn't" (quoted in Montgomery 1995, p. 255).

A large component of ARENA's relatively successful electoral strategy in the postwar era has been instilling fear of the consequences of voting for the party's opponents. The editors of *Estudios Centroamericanos (ECA)* have observed, "ARENA's [1997] electoral propaganda reinforces the existing fear in a population that always lives in the grip of traumas caused by a long and cruel civil war. The images and language ... are aimed at terrifying the electorate even more" (Editorial 1997b, p. 16). The editors also argued that such verbal aggression contributed to the physical violence that resulted in over a dozen deaths during the campaign season. Even during the 2004 presidential election, the party continued to rally its voters around its historic theme of burying the communists.

It is also important to point out that high-ranking military officers have expressed disagreement with the new military doctrine, which limits the role of the Armed Forces to that of protecting national security from external threats. Colonel Vaquerano, the head of the Military Doctrine and Education Command, defined National Security to include defense against "threats from its very interior" (Vaquerano 1995, p. 30). By making this statement, the colonel clearly violated the spirit of the new military doctrine contained in the peace accords, which eliminated the Armed Forces' role in internal security. His statement also raises the concern that the military may once again interpret dissenting expression as one of the internal threats to the nation. This would be extremely dangerous, of course, because previous Salvadoran governments have used such interpretations to justify eliminating their opponents.

Laws Allowing the Arbitrary Restriction of Expression

Like many other countries in the region, El Salvador has a contempt law. "Persons who offend the honor or decorum of a public official in the performance of his official duties or by reason of those duties" can be imprisoned for six months to four years under Article 339 of the criminal code. The law also stipulates that the maximum sentence is reserved for those who offend high ranking officials such as the President and the Vice President (Inter-American Commission on Human Rights 1999a).

The Inter-American Commission on Human Rights has condemned laws such as this which "limit the expression of ideas" and serve to silence "unpopular ideas and opinions." The same institution also objects to the fact that such laws serve to make public officials less subject to criticism than are ordinary citizens (Inter-American Commission on Human Rights 1999a). According to the Rapporteur for Freedom of Expression, contempt laws produce "a chilling effect" on freedom of expression, even if they are rarely enforced (Cantón 2001).

The National Civilian Police (PNC) clearly demonstrated the threat that such laws pose to freedom of expression when police agents arrested *CoLatino* Director Francisco Elias Valencia in 1996. The police charged the journalist with offending PNC Deputy Commissioner González Garciaguirre by publishing an exposé accusing the official of corruption. González Garciaguirre offered to drop the charges if Valencia would apologize and reveal the newspaper's sources within the police force (CL, 13 July 1996). Complicating matters further, the PNC refused to allow access to the files that could be used to prove that González Garciaguirre was indeed disciplined because of corruption. Journalists throughout the country cried out against the arrest. The Journalists' Association of El Salvador (APES) referred to the incident as a "flagrant violation of freedom of expression" and an attempt "to violently cut off the press's oversight role" (PG, 13 July 1996).[2]

These laws also enable Salvadoran officials to provide themselves with impunity by denying access to what should be public information. In fact, the Committee to Protect Journalists (CPJ) identified this problem as "the number one worry of journalists in El Salvador" (CPJ 2000). This statement is consistent with my own research. Almost all of the journalists I interviewed told me that the lack of legal guarantees for freedom of information was one of the most serious obstacles to their work. Channel 12 News Director Mauricio Funes, for example, complained, "there are still government officials who consider their official work to be a private concern. They refuse to respond to questions from the press. They keep their files secret" (Funes 2000).

Such restrictions on access to information also limit freedom of expression. According to the Inter-American Commission on Human Rights, "bad government needs secrecy to survive" because "information allows people to scrutinize the actions of a government and is the basis for a proper, informed debate of those actions." Without such information, journalists and opposition groups cannot effectively perform the necessary oversight to ensure that state actors obey the law. The Inter-American Commission on Human Rights has also established norms regarding the conditions in which governments may be allowed to keep information secret: restrictions must be based upon legitimate public goals according to the law; release of the information must threaten to cause substantial damage to those goals; and the damage must be greater than the public benefits of releasing the information. The Commission has specifically prohibited "restrictions intended to protect governments from embarrassment or the exposure of wrongdoing" (Inter-American Commission on Human Rights 1999b).

The Salvadoran public needs access to information about the Armed Forces because of the military's role in human rights abuses throughout the nation's history. In 1993, Defense Minister Corado responded to a question regarding the number of troops in the armed forces by stating, "that information cannot be given in public." He even told the press that he would not give this information to the Legislative Assembly (DH, 21 Oct. 1993). Yet this information was vital with regard to the provisions of the peace accords relating to troop reductions. Without this information, Salvadorans could not effectively debate the issue of whether or not the military leadership had complied with its obligations under the accords.

The new civilian police force has also been reluctant to allow access to information. Gustavo Palmieri of the Foundation for the Study of the Application of Law (FESPAD) has written, "There is still no clear institutional position with regard to the publicity of a large part of the information from the PNC.... Many of the reports, studies, evaluations and statistics continue to be thought of as secrets" (Palmieri 1998, p. 324). An editorial cartoonist for *El Diario de Hoy* expressed the media's frustration with the PNC's attempts to control and limit information. His drawing showed a television with the image of a police agent holding his hands to block the camera. The caption reads, "Do not adjust your television. This is not an interruption of the signal, but of the information" (DH, 27 June 1996).

Article 272 of the criminal procedures code—known as the gag law (*ley mordaza*)—also serves as a barrier to expression by giving judges excessive discretion to declare a case in reserve, i.e., to exclude the media and the public from the trial. The CPJ has found that judges frequently use this power (Smeets 2000b, 2000a). The rationale behind this law is that judges must have the ability to limit press coverage in order to protect the right to the presumption of innocence. While there certainly are cases in which this becomes necessary, Salvadoran journalists believe that judges often invoke the law for other purposes. In fact, APES has argued that excessive secrecy in the courts also undermines the rights of the accused by preventing public scrutiny of judicial procedures (DH, 27 Sept. 1995).

It is important, however, to acknowledge the significant contribution to access to information by the Office of the Human Rights Counsel (PDDH). The institution's primary functions include disseminating relevant information from its investigations of human rights abuses, including the role of other state agencies in these violations. As indicated in subsequent chapters, the PDDH has provided the media with crucial information about topics such as retardation of justice, cover-ups, clandestine police structures, and witness protection. This was especially true during the tenure of Dr. Velásquez de Avilés, who told me, "one of my policies was precisely an open door policy with social communicators, on the understanding that the ability to be informed is a constitutional right of the citizenry" (Velásquez de Avilés 2000). Many of the journalists I interviewed confirmed this account. The availability of this information facilitated public discussion of these issues in the media.

Journalists did not receive a similar level of support, however, from the next Human Rights Counsel, Eduardo Peñate Polanco. APES President David Rivas served as the PDDH's Communications Director under Dr. Velásquez de Avilés. In 1998, however, he resigned precisely because the new Human Rights Counselor was restricting the media's access to information (CL, 31 Dec. 1998). Media professionals, such as Channel 33 News Director Narciso Castillo, lost their confidence in the PDDH as a source under Peñate Polanco (Castillo 2000b). Without this source of information about state activities, journalists could not effectively carry out the oversight functions which are critical for holding public officials accountable for abuses of power.

Violence as an Obstacle to Expression

Human rights abusers have continued to use threats of physical violence to hamper expression in postwar El Salvador. UCA Vice Rector Rodolfo Cardenal told me, "there are death threats constantly" (Cardenal 2000). Similarly, a source at the U.S. Embassy working on labor and human rights issues reported that he could not think of any of his contacts who had not received threats (U.S. Embassy labor source 2000). While such threats would have a chilling effect on freedom of expression in stable democracies such as the U.S., their impact is much stronger in a nation such as El Salvador, where most acts of physical violence continue to go unpunished.

Impunity has been an important factor in the continuation of these threats. In 1993, the United Nations Observer Mission in El Salvador (ONUSAL) reported that the Salvadoran government was failing to conduct "serious investigations into the death threats, and the result has been impunity for the perpetrators" (ONUSAL Human Rights Division 1993c, 89). In 1995, the (nongovernmental) Human Rights Commission of El Salvador (CDHES) found that the courts frequently refused even to take statements from threat victims whom the judges felt were not credible because the judges considered them to be "communists" or "guerrillas" (CDHES 1995, p. 16). In 2000, Cardenal complained of a vicious circle in which "threats are not investigated. They are considered something ordinary, common. This, then, allows the threats to continue" (Cardenal 2000). As we shall see in the coming chapters, Salvadorans who expressed themselves against impunity have frequently received such threats.

As discussed in Chapter Two, smear campaigns have the power of threats because the media and powerful political figures have slandered dissidents who would later be abducted or murdered. This is consistent with the PDDH's definition of a death threat as "the intentional action that, in an expressed or hidden manner, seeks to create the justified fear that the individual will suffer attacks against his life" (Rodríguez Cuadros 1997, p. 58). An example of such smear campaigns would be the frequent government charge that human rights advocates defend criminals and seek to undermine the nation's institutions (Amnesty International 2001b). FMLN leader Fabio Castillo has accused ARENA of using "verbal violence" during the 2000 elections. He blamed this "dirty campaign," in turn, for legitimizing the physical violence directed against FMLN members prior to the elections (Castillo 2000a). I have found no evidence of a single case where state officials or media professionals have been punished for endangering the lives of human rights advocates by slandering them in this manner.

Death squads have continued to impede freedom of expression during the postwar era. As discussed in Chapter Seven, these paramilitary organizations continued to murder opposition figures during the first several years following the end of the civil war. Even after the politically-motivated killings subsided in 1994, however, the death squads continued to terrorize Salvadorans into silence. In 1997, for example, the PDDH reported on the continued existence of paramilitary structures in the town of Zacatecoluca. It found that the family of Marta Elena Rosales Montenegro had been threatened by figures linked to the military since 1979. The report registered a total of one hundred fifty acts of intimidation against Rosales Montenegro alone. The PDDH investigation revealed that this particular death squad had continued threatening "many residents" in the area. The agency also faulted the PNC for not carrying out a sufficient investigation of Rosales Montenegro's complaints (Velásquez de Avilés 1997b, pp. 157–9).[3]

Death squads have also continued to threaten prominent individuals. In June 1996, the Roberto D'Aubuisson Nationalist Force issued death threats against fifteen public figures, including journalists and religious leaders, among others. The faceless group also denounced "the nefarious foreign press" in its communiqué. The death squad warned them that their "time has come to an end" because they "defame and discredit honorable individuals" (PG, 27 June 1996).

Postwar death squads have not limited their actions to threats and other forms of intimidation. In October 1996, for example, masked men attempted to kidnap Madeleine Lagadec Pro Human Rights Commission (CPDH-ML) staff member Eliezar Ambelis while he was traveling in the department of San Vicente. An anonymous caller warned the CPDH-ML's office, "your office has to disappear. Be careful" shortly after this incident. Ambelis had received a death threat in September which warned him, "We don't like you fucking about with your talks in the communities" (Amnesty International 1996b). It is therefore clear that the perpetrators were specifically targeting the right to freedom of expression in this case.

A leader of the CPDH-ML told me that this incident was far from unique. She stated that there have been many abductions or attempted abductions of nongovernmental organization (NGO) leaders. "The death squads still exist," she said, "but they do not act on the large scale as they used to" (Female CPDH-ML leader 2000).

It is very difficult, however, to estimate the true impact of death squad violence. As the president of the Committee of Family Members of Victims of Human Rights Violations in El Salvador (CODEFAM) explained, "you can express yourself about an event, but the security of your life is not guaranteed" because of the possibility of "a reprisal disguised as crime" (Mendoza Zamora 1999). This statement shows how a relatively small number of death squad attacks can have a chilling effect on freedom of expression.

Death squads have been closely related to another manifestation of impunity: espionage. In 1994, Human Rights Watch warned that files from the disbanded National Intelligence Department (DNI) were missing. The NGO compared this situation to that of 1979, when Roberto D'Aubuisson obtained copies of state intelligence files which were then used to identify targets for the death squads (Human Rights Watch/Americas 1994, p. 13).The following year, Mirna Perlera de Anaya of the CDHES claimed that the files were still under the control of figures associated with the DNI (Perla de Anaya 1995, p. 45). These files therefore constituted a serious threat to those individuals whom the DNI had labeled as subversives because they had dared to express themselves against human rights violations during the war.

Another cause for concern has been the military's continuing involvement in domestic intelligence activities, a very serious violation of the peace accords. In the summer of 1994, UN Secretary General Boutros-Ghali warned that active duty military personnel continued to conduct domestic espionage (Boutros-Ghali 1995k, pp. 577–8). A related problem concerns the transfer of military personnel into the new State Intelligence Agency (OIE). The government thus increased the likelihood that human rights violators would target dissidents for surveillance through its failure to prevent and correct these violations of the peace accords.

Phone tapping is illegal in El Salvador under any circumstances. Nevertheless, this practice has continued throughout the postwar era. In the midst of high profile death squad murders of FMLN leaders during the 1994 electoral period, telecommunications union leader Humberto Centeno revealed evidence of widespread phone tapping by the National Administration of Telecommunications (ANTEL), the government-owned phone company. He even presented secretly recorded conversations of figures such as FMLN presidential candidate Rubén Zamora, President Cristiani, and ARENA presidential candidate Armando Calderón Sol. Centeno also expressed his belief that the death squads were using this information to plan their attacks (Mejía 1994, p. 6; PG, 23 Oct. 1993). The fact that death squads might be listening in on any phone conversation obviously discourages people from discussing political issues via this medium. Indeed, Salvadorans could risk their lives by merely discussing their plans for the day over the telephone because death squads could intercept that information and use it to establish an ambush.

In 2000, Channel 12 owner Jorge Zedán brought the issue of electronic espionage back to public attention by complaining that his phone was tapped. *El Diario de Hoy* responded by launching its own investigation. The Legislative Assembly reacted to the newspaper's reports by holding hearings on the issue. The former Superintendent of Electricity and Telecommunications, Orlando de Sola, testified that he had seen the room in the Presidential House that the OIE used for phone tapping. He also indicated that the Telecom corporation was involved. Unknown assailants abducted Zedán and held him for five days while the hearings were being held. The victim decided not to file a complaint with the Attorney General's Office. To my knowledge, no one has been able to clearly establish the motive for this abduction (PG, 21 July 2000; Mejía 1994, p. 6; CPJ 2001; DH, 4 Nov. 2000). It is certainly possible, however, that Zedán's abductors decided to kidnap him on the basis of a tapped telephone conversation. They may also have used the information they gathered to identify a time and place where he would be vulnerable.

The hearings revealed that Zedan was far from the only person whose phone had been tapped. Others targets included the Office of the Attorney General, the Federation of Association and Independent Unions of El Salvador, the Salvadoran Bank Association, the home phone of *El Diario de Hoy* Director Lafitte Fernández, and the gay rights NGO Entre Amigos. Over two hundred phones had been tapped (IAPA 2001; DH, 8 June 2000). APES President David Rivas—who was also targeted by the espionage—argued that the phone taps were intended to limit freedom of the press. He also reported that he knew journalists who could not speak freely at work nor conduct interviews because of the spying (Rivas 2000).

Human rights abusers have used the impunity they enjoy to discourage witnesses from expressing themselves and cooperating with investigations. According to Narciso Castillo, "This is a nation without witnesses. There are never witnesses. Every Salvadoran knows that what he should say is 'I don't know anything.' The first thing that they say to you, 'I did not see anything, I don't know,' because they are afraid. Many witnesses in court cases have died here" (Castillo 2000b). While this is a slight exaggeration—the following chapters will discuss the crucial role of some very brave Salvadorans who refused to remain silent—it is nonetheless very close to the truth.

This lack of witnesses is not simply a cultural legacy of the war. Rather, it reflects the reality of impunity in postwar El Salvador. According to one reporter, "I believe the witness protection program in El Salvador exists in name only" (Two TCS reporters 2000). Even Supreme Court of Justice Magistrate Anita Calderón de Buitrago acknowledged, "we don't have enough economic resources to protect those individuals." "Protection," she continued, "is not only having a police agent at the door of the witness's house or accompaniment by a guard during the trial. Because something could happen after the trial" (Calderón de Buitrago 2000).

Furthermore, there have been serious flaws in the witness protection mechanisms that do exist. The PNC's Division for the Protection of Important Persons (PPI) is composed of bodyguards who do not receive training in the police academy (Stanley 1996b, p. 21). As discussed in Chapter Nine, PPI bodyguards have taken part in the intimidation of the witnesses they are supposed to protect. Even when this is not the case, the witness's willingness to trust police for protection has been undermined when threats have come from other police units (Meléndez 2000). During the investigation of the murder of radio announcer Lorena Saravia, for example, a key witness who had information on procedural fraud committed by the police investigators fled the nation after receiving threats from other police agents (PG, 28 May 1998). Without credible protection, it is very understandable that relatively few Salvadorans have been willing to risk expressing themselves against powerful wrongdoers.

Salvadorans who take an active role in the pursuit of justice for abuses against their relatives have faced similar obstacles. As a human rights activist explained, "the people that decide to complain know that they are risking their lives. Out of one hundred cases, two or three individuals decide to do so" (Male CPDH-ML leader 2000). Those that do speak out tend to be from more affluent backgrounds than the majority of Salvadorans. Paulita Pike, the president of the Association of Victims of Human Rights Violations of El Salvador (AVIOLESAL), told me, "you have to be willing to get death threats. Everybody in this group has had death threats. Everybody in this group has had bodyguards" (Pike 2000). Her group includes Salvadorans such as the García Prietos and the Vilanovas, families who are much better off than most Salvadorans. As a result, they are able to pay for security measures which would be prohibitively expensive for most Salvadorans.

Witnesses and victims' relatives must also evaluate these risks associated with expressing themselves in relation to their perception of the likelihood that state institutions would function properly and achieve results. In a 1998 survey, for example, 50.7% of those respondents who did not report crimes explained that they did not believe that the authorities would do anything. Indeed, 57% of subjects who did report crimes stated that the authorities had not done anything, while only 16.5% of the same group were satisfied with the authorities' actions (IUDOP 1998a, pp. 794–5). This has resulted in a vicious circle in which impunity has bred distrust in state institutions, which has then led to further impunity.

Many of the media's sources have also been affected by fear and impunity. As one journalist explained, "when it concerns a delicate case," the source "becomes a target for any type of intimidation or any kind of attack" (Arguda 2000). An investigative reporter who has worked on such cases as the Vilanova and Saravia murders told me that fear has affected her sources "most of the time" (Currlin 2000).

Media sources have faced threats and reprisals even when responsible journalists have not identified them in their reports because they may be forced to do so at a later time. In February 1998, the Legislation Committee in the Assembly shelved a proposed reform of the criminal process code that would have explicitly guaranteed that journalists could not be forced to reveal their sources, after giving it only fifteen minutes of consideration (EM, 13 June 1998). As a result, journalists I interviewed in 2000 were still worried that they might be forced to reveal their sources (Driotes 2000; Flores Allende 2000).

Journalists themselves have also suffered from the impact of impunity. A television reporter explained to me, "there are no precedents for respecting the work of journalists when their rights have been violated. Things always go only as far as the authorities want them to go" (Female reporter from Canal 33 2000). In the fall of 1999, a well-known journalist from this reporter's television station, José Solórzano, discovered that the brakes on his car had been cut after his interview with Hilda Jiménez, the mother of Katya Miranda, a young girl who was raped and murdered while staying at the beach compound of her influential family.[4] A suspicious black vehicle with black windows had been following Solórzano when he discovered the problem. His boss, Narciso Castillo, speculated that the attack was meant to "terrify" the journalist rather than kill him (DH, 31 Oct. 1999). Opposition groups, including the FMLN, have also been accused of threatening reporters (see APES 2002).

Journalists have also suffered attacks while in the field. In 1996, for example, riot police brutally beat a Channel 12 cameraman while he was covering a disturbance caused by demobilized civil patrol members (PG, 18 Oct. 1996). Riot police shot *El Mundo* photographer Walter Santos López with rubber bullets at close range while he was covering a confrontation between the police and striking health workers in March 2000. Santos López was with photographers from other papers and was clearly identified as a journalist at the time of the attack. The Office of the Human Rights Counsel (PDDH) report on this incident recalled that a demonstrator had been killed by rubber bullets under similar circumstances in the past (PDDH 2000). By hampering the freedom of journalists covering such events, the police have also violated the protesters' right to expression because they depend upon media coverage in order to reach wider audiences.

Human rights violators do not need to physically attack reporters, however, to create self-censorship in the media. Channel 12 News Director Mauricio Funes has explained, "journalism has not gotten very involved in attempts to dig into the secrets of power and find human rights violators." "That is why," he continued, "there have not been so many reprisals" (Funes 2000). The restrictions on freedom of expression therefore go beyond the visible violence directed against individuals who dare to speak out.

Salvadoran authorities have also used excessive violence against demonstrators. The PDDH found, for example, that police leaders caused a March 2000 confrontation between striking healthcare workers and riot police, despite the fact that the protest leaders had already agreed to disperse. Furthermore, the PDDH classified the police's actions against the strikers as "a disproportionate use of force" (PDDH 2000). The police have also justified the use of violence on the basis of a 1995 law that allows them to arrest any demonstrator who comes within four meters of the police line. Unionists have claimed that police agents have intentionally moved closer to the demonstrators in order to use this provision to provoke violence (PG, 3 Feb. 1995: 28; Berríos et al. 1999).

Salvadoran law has encouraged this type of police repression by giving labor courts broad discretionary power to declare strikes illegal. As a result, judges have ruled that very few—if any—strikes were legal in postwar El Salvador. Once a judge rules that a strike is illegal, the government has justification to send in the Unit for Maintaining Order (Silva 2000; William 2000; Fundación Friedrich Ebert Stiftung 1994, p. 11).

The End of a Cycle?

As discussed in Chapter Two, Salvadoran history has seen a series of cycles of limited political openings followed by increased repression. Salvadorans have certainly pushed the opening that followed the 1992 peace accords far beyond that of any previous period of liberalization. Yet there have already been signs of regression during recent years.

The first major setback for freedom of expression was the election of Eduardo Peñate Polanco as the Human Rights Counsel in 1998. Both ARENA and the FMLN backed him initially despite the fact that he was facing charges and investigations by the Supreme Court of Justice, the National Judicial Council, and the PDDH itself regarding his performance as a judge (Villacorta Zuluaga 1998, p. 676). The FMLN attempted to withdraw its approval but did so too late. While Salvadorans had filed an average of 170.3 denunciations per month when Dr. Velásquez de Avilés was in office, they filed only 97 per month under Peñate Polanco. The office also issued fewer resolutions, from a monthly average of 85.5 under Dr. Velásquez de Avilés to a rate of 5.16 per month under Peñate Polanco (SAPRIN et al. 1999, pp. 143, 145). Peñate Polanco also came into conflict with his subordinates at the PDDH. This, in turn, led to the termination or resignation of many of the office's personnel, including Communications Director David Rivas; the Head of Economic, Social and Cultural Rights Office, Antonio Aguilar Martínez; and the Assistant Counsel for Women, Aracely Zamora (DH, 23 Apr. 1999; CL, 31 Dec. 1998).

It took a long, drawn-out fight to finally force Peñate Polanco to resign in January 2000. Many Salvadoran individuals and institutions engaged in heated criticism of the Human Rights Counsel throughout his stay in office. "If it were not for the press," Ruben Zamora explained, "Peñate Polanco would probably have finished his term in peace" (Zamora 2001). David Morales, the head of investigation at the PDDH, made a similar argument in which he credited "the civil society organizations, above all the NGOs" for pressuring the legislators to act (Morales 2000). Even ARENA Legislative Deputy Walter Araujo stated that his party opposed Peñate Polanco because of the Counsel's lack of credibility among human rights organizations (DH, 16 July 1999).

While the removal of Peñate Polanco from office was certainly an important victory, it was not sufficient to undo the damage to the PDDH. The Assembly was unable to agree upon a new Counsel until Peñate Polanco's term would have ended in the summer of 2001—almost a year and half after he resigned. The office remained in limbo with Assistant Counsel Valladares Melgar serving as acting Counsel until the Assembly appointed a successor. According to the U.S. State Department, the Salvadoran public has begun to regain its confidence in the PDDH since Dr. Beatrice Alamanni de Carrillo took office (U.S. Department of State 2002).

The election of President Francisco Flores (also from ARENA) in March 1999 has proven to be yet another setback for freedom of expression. Flores has moved to control and manipulate the media's coverage of his presidency. The Inter-American Press Association (IAPA) found that Flores would meet with only those journalists who agreed to a strict set of conditions. He required them to give advance notice of what questions will be asked, surrender their recording equipment during the meetings, and guarantee that almost everything remain off the record (IAPA 2000). These restrictions demonstrate a profound hostility toward freedom of expression and the media's role as public watchdogs.

There have also been increased signs of espionage directed against Salvadoran dissidents. As mentioned earlier in this chapter, there was a major scandal regarding phone tapping in the summer of 1999. A series of suspicious break-ins directed against the offices of human rights organizations began earlier that year. The intruders took records, membership lists, and computer files. The fact that they did not take easily accessible cash has demonstrated that these events were not the result of common crime. As of April 1999, intruders had broken into the Lutheran

Church's human rights office four times (Amnesty International 2001a; PDDH 1999a; CODEFAM 2000). According to the Solidarity and Exchange Center (CIS), NGOs suffered at least twenty such incidents during 1999 (Herzog 1999).[5]

The political space available in El Salvador has been shaped by various external factors, such as the U.S. government's support of the negotiations and the peace process. The international context changed dramatically, however, following the terrorist attacks on the World Trade Center and the Pentagon on September 11, 2001. While it is certainly true that the Bush Administration has not focused on El Salvador as part of its war on terrorism, the aftermath of the attacks has nonetheless had a negative impact on democratization there. The Salvadoran government fired the security workers at the nation's main airport and replaced them with a mixture of police and military troops. The soldiers involved have included members of the special forces, the Military Police and the Border Agents (DH, 12 Oct. 2001). As will be discussed in Chapter Six, the Military Police is the renamed Treasury Police and the Border Agents are the renamed National Guard. Both of these institutions had important links with the death squads during the war. Another troubling sign came in 2003, when ARENA's Vice President of Ideology, Mario Acosta Oertel, told *El Diario de Hoy* that the FMLN was "a branch of the axis of evil"—a reference to President Bush's label for Iraq, Iran, and North Korea (DH, 9 May 2003).[6]

Implications for the Impact of Expression

The political opening during the postwar period has certainly gone far beyond any previous period of liberalization in Salvadoran history. Nonetheless, Salvadorans have been faced with significant obstacles to using freedom of expression to protect other human rights. The government has continued to foster impunity. Those who violated human rights during the war were protected from prosecution by two amnesty laws. Human rights violators have continued using violence in the form of threats and physical attacks against witnesses, victims' relatives, and the media. As a result, only those Salvadorans who have been willing to risk their lives have spoken out against continuing human rights abuses and impunity during the postwar era. When evaluating the impact of freedom of expression on the protection of other human rights, we must keep in mind that the majority of Salvadorans have been unable to express themselves about human rights abuses.

As discussed in Chapter Two, impunity was not the only factor which prevented Salvadorans from exercising their right to freedom of expression prior to the 1992 peace accords. The dominant media have traditionally limited freedom of expression through their pro-government bias and their hostile attitude toward human rights. Chapter Four examines the degree to which they continued to do so in the postwar era.

4

The Dominant Media Continue to Hinder Freedom of Expression

There have been important improvements in the Salvadoran media as the papers and television news shows opened themselves up to previously excluded groups and individuals. The fact that many groups—particularly human rights organizations, unions, and poor communities—remain excluded, however, has hindered freedom of expression. Despite attempts to establish alternative media outlets, the industry has remained concentrated in the hands of the same right-wing figures who owned it during the war. A new generation of journalists has begun uncovering important human rights stories, but many have had to continue censoring themselves according to the political affiliations and economic interests of their employers. The 1999 Journalists' Association of El Salvador (APES) ethics code has yet to have a noticeable impact on the media's behavior.

The Postwar Opening Within the Media

As indicated in Chapter Two, a new generation of Salvadorans has made its presence felt in the postwar media. Around 1995, the average age of journalists working for *El Diario de Hoy* dropped by over twenty years. These young media professionals brought with them their formal training in the profession, in contrast to the "empéricos"—journalists without professional training—whom they replaced (Janus 1998, p. 15).

Some members of this new generation have won high praise for the quality of their work. Florentín Meléndez, for example, stated that these journalists have set "very important precedents in the area of investigation of human rights violations."[1] He emphasized, "areas that the media used to not investigate are now investigated" (Meléndez 2000). Similarly, former guerrilla radio director Carlos Henríquez Consalvi has remarked, "we have seen many cases of human rights violations after the war that have been resolved thanks to young journalists" (Consalvi 2000).

While many Salvadorans would agree that there has been important progress in the postwar media, others have maintained that statements such those above overestimate the actual progress. Channel 33 News Director Narciso Castillo, for example, recognized "an incredible difference" from the wartime media. "They are much more open," he continued, "but still not [open] enough" (Castillo 2000b). Some observers have suggested that the improvements in *El Diario de Hoy* have been the result of conflict within the National Republican Alliance (ARENA) rather than genuine openness. Furthermore, a report commissioned by the United States Agency for International Development (USAID) found that "investigative journalism has not developed at the rate expected" (Janus 1998, pp. 15–6, 7).

APES president David Rivas told me that he was forced to resign from his job at Megavisión in July 1999 because of conflicts with the news director. Rivas claimed that his superiors were attempting to tell him whom he could and could not interview. He also stated that management had been pressuring him to engage in sensationalism. He reported difficulty finding work because he had worked in the Office of the Human Rights Counsel during the tenure of Dr. Velásquez de Avilés and was thus perceived as a "leftist." While Rivas certainly recognized the important developments within Salvadoran media, he did not share the optimistic views discussed above. "It is not possible to say that we enjoy complete freedom of expression. We have to continue struggling so that these spaces truly open once and for all" (Rivas 2000).

The Highly Concentrated Structure of the Postwar Media

The postwar political opening has not resulted in a significant shift in the ownership of the media. Six years after the war ended, a USAID report found, "one man, Boris Esersky, virtually owns the television sector" through Telecorporación Salvadoreña (TCS).[2] This corporation also has interests in cable television, public relations, advertising, and magazines (Janus 1998, pp. 10, 17). This market position has given Esersky political leverage, which he has used, in turn, to further TCS's economic interests. One example of this influence was his ability to pressure the government into not privatizing state-run Channel 8, thus preventing the emergence of potential competitors. As a result, Rick Rockwell and Noreen Janus have commented, "the era of the media cacique [strongman] is still going strong" (Rockwell and Janus 1999, p. 129).

It is widely acknowledged that TCS's Cuatro Visión has been the most popular television newscast in El Salvador. It has achieved high ratings through its focus on blood and violence. This, in turn, has cost the program respect among most journalists. One reporter told me that he had turned down relatively high-paying offers from this program because working for it would damage his professional reputation (Arguda 2000). Nonetheless, the public has continued watching Cuatro Visión and other media outlets have engaged in sensationalism to compete with the news program.

In a sense, TCS is its own toughest competitor because each channel (2, 4, and 6) has a separate news division. There is also a TCS newscast which is broadcast simultaneously on all three of its stations. Together, the three TCS channels had 85% of the viewing audience in 1994 (Spence, Dye et al. 1994, p. 9). This figure has since risen above 90% (Janus 1998, p. 12).

TCS has been able to maintain its lock on the market through vertical integration. The corporation has removed its only serious competitors—Channel 12 and Channel 33—from its cable lineup. TCS has also used its strong presence in the advertising and public relations businesses to its advantage in order to deprive its competitors of revenue (Janus 1998, pp. 18, 21). This has put Channel 12 and Channel 33 in the vulnerable position of having to rely on advertising from the very government that they may wish to criticize. This is especially problematic because, as discussed below, the ARENA governments have withheld advertising to punish critical media outlets.

In sharp contrast to TCS, Channel 12 has continued to experience economic hardship. The situation improved somewhat when Mexican TV Azteca bought 75% of the station in 1997. The situation took a turn for the worse in June 2000, however, and Jorge Zedan admitted that Channel 12 had lost somewhere between two and three million colones ($230,000 to $343,000) that year. The situation deteriorated further when TV Azteca announced its intentions of selling the corporation's interests in the station (Janus 1998, p. 1; PG, 28 Apr. 2000; U.S. Embassy press source 2000). There have been rumors that TCS was interested in acquiring controlling interest in Channel 12. As of this writing, however, TV Azteca has not yet found a buyer.

The Salvadoran newspaper market is only marginally more diverse.

It has continued to be dominated by the same two dailies, *El Diario de Hoy* and *La Prensa Gráfica*. The families who established each paper continue to own them. Both papers have averaged a circulation of roughly one hundred thousand copies each (Janus 1998, p. 10). In comparison, *El Mundo* and *CoLatino* have had daily averages of roughly twenty thousand copies each. A fifth daily paper, *Más*, has appeared in recent years with an average circulation of about forty thousand (U.S. Embassy press source 2000).[3] This does not represent diversification, however, because *Más* is published by *El Diario de Hoy*. It is also important to point out that this paper has a reputation for being very sensationalist.

There are, of course, some small—very small—alternative media. *CoLatino* has continued publishing as an employee-owned business since 1989.[4] A USAID report found, "It often carries stories covered nowhere else." It has not, however, been able to expand its small circulation during the postwar era (Janus 1998, p. 11). Nor has the paper attracted significant advertising outside of its classified section. In fact, *CoLatino* has continued to provide opposition groups with free space for political announcements (Valencia 2000).

YSUCA—the radio station at the Central American University (UCA)—is another alternative media outlet that has survived in the postwar era. This station has specifically sought to include information and views from disadvantaged Salvadorans. It has even had a weekly human rights program. This station is quite unique, however, because its connection to the Jesuit university has given it some independence from the forces of the market.

Channel 33 is owned by another school, La Universidad Tecnológica. News Director Narciso Castillo told me that this relationship has allowed the all-news station to be more independent than other media outlets. Castillo has recognized, however, that serious limitations have persisted. "I could launch a stronger, more direct struggle for freedom of expression," he stated, "as *CoLatino* does, for example. But you [can] see what *CoLatino* is like" (Castillo 2000b). As discussed above, *CoLatino* has very little advertising revenue and reaches a relatively small audience.

The Difficulty of Creating New Media Outlets

Perhaps the power of TCS, *La Prensa Gráfica*, and *El Diario de Hoy* has been demonstrated best by the failed attempts to establish new media outlets. According to an USAID report, "the links between the media and the center of political power make it difficult to start a new media" (Janus 1998, p. 10). Foreign journalists who stayed on after the war tried to work with Salvadorans to create such a new voice, *Primera Plana*. This weekly newspaper began publishing in 1994 with financial assistance from international donors. The goal, however, was to make the paper self-sufficient and switch to a daily format. Hemisphere Initiatives praised the paper, stating that *Primera Plana* "did not shrink from criticizing, even burlesquing, political leaders, including leftists" (Spence et al. 1997, p. 13).

Primera Plana ceased publishing after nine months. Some observers have explained that the paper failed because it could not attract sufficient advertising revenue (Smeets 2000b). Its former business manager, Richard Paulo Luers, told me that the real problem was that the paper's management could not convince any local investors to put their money into the project. The reason he gave me for this, in turn, sounded like something out of a Hollywood gangster movie:

> People talk a lot about free competition. It doesn't exist very much in this country. It's all in the realm of two most important business interests and two or three competing families. Everybody respects each other's turf. For example, one of the guys who owns one of the TV companies said he really tried to get people in touch with us to invest in our newspaper. But he said, "I can't do it [myself] because if I do, the owners of the newspapers are going to put on [another] TV channel to fuck me. So I can't fuck with them because then they'll fuck with me" [Luers 2000].

It is important to recognize, however, that *Primera Plana* did make some crucial contributions to the development of the Salvadoran media during its short existence. Luers explained that the paper's management intentionally hired young journalists straight from the universities. They did so because they wanted reporters who had not been submerged in the dominant media culture of the time. While these reporters were unable to continue working at *Primera Plana*, they were able to bring their valuable experience to other media outlets. Observers have also credited the paper with introducing investigative journalism in El Salvador (Luers 2000; Smeets 2000b).

Local activists began organizing community radio stations shortly before the war ended. They conceived of this movement as "an alternative to a radio culture that does not address their needs and problems." They wanted to create radio stations "without financial motives," but rather "aimed at promoting communication spaces, linked to a plural and democratic exercise of freedom of expression" (Velásquez de Avilés 1996a, p. 9). The stations' activities included human rights campaigns (Pérez and Ayala Ramírez 1997, p. 67).

Despite these modest and positive goals, both the ARENA government and the dominant forces within the media industry opposed the community stations. According to APES president David Rivas, the problem was that the government considered them to be leftists aligned with the Farabundo Martí National Liberation Front (FMLN). A Freudian slip by National Administration of Telecommunications (ANTEL) President Juan José Domenech during a television interview supports Rivas's account. "The radio stations," he began, "who call themselves Communists, communi—uh, community, according to ANTEL, they are totally outside of the law" (Bollerslev 1996, p. 16). The community stations also came into conflict with the economic interests of commercial radio.

The radio stations affiliated with the Association of Participatory Radio and Programs of El Salvador (ARPAS) and the COMUNICA Foundation formally applied for FM frequencies from ANTEL. Human Rights Counsel Velásquez de Avilés found that the state agency's responses were neither timely nor satisfactory. Frustrated by the delay, the stations then began illegal trial transmissions. In August 1995, ANTEL announced that it was technically unfeasible to assign frequencies for the radios and began legal proceedings against several of them (Velásquez de Avilés 1996a, pp. 4–5). In December, ANTEL closed the stations, confiscated their equipment, and imposed fines. It carried out most of these actions without legal search warrants. The authorities used violence against at least one group which resisted (Pérez and Ayala Ramírez 1997, p. 73).

The community radio stations achieved a partial victory when the Supreme Court of Justice found that the seizures had been illegal and ordered ANTEL to return the equipment. At the same time, the court ordered the radios to cease broadcasting until they obtained licenses. Ten out of eleven stations were unwilling to wait and resumed transmissions (U.S. Department of State 1997).

The radios suffered a further setback with the approval of the 1996 telecommunications law, which ARENA passed without any votes from the opposition parties. The National Conciliation Party and the Christian Democrats claimed that the commercial media had attempted to buy their votes with promises of free air time (Pérez and Ayala Ramírez 1997, p. 75; DH, 8 Nov. 1997). The law established that the government would assign frequencies to the highest bidder. YSUCA director Ayala Ramírez complained that the new law did not recognize the category of nonprofit media organizations. He also argued that it would continue to protect the media monopolies (Ayala Ramírez 1997b, p. 50; 1997a, p. 27; Pérez and Ayala Ramírez 1997, p. 76).

In 1996, a technical committee set up to resolve the problem found that there was enough space for the radios within the FM spectrum (Pérez and Ayala Ramírez 1997, p. 75). The Office of the Human Rights Counsel (PDDH) also found that there were frequencies available for the community stations (Velásquez de Avilés 1996a, p. 6). The following year, however, the Christian Democrats, ARENA and the National Conciliation Party approved reforms to the telecommunication law, establishing that there would be a 400 MHz separation between FM stations, thus decreasing the possibilities of finding space for the radios on the FM dial. ARPAS charged that the media oligopoly was behind the changes (Pérez and Ayala Ramírez 1997, p. 81).

As of 2000, there were over twenty community radio stations associated with ARPAS, although some of them had not resolved their legal status. Those stations that have achieved legal permission to broadcast have done so through the purchase of frequencies rather than through legislative reform. As a result, the stations have had to operate more like commercial radios (ARPAS leader 2000; Ayala Ramírez 2000).

Self-Censorship Within the Media

Since the end of the war, the government no longer directly censors the media. This does not mean, however, that there is no longer any form of censorship. Many journalists openly told me that there was still censorship within the media itself. Journalists have sometimes censored themselves because of the political position of their employers. Quite often, however, they have censored their own work in order to avoid reprisals from advertisers, including private industries, government entities, and political parties. It is difficult for outside observers to see self-censorship, however, because journalists usually censor themselves without any overt pressure. In other words, Salvadoran journalists have been aware what topics they should avoid. The power of advertisers has been very clear in El Salvador, however, because of the negative impact that they have had on the more open media outlets.

Most Salvadorans I interviewed indicated that there was self-censorship within the media. More specifically, thirteen of the fourteen reporters I spoke with mentioned self-censorship as a barrier within the profession. Even some of the news directors acknowledged the existence of this practice.

Only one news director explicitly told me that self-censorship was not a serious problem. Julio Rank of *El Noticiero* (a TCS newscast) explained that even if one media outlet succumbed to pressure to limit coverage from its sponsors, its competitors would publish the information (Rank 2000). I must point out that I would probably have heard similar arguments if I had had the opportunity to interview more news directors from the large, mainstream media outlets.[5]

It would be wrong to ignore the important progress within the media since the war ended. According to APES President David Rivas, "there is more objectivity. The journalists give more space to the left. They give more space to the right. There is more debate. There is more dialogue and more discussion." He also pointed out, however, that the sponsors have continued to set the media agenda according to their interests (Rivas 2000). Similarly, one reporter praised *El Diario de Hoy*'s investigative work on issues such as a scandal regarding cesarean births at the public hospitals. The same journalist still recognized, however, that the paper has continued to support the dominant sector of society.[6] One reporter from a media outlet strongly associated with the far right said that her superiors kept their politics to the editorials and did not interfere in her work. Nonetheless, the same respondent later stated that reporters are pressured to censor themselves.

The theory that free competition creates disincentives for self-censorship does not fit the reality of El Salvador because of the high degree of concentration of ownership within the industry. An editorialist for *El Diario de Hoy* gave TCS the nickname "Tele Censura" because of the important issues it has failed to investigate. TCS has been able to do so without worrying about the competition because of its ability to channel revenue to its stations through its own advertising subsidiary (Janus 1998, p. 21, 23)[7]. In other words, free competition does not truly exist in El Salvador.

One source of self-censorship has been the political affiliation of the media owners and directors. As David Rivas explained, "Why do the media censor themselves? Because the owners of the principal media in El Salvador have organic ties to the governing party, ARENA" (Rivas 2000). Even a right-wing deputy and former military officer admitted that "big capital" has not allowed certain issues to be aired (Almendáriz Rivas 2000).

A blatant example of the limits that media owners impose on their journalists took place after the elections in March 2000. *El Diario de Hoy* removed Juan José Dalton from the paper's editorial board because he wrote an article criticizing ARENA. He then resigned from the paper altogether (CPJ 2001). The case of Dalton is unique simply because most Salvadoran journalists know better than to contradict the political position of their employers.

Another important source of self-censorship relates more directly to the argument that competition prevents censorship. What is the most important form of competition between the media? The obvious answer is that they compete for profits, which in turn come mainly from advertising revenue. Rather than promoting openness, however, sponsors actually encourage self-censorship. Janus has reported that the journalists she interviewed identified the role of advertisers as the most important barrier to expression (Janus 1998, p. 21).

The journalists I interviewed expressed similar beliefs. One reporter explained, "there is a tendency in the press in general to favor the government and institutions that violate human rights (private enterprise, for example). When a media outlet is very suspicious, it runs the risk of the advertising being suspended." Channel 33 News Director Narciso Castillo explained that private industry has used this capability to influence media coverage to favor ARENA because "all of the business owners are from ARENA" (Castillo 2000b). Even the national editor at *La Prensa Gráfica* complained that the media industry has placed profits over the duty to inform the public (PG, 26 July 1998).

El Diario de Hoy appeared to violate this rule when it broke the phone tapping scandal in the summer of 2000 (see Chapter Three). The Committee to Protect Journalists (CPJ) referred to this as "a daring move in a country where advertisers are normally off limits." Telecom—the phone company implicated in the scandal—reaffirmed the rule, however, by pulling its advertising from the paper (CPJ 2001). This was especially significant because the company was the paper's third most important sponsor (IAPA 2001).

Advertisers do not usually need to flex their muscle in such a blatant manner, however. According to Narciso Castillo, roughly twenty media outlets sent reporters to the Legislative Assembly when fifty pilots were denouncing labor abuses by the airline TACA. Yet only two media outlets actually reported on this issue. "Why didn't the others release the information?" he asked rhetorically. "Because," he answered, "TACA is their sponsor" (Castillo 2000b).

Private businesses are not the only sponsors who have sought to control the content of the media. The government has also used this tool to indirectly censor news coverage. This is very important given that the state is one of the main advertising clients in the nation (Rivas 2000). Government entities place public service announcements, statements on current events (strikes, demonstrations, legislation, etc.), and thinly disguised propaganda for the ruling party. Channel 12 News Director Mauricio Funes has explained, "If a [news] program allows the broadcast of information denouncing human rights violations, abuses of public power, the arbitrary use of power, or impunity ... it is always possible to use the instrument of pressure or blackmail that continues with this policy of withdrawing the [public] advertising investment" (Funes 2000). According to a representative of Radio Doble C, "there is fear of being against the government" because "they tie up the purse" (DH, 16 Aug. 1996). It is important to point out that Salvadoran President Armando Calderón Sol signed the Declaration of Chapúltepec in July 1994. By doing so, he explicitly acknowledged "the granting or withdrawal of government advertising may not be used to reward or punish the media or individual journalists."[8] Yet his government continued to do so.

Political parties have also used their advertising budgets to reward and punish the media. The public became aware of one such instance during the 2000 electoral campaign. Channel 33 published a survey by the Universidad Tecnológica (its owner) showing that the FMLN was ahead of ARENA. According to the station's news director, Narciso Castillo, ARENA promptly withdrew its advertising from the station (Castillo 2000b). ARENA has had extra leverage when using this threat because the ruling party has had the largest advertising budget. During the 1994 elections, ARENA spent roughly $250,000 for television spots on channels 2, 4, 6, 12, and 21. The next largest advertising budget was that of the Christian Democratic Party, which spent about $132,000 on the same stations. In contrast, the FMLN/Democratic Convergence coalition spent only $57,000 (Spence, Dye et al. 1994, p. 10).

The ruling party has compounded this problem by misusing state resources for its own electoral ends. During the 1994 elections, the Salvadoran government spent almost $177,000 for television ads on channels 2, 4, 6, 12 and 21 (Spence, Dye et al. 1994, p. 10). ARENA has used these ads, in turn, as part of its campaign strategy by presenting the accomplishments of the incumbent. The government has even used the same images and slogans as ARENA's commercials, including the "thumbs up" sign of 1994. Spence and Vickers have pointed out that the government has contradicted its stated ideological commitment to freedom of the market through its saturation of the media; sometimes almost half of a program's ads have been part of the government's efforts to promote ARENA (Spence, Dye et al. 1994, p. 9; Spence and Vickers 1994, pp. 18–9; CIDAI 1999, p. 74). Taken together, ARENA and the government spent almost $428,000 for spots on channels 2, 4, 6, 12, and 21 during the 1994 campaign. This resulted in a roughly 7.5 to 1 spending advantage over the leftist coalition.

Some sources have reported that advertisers exercise their power to censor the news through phone calls to the media. According to APES President David Rivas, for example, "there are businessmen who simply pick up the telephone, call, and ask that information not be released." "There are still very powerful political sectors in the media," he explained, "that can influence the firing of a journalist. There are journalists who arrive at a media outlet and fear that the politician whom they have interviewed is going to call to demand [their dismissal]" (Rivas 2000).

In most cases of self-censorship, however, the advertisers have no need to make such phone calls. When I asked one reporter about threats from sponsors, she replied, "Maybe we don't get the threat. We know, for example, that we're going to do something that's going to involve a client of ours [and] we may not be allowed to get it out." Another reporter explained, "Perhaps if I have not had direct problems, it is because of the fact that one knows when to limit oneself." Even an article in *La Prensa Gráfica* reported that one journalist works in a media outlet where, "the censorship is so great that the press chiefs do not wait for the advertisers to call to stop information. Rather, they eliminate 'what is inappropriate' through their own initiative" (PG, 26 July 1998).

Perhaps some journalists would be willing to risk losing their jobs if they believed that they could find work elsewhere. A USAID report has indicated, however, that journalists fired by TCS have been blacklisted and therefore have been unable to find work in the field (Janus 1998, p. 18). One Salvadoran journalist claimed that the records of reporters who have covered sensitive topics such as death squads had been "stained" by such work. Other media outlets have therefore closed their doors to these reporters.

The impact of self-censorship can also be demonstrated by the record of what has happened to media outlets which have not censored themselves as much as their competitors. When I asked News Director Mauricio Funes about Channel 12's reputation as one of the freest media organizations, he replied, "I would not say that we are the freest or one of the freest media." "We are one of the few media," he continued, "under less control. Because saying that we are the freest means that there is a climate of freedom" (Funes 2000). Funes has recognized that Channel 12 is also under pressure from sponsors, but explained that the station's owners have promised not to give in. The station has paid a serious cost for such integrity. According to Funes, the reason why TV Azteca decided to sell its interests in Channel 12 was that "a media enterprise that does not make this kind of agreement with power is not so profitable" (Funes 2000). Within this context, only nonprofit media can afford to tell the truth. As demonstrated in the discussion of community radio stations, however, the dominant media and the Salvadoran government have sought to reduce or eliminate the nonprofit sector of the media industry.

Other relatively independent media outlets have also faced economic hardship. Channel 33 was forced to cut back its 24-hour news coverage to 6:00 A.M. to 10:00 P.M. and to make itself available for infomercials (Janus 1998, p. 13). *Tendencias* had to stop publishing for two months in 1998 (Turcios 1998). It went out of business sometime after I left El Salvador in March 2000. There is also, of course, the case of *CoLatino*. According to Valencia, the paper carried paying ads only one out of the first four days in February 2000 (Valencia 2000).

It is certainly true that the media practices self-censorship in many nations, including the U.S. (see Herman and Chomsky 1988, for example). The information given above, however, demonstrates that this phenomenon is particularly strong in El Salvador. As Channel 33 News

Director Narciso Castillo explained, "I am sure that the owners of the *New York Times* and the *Washington Post* also interfere. But here it is very much more evident. It is much stronger" (Castillo 2000b). A reporter working for a wire service also claimed that these pressures have more impact on the Salvadoran media than their international counterparts. "I believe," he stated, "that the people who work with the international media have more freedom, as has always been the case in this nation."

The Government Sets the Agenda

As indicated above, media professionals have produced some very important examples of investigative journalism in postwar El Salvador. These reports, however, have been the exceptions. The defunct newspaper *Primera Plana* represented an attempt to set an example of professional investigative journalism. According to the paper's business manager, the majority of the Salvadoran media in 2000 continued to have a "very strong understanding that, basically, news is what the government says." He went on to explain, "ninety percent of the legwork these poor little reporters do is go[ing] to press conferences and get[ting] official statements" (Luers 2000). The national editor at *La Prensa Gráfica* gave a similar description of the media in 1998. According to him, the majority of media gave their reporters a list of press conferences every morning. The result, he said, was that the sources rather than the journalists got to decide what was newsworthy (PG, 26 July 1998).

As a result, the media have not paid adequate attention to some important issues. According to the Foundation for the Study of the Application of the Law (FESPAD), "some types of events are generally published ... such as in the case of the death of police agents in confrontations, while others rarely become known, as in the case of [police] mistreatment, arbitrary arrests, torture in police facilities, etc." (FESPAD 1998, p. 19). One media critic has argued that important issues including human rights are not covered precisely because government officials and political parties do not give press conferences regarding these topics (Cantarero 1998). One government agency has given many conferences on this topic, of course, the Office of the Human Rights Counsel (PDDH). This was especially the case during the tenure of Dr. Velásquez de Avilés as Human Rights Counsel. As discussed below, however, the office's relationship with the media deteriorated under the leadership of Eduardo Peñate Polanco.

Limited Access to the Media

Access to the media is closely related to the issue of setting the media's agenda. The journalists' reliance upon official sources and information from government press conferences has led them to neglect other actors, such as unions and social movements. They have also favored middle and upper-class Salvadorans over the campesinos and urban poor, thus reaffirming that freedom of expression has remained a privilege rather than a universal right.

While the fact that media can publish the information that they choose is a crucial component of freedom of expression, it does not fully establish freedom of expression as a universal human right. Common Salvadorans need the media's assistance in order to amplify their voices so that they can reach a broad section of the population. These Salvadorans can draw upon other mechanisms of expression, such as strikes and protests. Yet relatively few of their fellow citizens will be aware of these events without adequate media coverage. Nor will most Salvadorans understand the reasons behind these activities if the media do not include this information in their coverage.

This means that freedom of the press—a component of freedom of expression—brings with it the obligation to facilitate the free expression of other members of society. The PDDH's manual for classifying human rights violations is very clear on this issue, stating, "freedom of expression requires that the media be virtually open to all without discrimination, or, more exactly, that there not be individuals or groups who, a priori, are excluded from access to such media (Rodríguez Cuadros 1997, p. 184). Article 13 of the APES ethics code also stipulates that journalists have a duty to "avoid excluding individuals, organizations, and any other source that deserves to be taken into account" (APES 1999, p. 6).

Previously excluded groups have certainly made progress in terms of media access during the postwar era. As many commentators have pointed out, even *El Diario de Hoy* contains statements from opposition politicians. Indeed, former FMLN comandante Salvador Samoyoa has written a weekly column in *La Prensa Gráfica*. While this opening is important, it is insufficient with regard to the criteria laid out by the PDDH and APES. Channel 12 News Director Mauricio Funes has argued that this opening has only gone halfway. He stated, "a systematic process of journalistic 'veto' continues to be observed against personalities who are not palatable for the owners of these media" (Funes 1995, p. 21). According to Funes, "what has changed with the signing of the peace [accords] is the content of the exclusion" in the media (Funes 1996, p. 20). One contributor to *Estudios Centroamericanos (ECA)* compared the appearance of former guerrillas such as Samoyoa to the Spanish Inquisition: "There has always been a place for the *conversos*[9] to practice their new faith" (Montonya 1997, p. 1016). In other words, the mainstream media have been willing to accept those leftists who have accepted the dominant paradigm.

Human rights organizations have had great difficulty gaining access to the media. According to Central American University (UCA) Rector José María Tojeira, "groups that do not have political connections, that aim to protect human rights are marginalized and left out by the big media" (Tojeira 2000). Nongovernmental organizations (NGOs) have indeed complained that the media has not been interested in their work. A founder of the Committee of Mothers and Family Members of Prisoners, the Disappeared and the Politically Assassinated (COMADRES) explained how her organization had repeatedly given press conferences without succeeding to draw media attention. She also claimed that the media corporations had policies against covering such conferences (de García 1999). Elmer Mendoza of the Committee of Family Members of Victims of Human Rights Violations in El Salvador (CODEFAM) reported having similar experiences. "*El Diario de Hoy* has never come to one of our press conferences," he explained. "*La Prensa Gráfica*," he continued, "may have come once or twice out of approximately twenty conferences. In terms of television, sometimes Channel 12, Channel 33, TCS—very few times (Mendoza Zamora 1999). Gloria Guzmán, one of the founders of the feminist organization Las DIGNAS, complained that even Channel 12 ignored the role of women's organizations during its review of 1999 (Guzmán 2000). The leader of one labor federation has also reported that the media has either distorted the organization's press releases or ignored them completely (Hernán Gutiérrez 1999). Without access to the media, groups such as these can only reach a very limited audience when they express themselves about human rights issues.

The dominant media outlets have also excluded specific individuals. According to APES President David Rivas, "there are still lists in some media organizations of individuals who do not have access to them. For example, Father José María Tojeira has never been on Telecorporación Salvadoreña's [interview] program *Frente a Frente*." "He has been on Channel 12," Rivas continued, "on Channel 33, but he has never been on Telecorporación Salvadoreña" (Rivas 2000).

Opposition groups have therefore had to continue to rely on paid ads in order to get their messages to the public. Yet the media has even discriminated against them in this area. According to Gilberto García of the Labor Studies Center, *El Diario de Hoy* charged double its normal rate for ads criticizing the government's handling of the health care strike in 2000 (García 2000). Some groups, such as the marginalized communities, have not been able to afford paid ads (Cuéllar 2000).

Media Bias and Misrepresentation

The dominant media outlets have continued to be associated with ARENA and the political right in general. In 1998, President Calderón Sol's communications secretary, Eduardo Torres, admitted that *El Diario de Hoy* and *La Prensa Gráfica* were biased in favor of the ruling party. "Both papers," he stated, "do not stray very far from our political project." He also explained, "both [papers] are identified with what is being done" by the government (DH, 31 May 1998). A USAID report came to a similar conclusion. The author stated, "in terms of ownership, content, and identity, they [the media] continue to be polarized, aligned primarily with the right." The same report found that *El Mundo* had moved further to the right when its original owners, the Borja family, regained control of the paper from stockholders (Janus 1998, pp. 10–1).[10]

There was a period during which new leadership moved *La Prensa Gráfica* toward greater independence. In 1993, *La Prensa Gráfica* replaced seventy percent of its editors, including the editor in chief. This change did not last, however, as the old leadership gradually regained power. These figures reversed much of the progress, going so far as to stop investigative journalism. Four of the paper's editors staged a strike in April 1998 to demand greater independence and a commitment to being the leading force in terms of quality within the media. The paper was willing to compromise over independence, but refused to give the strikers sufficient assurances that it would be committed to improving the quality of its reporting. The four editors resigned in protest and went to work for *El Diario de Hoy*. *La Prensa Gráfica* then hired Cecilia Gallardo de Cano as its new managing editor. This move did not bode well for the paper's political independence, given that she had been the Education Minister in the ARENA government when *La Prensa Gráfica* offered her the job. The political nature of this choice became even more apparent in light of the fact that she had no previous experience in journalism (Villacorta 1998, pp. 22–4; CL, 24 Apr. 1998).

Gallardo de Cano was far from the only former government official to work in the media. President Calderón Sol's communications secretary, Eduardo Torres, for example, became an editor at *El Diario de Hoy*. The revolving door has also moved in the opposite direction. One of the editors who left *La Prensa Gráfica*, Flavio Villacorta, became the head of the State Intelligence Organization (OIE) when President Francisco Flores took office in June 1999 (Smeets 2000b). Such close political ties between journalists and public officials create obvious problems with regard to the media's duty to inform the population about misdeeds within the government. The crossover between journalist and government officials also undermines the state's ability to provide equal protection for the rights of all media organizations.

The dominant news organizations have demonstrated that they have remained biased in favor of human rights violators through their coverage of well-documented events in Salvadoran history. In 1992, for example, *La Prensa Gráfica* reported that ARENA leader Calderón Sol praised Roberto D'Aubuisson "as one of those who contributed to the democratic process" (PG, 3 Feb. 1992). As William Gamson has pointed out, journalists frame news stories such as this through the information they include, as well as the facts which they leave out (Gamson 1989, p. 158). In this case, the reporter failed to mention D'Aubuisson's involvement in the assassination of Archbishop Romero and his leading role in organizing the death squads, facts which clearly undermine the presentation of D'Aubuisson as a democrat. This omission, in turn, benefits the political party D'Aubuisson founded, ARENA.

In March 1992, *El Diario de Hoy* published an article on the march commemorating the anniversary of Romero's death. However, the paper buried information regarding the purpose of the demonstration deep within the piece. Most of the article focused on complaints that the demonstration had blocked traffic. The paper did not even mention Romero in the headline. The reporter gave no indication that he or she had tried to get the demonstrators' side of the story. When the article finally mentioned the anniversary, it made a vague reference to "the death of Archbishop Oscar Romero" (DH, 25 Mar. 1992). This phrasing failed to provide the reader with any information about how Romero died or who killed him. He could have died of natural causes. Or he could have been murdered during a robbery. The television coverage by TCS and Teleprensa also failed to provide this information (TCS Noticias 1992; Teleprensa 1992).

Not all of the media's coverage was this biased, however. In 1993, Channel 12 clearly stated that the Truth Commission had linked D'Aubuisson to the assassination. It also showed footage of marchers shouting, "Who gave the order to murder Monseñor Romero?—D'Aubuisson!" (Al Día 1993c). As we have seen, however, advertisers have punished Channel 12 for mentioning information left out by the dominant media.

In 1995, *El Diario de Hoy* improved its coverage of the Romero anniversary somewhat. The paper reported he was "shot to death by unknown subjects" (DH, 25 Mar. 1995). *El Diario de Hoy* was nonetheless misleading its readers, given that Romero's killers were not unknown subjects. The Truth Commission had confirmed information that had already been widely known: D'Aubuisson ordered the killing. The Truth Commission had also named the trigger man. Both *El Diario de Hoy* and *La Prensa Gráfica* used similar phrasing to avoid the truth in their coverage of the twentieth anniversary of the assassination in March 2000 (DH, 24 Mar. 2000; DH 25 Mar. 2000; PG 25 Mar. 2000).

The two leading papers engaged in similar misrepresentation during their coverage of the 1989 massacre at the UCA. *La Prensa Gráfica* placed the headline "Accused soldiers sentenced to 30 years in prison" on an article regarding the sentencing of the two officers convicted of killing the six priests and two women. The paper reported, "a supposed military commando unit murdered the Jesuit fathers" (PG, 24 Jan. 1992). This phrasing was highly misleading, given that the news story is about the two officers whom a jury found guilty of the killings. About one year later, the same paper reported on the judicial hearings regarding the application of the 1993 amnesty to these soldiers. Once again, *La Prensa Gráfica* referred to these convicted criminals as "implicated" in the killings (PG, 1 Nov. 1993).

The dominant media also tried to divert attention away from the military figures who killed the Jesuits by implying that the FMLN was to blame for the massacre. In an article published in 2000, *El Diario de Hoy* placed the massacre in the context of the FMLN "unleashing the bloody 'offensive to the top' upon the civilian population." The paper quoted statements from Defense Minister Martínez Varela, who said he regretted the deaths but placed them "in the context of indiscriminate violence generated by the [FMLN's] ambition to reach power through arms" (DH, 8 Jan. 2000).[11] The paper was misleading the public, however, because the violence was not at all indiscriminate. The trial of this case, as well as the Truth Commission report, clearly demonstrated that the military leadership had developed a well-prepared plan for carrying out this massacre.

By focusing on the guerrilla offensive, the paper created the impression that those resisting the FMLN—the Armed Forces—were heroes. The reporter emphasized this suggestion through his or her claim that the guerrillas were attacking the civilian population. This is a serious misrepresentation given that the clear goal of the offensive was to attack the Salvadoran state. The reporter also frames the issue by failing to include the fact that it was actually the Salvadoran military that attacked the civilian population (see Chapter Two).

As in the coverage of the Romero assassination, the television news programs appeared to be less biased than the two dominant newspapers. TCS's *El Noticiero* on Channel 6, for example, actually quoted the Vice Rector of the UCA, Rodolfo Cardenal, during its coverage of the Truth Commission. He claimed, "the most important thing in the report is not the names, but rather that the report shows us that the Army, the Judicial System, the State as a whole failed to fulfill its constitutional mission." The report clearly stated that the Truth Commission had implicated six high-ranking military officers in the UCA massacre (El Noticiero 1993c).

There have been signs that the impact of dominant media's bias toward the government has increased in recent years. While ARENA maintained the presidency in 1999, it lost significant ground to the FMLN in the Assembly during the 1997 and 2000 elections. According to the Committee to Protect Journalists (CPJ), the right-wing media owners and managers have felt threatened by the left's advances and have responded by reasserting tighter control over their journalists (CPJ 2001). Rubén Zamora agreed that this was happening. "They are trying," he stated, "to prevent the possibility of an opposition or leftist victory" (Zamora 2001). This has created another major setback in the struggle for freedom of expression.

Professional Ethics and Yellow Journalism

Journalists need professional ethics in order to respect the rights of others while they collect and publish the information that the public needs. As discussed above, Salvadoran law does not explicitly recognize journalists' right to protect the identity of their sources. In the example of the defamation suit against Valencia, it would have been completely unethical for the *CoLatino* director to reveal his sources because doing so would have clearly endangered their jobs in the National Civilian Police (PNC). Many Salvadoran journalists still have incomplete knowledge of professional ethics, however. According to journalism Professor Guillermo Mejía, "professional ethics is still a taboo subject. It is not discussed as it should be" within the universities and the industry (Mejía 2000).

APES took an important step toward remedying this problem through the creation and publication of an ethics code in September 1999. The code covers issues such as distinguishing between fact and opinion, publishing only established information, respecting the privacy of others, and the presumption of innocence (APES 1999, pp. 6–8). This code is certainly useful in the sense that it provides a normative framework that journalists can have easy access to while they work. It is also useful as a tool to measure the media's performance in the rest of this study. There are no mechanisms, however, for enforcing the code. Indeed, there is evidence that media owners and management are quite hostile toward the ethics code. One journalist reported she has heard of media owners telling their employees, "Fine, you accept the ethics code today and tomorrow get out of here."[12] Channel 12 News Director Mauricio Funes explained, "It was vetoed by the media owners." He then added that journalists would probably be safer ignoring the code, "because there are always conflicts between ethics and profitability" (Funes 2000).

One manifestation of this conflict has been yellow journalism. Article 9 of the APES ethics code states, "the morbid description of violence should be avoided. The images of crimes or accidents should be made and broadcast with due consideration for the victims and their relatives" (APES 1999, p. 5). According to YSUCA Director Ayala Ramírez, "truth and objectivity in information remain subordinate to profitability and marketing" (Ayala Ramírez 1999, p. 932). Janus came to a similar conclusion, reporting, "the drive for increased profitability is associated with a trend toward greater commercialism in the media—more sensationalism and more dependence on the ratings" (Janus 1998, p. 24). The most-watched news program, TCS's Cuatro Visión, has also been the most sensationalistic. The television show has achieved high ratings through its focus on blood and violence.

The fact that journalists are not required to obey an ethics code means that they are free to express themselves without any obligations or duties besides those imposed by their employers and the market. Such freedom does not enhance the right to freedom of expression, however. As we have seen above, media owners and advertisers have placed substantial restrictions on news coverage. Journalists could potentially have greater freedom under an ethics code which legitimizes the commitment to truth and accuracy over loyalty to employers and the bottom line.

Media Barriers Undermine Human Rights Advocates

The Salvadoran media have made important improvements during this period, such as the beginning of investigative journalism and the use of greater diversity in sources. New media outlets such as *Primera Plana,* however, have not been able to establish themselves and to challenge the dominant news corporations. Nor have previously existing alternatives such as *CoLatino* and Channel 12 been able to grow strong enough to challenge *El Diario de Hoy* and TCS. While the government has not engaged in overt censorship, it has continued to punish critical media organizations by withholding ads. The media have also censored themselves in response to boycotts by private enterprise and political parties such as ARENA. While journalists have become more professional during this period, they have continued to allow official sources to set their agenda. They have also engaged in sensationalism for the sake of profit. The large media outlets have continued to be biased against the left in their coverage of human rights issues.

The remaining chapters of this project assess the impact of human rights advocates' attempts to use freedom of expression to protect other fundamental rights in postwar El Salvador. It is important to keep in mind the continued existence of barriers to freedom of expression within the media—as well as the impunity which individual human rights violators and repressive institutions continue to enjoy—when evaluating the impact of their efforts. The next two chapters examine the implementation, violation, and perversion of key human rights provisions of the 1992 peace accords: the identification and removal of human rights abusers from the military; the independent investigation of wartime violations; and the replacement of the repressive military security forces with a new civilian police force. Chapters Seven, Eight, and Nine then examine specific cases of human rights violations in the postwar era.

5

Dealing with Wartime
Human Rights Abuses

This chapter addresses most directly the debates over the role of citizen participation in democratization and over how governments should deal with those individuals and structures responsible for widespread human rights abuses during previous authoritarian periods. The cases examined in this chapter show that opposition groups within El Salvador obtained mixed results from their attempts to use the right to freedom of expression to end the impunity traditionally enjoyed by human rights violators. These groups were unable to block the government's passage of two amnesty laws in 1992 and 1993. They did succeed, however, in using expression to help the Ad Hoc Commission identify military officers to be removed from service for human rights violations. They also contributed to the Truth Commission's investigation of past atrocities. Salvadoran opposition groups also achieved partial success with their calls for compliance with the recommendations made by both commissions.

The National Republican Alliance (ARENA) government passed the 1992 amnesty law before the Ad Hoc Commission and the Truth Commission began their investigations. Salvadoran nongovernmental organizations (NGOs), religious organizations, and unions cried out against this legislation. They claimed that the government's stated rationale for this legislation—forgiving and forgetting past abuses—clearly went against the purpose of these commissions, which was to establish accountability. These groups were unable to prevent passage of the legislation.

Pro-rights forces in El Salvador did, however, have an important impact on the work done by the bodies created under the peace accords for the purpose of addressing wartime human rights abuses. Both the Ad Hoc Commission and the Truth Commission relied heavily on expression from witnesses, civil society organizations, and the media during their investigations. Despite the binding nature of the recommendations made by these commissions, the Salvadoran government resisted implementing them and did so only slowly—if at all. Indeed, President Cristiani failed to remove the highest ranking military officers identified as human rights violators by the Ad Hoc Commission until seven months after the deadline established in the peace accords. While we should not minimize the role of international diplomats who pressured the government to comply, we should also recognize that democratic forces in Salvadoran society helped bring about international pressure by exercising their freedom of expression. Opposition forces in El Salvador also used public expression to create domestic pressure for compliance, especially when they discovered that some Farabundo Martí National Liberation Front (FMLN) leaders were willing to allow human rights violators identified by the Ad Hoc Commission to retain their high-ranking positions within the Armed Forces. Those individuals and institutions that cooperated with the commissions and those that called for implementation of the resulting recommendations faced serious risks of retaliation. The dominant media further reduced pressure for compliance with the recommendations through its biased coverage of both commissions.

The ARENA government and its allies quickly followed the publication of the Truth Commission Report in March 1993 with a second, broader amnesty law designed to protect the human rights violators identified within the report. The opposition complained that such a measure should come only after the government had implemented the Truth Commission's recommendations. The government, however, worked to pass the legislation as soon as possible because the report linked ARENA to human rights abuses. It was able to do so because ARENA and its allies still controlled a majority in the Assembly. The large media outlets also supported the Cristiani Administration's position on this issue.

The 1992 Amnesty Law

The Ad Hoc Commission did not officially begin its evaluation of military officers until May 19, 1992. The Truth Commission was installed on July 13, 1992. In contrast, the government and its allies began efforts to pass an amnesty law even before the peace accords were signed. The Assembly approved the National Reconciliation Law on January 23, 1992—just a week after the official signing of the accords.

This legislation did not provide for a complete amnesty, however.

Article 6 of the law provided that it would not apply to "those individuals who, according to the Truth Commission, have participated in grave acts of violence." It also stated that those prisoners who had already been found guilty in court would not benefit from this law. This first amnesty law did, however, remove all criminal and civil liability for all individuals who did not fit into these two categories. The legislation further stipulated that the Assembly could revisit the issue of those cases not covered by this amnesty six months after the release of the Truth Commission Report (DH, 16 Mar. 1993).

Human rights NGOs objected that this amnesty would undermine the Truth Commission's investigation. The government justified the law by arguing that an amnesty was needed to forgive and forget. The NGOs argued that this rationale went against the very purpose of the Truth Commission—establishing the truth about past violations. They also objected to the fact that judges would be allowed to apply this amnesty prior to the publication of the Truth Commission Report. The NGOs questioned what would happen if the amnesty had already been applied to someone mentioned in the Report (CDHES et al. 1992, p. 304).

Despite these protests, the Assembly unanimously approved the first amnesty law. One reason why the human rights advocates' public denunciation failed to stop this amnesty was that the Democratic Convergence—the small leftist coalition that had taken part in the 1989 and 1991 elections—was on board from the beginning. Rubén Zamora—who would run for president on the FMLN/Democratic Convergence ticket in 1994—was actually one of the authors of the National Reconciliation Law (Asamblea Legislativa de El Salvador 1992, p. 184). In this sense, we may interpret the passage of this amnesty law as one of the inter-elite pacts advocated by scholars such as Huntington (see Huntington 1993, p. 169). In this case, opposition groups were not able to use their right to expression to block the formation of this pact.

We must also realize, however, that ARENA had wanted a complete, unconditional amnesty right away (PG, 22 Jan. 1992). Zamora and other leftist politicians therefore helped limit the scope of the amnesty through their willingness to participate in drafting this law. It is also important to remember that ARENA controlled both the Assembly and the Presidency at this time. Therefore, leftist politicians would not have been able to block the passage of a more encompassing amnesty if they had not traded their support in exchange for limitations.

While ARENA and its allies could have passed the amnesty in the Assembly without help from the media, they needed to justify their actions to the public in order to avoid being held accountable at the ballot box for protecting themselves from prosecution for their crimes. The dominant media helped shield the government from such a backlash through their biased coverage of the issue. The Truth Commission report eventually found that the state and its allies committed eighty-five percent of human rights violations during the war, while the FMLN was responsible for only five percent. Yet the major Salvadoran newspapers presented the first amnesty law as primarily benefiting the former guerrillas (PG, 24 Jan 1992; PG, 30 Jan. 1992). Meanwhile, the Central American University (UCA) had to purchase a paid ad in order to make its argument that the amnesty would benefit military figures who committed violations (UCA 1992a, p. 23). In this context, the government and its allies appeared to be generous peacemakers who were forgiving of the supposedly widespread violations committed by the FMLN. In reality, however, they were war criminals seeking to protect themselves from justice.

The Ad Hoc Commission's Evaluation of Military Officers

The Ad Hoc Commission was one of the central components of the peace accords' attempts to end impunity. The Cristiani Administration and the FMLN authorized this body to evaluate military officers in terms of respect for human rights. They also empowered the commission to make binding recommendations regarding the removal or transfer of officers it found unfit for continued service (Government of El Salvador and FMLN 1995c, p. 195). The removal of human rights violators from military command became even more crucial once the 1992 amnesty reduced the likelihood that they would ever face criminal prosecution. While war criminals would not be imprisoned, they would at least lose the privilege of continuing to command the state structures they had misused. This would then reduce—though certainly not eliminate—their ability to commit human rights violations in the future.

The Ad Hoc Commission had only three months to investigate over two thousand officers. This task became even more difficult because government agencies such as the Defense Ministry provided the commission with little relevant information (Spence et al. 1992, p. 10; Molina Olivares 2000). Without cooperation from state authorities, the Ad Hoc Commission turned to civil society for the information it needed.

I had the opportunity to ask Commission member Eduardo Molina Olivares about the importance of information provided by human rights groups. "It was important," he replied, "because they had data on the ground [about] the El Mozote case, Las Hojas, San Sebastián" and many other cases. Human rights groups also helped the Ad Hoc Commission communicate with Salvadorans who had witnessed these abuses. The commission also relied upon media coverage of human rights violations (Molina Olivares 2000).

The Ad Hoc Commission officially presented its report in September 1992. Given the time and data constraints, it was only able to evaluate roughly ten percent of all officers (Spence et al. 1992, p. 5). Without the assistance from civil society, however, the Ad Hoc Commission would have been able to evaluate far fewer military commanders than that. The government and the FMLN had agreed that the names of the officers identified in the document were supposed to be kept confidential. Nonetheless, the (nongovernmental) Human Rights Commission of El Salvador (CDHES) published a leaked list of names in its newsletter.

Given that all three members of the commission were Salvadorans, many observers had serious doubts that they would have the courage to recommend the removal of powerful officers. As Truth Commission member Thomas Buergenthal has explained, "There is strong evidence to suggest that the government and the military only agreed to the establishment of the Ad Hoc Commission because they were convinced that it would not dare to discharge its responsibility honestly. At most, they thought the Commission would call for the dismissal of a few low-ranking officers" (Buergenthal 1995, p. 304).

With help from civil society, however, the Ad Hoc Commission was able to go far beyond these expectations. It recommended the removal of eighty officers—including Colonels and Generals—and the transfer of forty others. (Farah 1992, p. 22; Spence et al. 1992, p. 3, 11). The commission paid a serious price for its willingness to challenge such powerful figures. Molina Olivares explained, "They accused me of being the head of the international Marxist conspiracy to do away with the Armed Forces" (Molina Olivares 2000). In this dangerous context, all three members of the Ad Hoc Commission had to spend time in exile (Al Día 1992c; Buergenthal 1995, p. 304).

The eighty officers it ordered removed from service represented only 3.5% of the officer corps, while those it ordered transferred constituted just 1.7% (Spence et al. 1992, pp. 3, 5, 10). Yet some observers saw the list of officers to be removed as a major step forward. According to UCA Vice Rector Rodolfo Cardenal, for example, "Quantitatively, the list of purged officers is not significant.... Nevertheless, the work of the three commissioners ... has profoundly impacted society and above all the military itself" (Cardenal 1992, p. 970). Legal expert Margaret Popkin has referred to the symbolic effect of the inclusion of the entire High Command on the list (Popkin 1993, p. 4). Without the information provided by human rights organizations and witnesses, the commission would have achieved far less.

The Government's Reluctance to Remove Violators from the Military

According to the peace accords, the government was supposed to remove the officers named by the Ad Hoc Commission within sixty days of receiving the group's report (Government of El Salvador and FMLN 1995c, p. 196). Given that the Ad Hoc Commission presented its report on September 22, 1992, this meant that the Cristiani Administration was obligated to implement the commission's recommendations by November 21st.

By the end of October, however, it became clear that this goal would not be met. The UN Secretary General sent representatives to El Salvador to discuss the delays. Following these talks, the Secretary General announced a new schedule—including delays in the demobilization of the FMLN's military forces—on November 6. On January 7, 1993, the Secretary General accepted the government's action regarding eighty-seven of the officers identified for removal, "even though a number of them do not conform in all respects with those recommendations." The Secretary General refused to accept Cristiani's decision to retain eight officers—including Defense Minister General René Emilio Ponce—until his presidential term expired in May 1994, however (Boutros-Ghali 1995c, p. 287; PG, 7 Jan. 1993).[1] The Cristiani Administration justified these violations on the grounds that the military command would fall apart and that their removal would cause destabilization (DH, 14 Jan. 1993). In other words, the officers would cause destabilization if the President—their official Commander-in-Chief—attempted to remove them.

The international community—including the U.S. government—increased pressure for Cristiani to remove Ponce and the others mentioned in the report. On April 2, the Secretary General accepted Cristiani's new proposal to place all of the remaining officers named by the Ad Hoc Commission on paid leave by June 30. Cristiani further promised that said officers would retire by New Year's Eve 1993. (Boutros-Ghali 1995b, p. 416). Boutros-Ghali reported on July 7 that the officers had indeed been placed on leave. He accepted this as compliance with the accords (Boutros-Ghali 1995d, p. 471).

The government thus implemented Ad Hoc Commission's recommendations over seven months behind schedule. While placing high ranking human rights violators on paid leave did remove them from active service, this solution can also be seen as rewarding them with a long paid vacation. By failing to follow the letter and spirit of this key provision of the peace accords, the Cristiani Administration missed a crucial opportunity to clearly establish civilian authority over the military. In other words, he reinforced military prerogatives and autonomy—key barriers to the consolidation of democracy.

Impunity and Media Bias Undermine the Ad Hoc Commission's Recommendations

By resisting civilian power, these high-ranking officers clearly demonstrated that they continued to enjoy impunity during the postwar era. They took advantage of their impunity to discourage Salvadorans from calling for their timely removal. These military leaders reacted to public demands for their removal in much the same manner that they reacted to opposition during the war—by slandering those who dared speak out against them. One Armed Forces press release referred to the NGOs calling for compliance as "tendentious, irresponsible and of unmentionable intentions" (Las organizaciones no gubernamentales... 1992, p. 817). Similarly, General Ponce referred to the CDHES as a "known leftist organization and virtual enemy of the Armed Forces" (DH, 8 Jan. 1993). It is important to remember that death squads frequently abducted and murdered dissidents whom military leaders had slandered in this manner during the war. Furthermore, these powerful military figures made these accusations in the context of continuing death squad activities during the early postwar period, as discussed in Chapters Two and Seven. These accusations were therefore the equivalent of death threats.

In order for Salvadorans to feel secure about their right to criticize the military, they must have some evidence that the civilian government will remain in power to protect them from retribution. Ad Hoc Commission member Molina Olivares, however, warned of a possible coup from his exile in the United States (Al Día 1992c). While the Salvadoran government and the Armed Forces repeatedly denied the possibility of a coup, the Cristiani Administration's claims that it was delaying compliance in order to prevent destabilization suggested otherwise. Even without a coup, however, it remained clear that the Armed Forces were not subject to civilian control. As UCA Vice Rector Rodolfo Cardenal explained, "a coup is, in practice, unnecessary" because "the High Command continues to decide matters of national policy" (Cardenal 1992, p. 971). Dissidents therefore had little reason to believe that the government would protect them from military retribution if they called for the removal of these officers.

The leading media outlets did not provide accurate coverage that might have supported compliance with this crucial component of the peace accords. In January 1993, for example, *El Diario de Hoy* reported that President Cristiani said that the Armed Forces had already complied. Yet the paper failed to mention that Secretary General Boutros-Ghali had just stated that Cristiani's decision to retain eight of the officers until his term expired clearly violated the peace accords. Nor is there any evidence that the reporter tried to get opposing viewpoints from NGOs, the FMLN, or the members of the Ad Hoc Commission themselves (DH, 8 Jan. 1993). These omissions framed the issue as leftists attempting to get more concessions out of the military than the FMLN won at the negotiating table.

Nor did the dominant media encourage or promote citizen oversight. Shortly after the peace accords were signed, an article in *La Prensa Gráfica* mentioned that the agreement contained provision for the purification of the Armed Forces. Nowhere, however, did the reporter mention **why** this was necessary, nor the criteria that the Ad Hoc Commission would use in order to do so (PG, 18 Jan. 1992). In another example, a television interviewer said that Cristiani did not have to comply with the Ad Hoc Commission's recommendations (Buenos Días 1992b). This was a very serious misrepresentation, of course, because Cristiani had promised to do so when he signed the peace accords.

Social movements also faced great difficulties as they tried to get out their message calling for compliance with the Ad Hoc Commission's recommendations. On October 31, 1992, for example, the Permanent Committee for the National Debate (CPDN) sponsored a large demonstration demanding that the indicated officers be removed on schedule. Both *La Prensa Gráfica* and *El Diario de Hoy* covered this event. Yet nowhere did they mention the issue of implementing the Ad Hoc Commission's recommendations. Instead, they focused on one small portion of the demonstration, a confrontation between the "mob" and a pair of innocent bystanders from Honduras. The papers also referred to the protesters as FMLN groups, terrorists, and subversives—a distortion given that organizations such as the Catholic and Lutheran churches supported the CPDN (PG, 2 Nov. 1992; DH, 2 Nov. 1992).[2] The pro-government media's decision to emphasize this incident and to ignore the purpose of the demonstration made it very difficult—if not impossible—for the human rights advocates to alert the public to the government's serious violation of the peace accords. This, in turn, helped reduce the domestic pressure on the government to fulfill its promise to remove those officers identified as human rights abusers.

The dominant media also presented biased images of the Ad Hoc Commission members. *El Diario de Hoy*, for example, quoted a colonel who referred to Commissioner Molina Olivares as "committed to slandering the Armed Forces and a declared leftist" and asserted that the Commission was totally ignorant of "the constitutional rights of the officers" (DH, 4 Dec. 1992). Yet the paper did not mention any opposing viewpoints nor did it give Molina Olivares the right to respond to this accusation. Nor did the press recall General Rubio's statement, "the individuals who are here [on the Commission] are honorable persons and no one can doubt how they are going to be or act" (Al Día 1992b). Rubio made the remark in May 1992, when most observers believed that the Ad Hoc Commission would not dare touch high-ranking officers.

The pro-government papers also attacked the Commission members on the editorial pages in much the same manner in which they had slandered opposition figures in order to justify human rights violations during the war. *El Diario de Hoy*, for example, labeled the Ad Hoc Commission as a front for the FMLN (DH, 7 Jan. 1993). Columnist Kirio Waldo Salgado referred to the Commission members as "enemies of the Armed Forces" and "reds." He further complained that Molina Olivares in particular was a founder of the Democratic Convergence and accused him of unspecified terrorist acts (Salgado M. 1993).

The dominant media further undermined political pressure for compliance with the Ad Hoc Commission's recommendations by presenting the FMLN—as well as the civilian opposition—as dangerous and justifying the military's repression during the war. *La Prensa Gráfica*, for example, based an article on a press release from the Armed Forces. This piece stated, "There is a smear campaign against the Armed Forces coming from extreme leftist groups through the organization that calls itself the Nongovernmental Human Rights Commission." This article also quotes the press release, which claimed that these groups "intend to destroy the armed institution that has patriotically fought to prevent the Marxist-Leninist aggression from implanting a totalitarian regime" (PG, 26 Nov. 1992). The writer did not, however, present any opposing viewpoints. Nor did he or she give the CDHES the opportunity to reply to the Armed Forces' smear campaign against the NGO. *La Prensa Gráfica* thus acted as the military's accomplice.

The leading papers published similar arguments in their editorial pages. Kirio Waldo Salgado wrote that the Armed Forces' only crime had been "to follow orders, to be subject to Civilian Power in the hands of the left (1980–1989) and—the most important—having prevented the communist subversion from taking State Power" (Salgado M. 1993). The supposedly leftist administration to which he referred was, of course, that of President Duarte, a Christian Democrat who failed to challenge the military. Another columnist similarly complained that the officers were being punished "for the 'crime' of having fulfilled the constitutional duty of saving their Homeland" from terrorists (González 1993). In other words, the crimes committed by these officers were not really crimes because the Marxist threat justified **any** actions the military leaders decided to take.

The pro-government media also echoed another one of the Armed Forces' complaints against the Ad Hoc Commission, the disingenuous call for balance. One columnist, for example, rhetorically asked if there would be an evaluation of FMLN leaders in terms of their human rights records and if they would be similarly punished (Araujo Cárdenas 1992). In reality, however, there was no need to have the Ad Hoc Commission evaluate the FMLN's leaders because the FMLN had already agreed to completely dismantle its military structure as part of the peace accords. In order to achieve true balance, the government would have had to dismantle the entire Armed Forces. By making such disingenuous calls for balance, the dominant media also ignored the fact that the Truth Commission was already in the process of investigation human rights violations committed by both sides.

The large media also reacted negatively toward international pressure for the removal of the officers identified by the commission. *El Diario de Hoy* referred to a statement that the U.S. government would condition its military aid on the removal of the officers as "an open confession of direct intervention by a foreign government in the internal affairs of another." The newspaper also complained when a U.S. Embassy source justified conditioning this aid by stating, "above all, the Salvadoran people want the implementation of this chapter of the accords." The writer dismissed this justification by rhetorically asking if the embassy had conducted a survey in order to ascertain whether the Salvadoran people wanted this (DH, 15 Jan 1993).

Calls for Compliance with the Ad Hoc Commission's Recommendations

Some Salvadorans pressured the government to remove the indicated officers despite the difficulties facing them. The Central American University (UCA) argued in late 1992, "Throughout the process of ending the armed conflict, President Cristiani has been folding to military pressure to avoid the cleansing" of the Armed Forces (UCA 1992c, p. 956). It also warned, "to accede to this intention" of keeping the officers on until they retired "means annulling one of the healthiest effects of the accords" (UCA 1992b, pp. 829–30). Similarly, Democratic Convergence leader Rubén Zamora complained in January 1993, "if the President of the Republic were really the Commander-in-Chief of the Armed Forces," he would have already removed the officers (El Noticiero 1993b).

Grassroots opposition forces also exercised their right to expression in order to generate pressure for compliance. The CPDN began pushing for compliance even before the first delays were announced. In September 1992, for example, the coalition also denounced the possibility of a military coup aimed at resisting the removals (YSU 1992b). The CPDN staged large demonstrations, such as the October 31 protest discussed above. Despite the difficulty in getting their message out to the public, these Salvadoran dissidents had an important impact on the eventual removal of the remaining officers identified as human rights violators by the Ad Hoc Commission. Representative McGovern recalled, "If everybody was quiet after the report was released, it would not have been a big deal. If that [domestic] pressure did not exist, you could bet your life [that] the powers that be would have just taken that report, put it on the shelf and let it collect dust" (McGovern 2001).

The peace accords contained another mechanism that depended upon expression by Salvadorans—the Truth Commission. This body reinforced the Ad Hoc Commission's recommendations when it published its report showing that officers such as Defense Minister General Ponce had been deeply involved in some of the war's most notorious human rights violations, including the 1989 massacre at the UCA. Observers have therefore credited the Truth Commission with forcing the remaining officers named by the Ad Hoc Commission to finally step down (Spence, Vickers et al. 1994, p. 15). This means that those Salvadorans who contributed to the Truth Commission's investigation by exercising their right to freedom of expression indirectly created the necessary pressure for the removal of the remaining officers identified as human rights abusers.

In the case of Argentina, McSherry found, "Public outrage emboldened political party leaders and allowed, even obligated, them to reject pacts offered by the armed forces" (McSherry 1997, p. 113). A similar dynamic took place in El Salvador when whistleblowers announced that some of the former guerrillas were considering making a pact to allow the remaining officers to serve until the end of Cristiani's term in 1994.

During the early stages of peace process, the FMLN retained a very important source of leverage, the option of suspending the demobilization of its own troops until it received a favorable response from the Cristiani Administration. In December 1992, however, it was leaked to the media that some sectors of the FMLN—especially Joaquín Villalobos and his followers—were willing to continue to dismantle the group's military structures without insisting on the removal of the remaining officers identified by the Ad Hoc Commission (IDHUCA 1993, p. 38; 1994b, p. 23). In exchange, Villalobos wanted the government to provide economic benefits for mid-level FMLN commanders (Holiday and Stanley 1997, p. 557; Popkin 2000, p. 107). These sectors of the FMLN also sought to prevent military unrest that might bring down the Cristiani government and thus end the peace process (Molina Olivares 2000). The United Nations announced that it would accept such an arrangement if both parties agreed to it (DH, 8 Jan. 1993). Giving in to military demands on such an important issue would have reinforced military prerogatives and allowed these war criminals to remain in positions from which they could continue violating human rights.

Villalobos and those FMLN leaders who agreed with him were acting in a manner consistent with the theory that democratization is best served through pacts among elites. As Huntington has advised the opposition forces in transitions to democracy, they were willing to make a deal which many of their followers would see as a betrayal of their interests. Their actions were also consistent with Huntington's advice that opposition elites should be willing to compromise on every issue except holding elections (see Huntington 1993, pp. 162–3,169). By seeking to prevent military unrest which could theoretically bring down the Cristiani government, Villalobos and his supporters were also acting in a manner consistent with the realpolitik approach advocated by authors such as Zalaquett (see Zalaquett 1995, p. 205). Essentially, they were willing to sacrifice the conviction that human rights abusers should be punished— however mildly—because they believed that the risk of military retribution would be too costly for them to maintain their convictions.

Some of the FMLN's most likely supporters, including NGOs, unions, universities, and its electoral allies, used public criticism to pressure the former guerrillas to insist that the government remove the officers. A group of human rights organizations issued a statement condemning the possibility of such a compromise on January 8, 1993. They referred to the suggestion of allowing the officers identified by the Ad Hoc Commission to remain as "an evident mockery of the accords." They also rejected the premise that the FMLN had the authority to renegotiate the provisions of the peace accords. According to these NGOs, the removal of these officers was a matter of national interest, rather than a problem between the government and the former guerrillas (CESPAD et al. 1993, pp. 135–6).[3]

Both the UCA and the University of El Salvador were important sources of support for the FMLN as it sought to establish itself as a political party. The former guerrillas therefore needed to demonstrate that they were acting in the best interests of the university communities. The University of El Salvador complained, "the FMLN, from day to night, has changed [its position] to opposing the purge and the demilitarization" (UES 1993, p. 133). The UCA protested, "not everything is negotiable and, certainly, the cleansing [of the Armed Forces] is not" (UCA 1992c, p. 955). The Jesuit university further warned the FMLN, "A party which negotiates away the truth and justice of dozens of thousands of victims cannot have any credibility" (UCA 1992c, p. 960). These statements sent a clear signal that the leadership of both universities were unwilling to tolerate the FMLN betraying the interests of its followers for the supposed greater good.

The FMLN did not have any previous experience in electoral politics. It did, however, have allies who participated in the 1989 and 1991 elections—the Democratic Convergence. Indeed, this group's leader, Rubén Zamora, would run for president on the FMLN ticket in 1994. The former guerrillas therefore had a very strong incentive against disappointing Zamora and his supporters. In early 1993, Zamora warned FMLN leaders that compromising would be "a very big problem for them vis-à-vis their base, because it was their people who suffered the most from (military) impunity" (Alder 1993).[4] In other words, betraying the interests of their supporters would cost the FMLN dearly at the ballot box.

Villalobos's critics were successful. According to Zamora, the public reaction to the possibility that the FMLN would accept this arrangement helped to prevent it from actually happening. "It made the FMLN immediately react," Zamora recalled, by "denying it" (Zamora 2001). Democratic forces in society had succeeded in using public expression to prevent opposition elites from making pacts which would undermine the democratic process.

The U.S. government certainly played an important role in persuading the Salvadoran government to eventually remove all of the officers cited by the Ad Hoc Commission. Ian Johnstone of the UN has identified the Clinton administration's decision to withhold military aid until the officers were taken off duty as a decisive factor (Johnstone 1995, p. 46). President Clinton could not have taken such action without the cooperation of Congress. According to Representative McGovern, Congressman Moakley took actions such as circulating a "Dear Colleague" letter urging full compliance with Ad Hoc Commission's recommendations. Moakley took such leadership, in turn, as the result of communication with Salvadoran groups about the issue (McGovern 2001). This clearly demonstrates how Salvadorans contributed to creating diplomatic pressure in favor of democratization by exercising their right to freedom of expression across national boundaries.

The Impact of Vetting the Officer Corps

On one level, the removal of 3.5% of the officer corps did not have a major impact on the Armed Forces. As discussed in Chapter Three, human rights violators such as the colonel charged with responsibility for the death of Madeleine Lagadec remained in the military and continued to rise through the ranks. Popkin concluded, "the new leaders represented continuity rather than a break with the past" (Popkin 1993, p. 5). The delays in removing officers, as well as the rewards given to some *retiring* officers, also created doubt regarding civilian control of the Armed Forces (Johnstone 1995, p. 33).

Doubt about the democratic character of a state is not always harmful, however. Indeed, those groups and individuals who criticized the government's attempts to violate this provision of the peace accords helped to increase public discussion of the issue of civilian control—something long overdue in Salvadoran society. It certainly would not have been helpful for the Salvadoran population—or the international community—to have the *illusion* that the military was acting in a manner consistent with the peace accords and democratization.

Eight years later, Ad Hoc Commission member Eduardo Molina Olivares acknowledged the limitations of the commission's work. He proudly told me, however, that the commission had set an important precedent (Molina Olivares 2000). Never before had such high-ranking military officers been formally identified as human rights violators. Nor had they ever had to consider the possibility that they would suffer any sanction, no matter how small, for their actions. As a result of the removal of these officers, however, powerful Salvadorans must weigh the possibility of being held accountable against any advantage they might seek through committing human rights violations. This, in turn, is a prerequisite for consolidating democracy by establishing democratic procedures as the proverbial "only game in town."

The eventual removal of the officers named by the Ad Hoc Commission also demonstrates the limitations of the realpolitik argument. Some sectors of the FMLN leadership had been willing to compromise on this issue for the greater good of preventing a military coup which would end the transition to democracy. While military hard-liners certainly complained about the attempt to hold them accountable, they did not overthrow the Cristiani Administration.

The Truth Commission Investigation

Without freedom of expression, most Salvadorans could not learn the truth about human rights violations during the war. Writing about his own nation, Argentina, Malamud-Goti has explained that the people living under authoritarian rule "inevitably hold widely varying versions of reality because these versions are based on the array of assumptions individuals make in their quest to make sense of what is happening around them." Without access to reliable information, Argentines engaged in "the constant flow of gossip" which they treated as the truth (Malamud-Goti 1996, p. 106). Thomas Buergenthal, who served on the Salvadoran Truth Commission, reported a similar situation in El Salvador. He described the nation as "awash in rumors of all sorts" (Buergenthal 1995, p. 305).

Even with the postwar opening, Salvadorans would have had great difficulty in working together to sort through rumors and disinformation. Writing about Archbishop Romero's weekly broadcasts, Ana Peterson explained, "in the face of powerful dominant group narratives, counter narratives require some type of 'institutional' support to enter the public imagination on anything other than a tiny scale" (Peterson 1997, p. 171). D'Aubuisson and his associates had murdered Romero precisely for the purpose of destroying this institutional support for the truth (see Chapter Two). The Salvadoran population continued to need such institutional support in the postwar era.

The Truth Commission provided this support. In contrast to the Ad Hoc Commission, this body had the mandate to publish its findings regarding wartime human rights violations. The government and the FMLN agreed, "The Commission shall have the task of investigating serious acts of violence that have occurred since 1980 and whose impact on society urgently demands that the public should know the truth." (Commission on the Truth for El Salvador 1995, p. 292). This was a much broader mandate than that of the Ad Hoc Commission.

The Truth Commission had another important mandate, one which distinguished it from previous truth commissions in other nations. The government and the FMLN empowered the body to make binding "legal, political or administrative" recommendations related to its findings. They further agreed to implement these recommendations (Commission on the Truth for El Salvador 1995, p. 174). Unlike the Ad Hoc Commission, however, the Truth Commission was not limited to making recommendations on a pre-specified set of issues, such as the removal of human rights abusers from the Armed Forces. By failing to provide such restrictions in the peace accords, the government and the FMLN made the Truth Commission potentially much more powerful than the Ad Hoc Commission.

The accords also clearly indicated that government and the FMLN had created this commission for the specific purpose of ending impunity. They agreed in the peace accords that "acts of this nature, regardless of the sector to which their perpetrators belong, must be the object of exemplary action by the law courts so that the punishment prescribed by law is meted out to those found responsible" (Government of El Salvador and FMLN 1995a, pp. 196).

According to the peace accords, the Truth Commission had only six months to carry out its research and issue its report. Human Rights Watch called this "an astonishingly short period of time" to investigate so many violations. The NGO also unfavorably compared this with the Chilean truth commission, which had nine months in which to investigate 2,279 cases (Human Rights Watch/Americas 1993, p. 7). The government and the FMLN eventually agreed to extend the Salvadoran Truth Commission's mandate by three months in order to allow the commissioners to process the information they had collected and to write up the report itself.

Given this constraint, the Truth Commission had to draw upon previous investigations. The Truth Commission's mandate authorized it to request "reports, records or documents from the Parties or any other information from State authorities or departments" (Government of El Salvador and FMLN 1995a, p. 174). Truth Commission member Thomas Buergenthal has reported, however, that state actors provided very little useful information. He stated, for example, that requests for military records "tended more often than not to be answered with explanations that the files had been destroyed, could not be found, or were incomplete" (Buergenthal 1995, p. 298). The government did provide many documents relating to human rights abuses committed by the FMLN. Buergenthal reported, however, "this material was for the most part useless for investigative purposes." He also stated that the FMLN was unable to provide relevant information about government violations (Buergenthal 1995, p. 302). Buergenthal has written that information provided by the U.S. government was not very useful either (Buergenthal 1995, pp. 298–9). The commission would therefore have to find alternative sources of information.

One obvious option within this context was for the commission to turn to those groups that had dedicated themselves to documenting human rights violations throughout the conflict—the NGOs. In its report, the Truth Commission does indeed thank "Salvadorian and international non-governmental organizations" because "without the cooperation of all these people it would have been impossible to penetrate the maze in which the truth often lay hidden" (Commission on the Truth for El Salvador 1995, p. 296).

By providing this information, the NGOs used their right to expression in order to directly influence the Truth Commission. It is also important to remember that these organizations had originally obtained their information from Salvadorans who had communicated with these groups. The human rights victims, their relatives, witnesses, and others who had given information to the NGOs thus had an indirect impact upon the commission through the NGOs' records and publications.

The Truth Commission explained how it used what it refers to as "secondary sources," including information from NGOs, in the methodological section of its report. The commissioners did not treat information from these organizations as sufficient evidence for establishing responsibility for human rights violations. They did, however, use NGO accounts to help verify information that it received from witnesses

(Commission on the Truth for El Salvador 1995, p. 300). According to Buergenthal, the commission also used information from NGOs as "useful background information" and "guideposts" for further investigation (Buergenthal 1995, p. 302). Without these guideposts, the Truth Commission would likely have gotten bogged down trying to investigate each and every case.

In October 1993, the (nongovernmental) Human Rights Commission of El Salvador (CDHES) gave the Truth Commission over six hundred pages of material documenting one hundred and ten of its best researched cases. The group also worked with foreign computer experts to systematize information from over nine thousand interviews conducted between 1979 and 1991. The NGO wanted to use this database to identify individual accountability in specific cases. According to Ball, one of the specific aims of this work was "to show the Truth Commission that the Salvadoran judiciary had taken essentially no action despite nearly 15 years of continuous legal activities on the part of the human rights NGO community" (Ball 1996, ch. 3.5.2; 2000, pp. 15–6).[5] The CDHES apparently achieved this objective; as discussed in Chapter Two, the Truth Commission did indeed find that the Salvadoran courts had served as an important institutional support for due process violations and impunity throughout the war.

Right-wing Salvadorans believed that information from the NGOs had a substantial impact upon the Truth Commission's findings. One op-ed piece in *El Diario de Hoy*, for example, complained that specific cases which the right cared about may have not "reached the hands of the members of the Truth Commission, given that the Archdiocese, Tutela Legal, and the Nongovernmental Human Rights Commission have only shouted in favor of the insurgents" (Zeldón 1993). In other words, the columnist believed that the Catholic Church and NGOs were having an important impact on the Truth Commission's investigation.

The Truth Commission did indeed cite Salvadoran NGOs in its report. In the chronology of violence that precedes the discussion of specific cases, for example, the Commission relied upon figures from Christian Legal Aid and the CDHES. The commission also credited NGOs as sources in cases such as the murder of four U.S. churchwomen, the Las Hojas massacre, the murder of agrarian reform officials including two U.S. advisors, and the death squad assassination of CDHES President Herbert Anaya (Commission on the Truth for El Salvador 1995, pp. 303, 393, 401, 409, 412).

Buergenthal has written that information from international NGOs was more useful than that coming from Salvadoran NGOs, at least in the beginning of the investigation (Buergenthal 1995, p. 302). While this may have been the case, it is important to recall that local NGOs, religious organizations, labor unions, and individual witnesses have provided much of this information to the international human rights organizations. Therefore, those Salvadoran groups and individuals who expressed themselves to international NGOs had an indirect impact on the commission.

Impunity Hinders Cooperation with the Truth Commission

Few individual witnesses were willing to come forward and provide information during the first three months of the commission's mandate. Although Buergenthal did not explicitly identify impunity as the reason for this reluctance, he did name several factors related to impunity. Salvadorans were hesitant to cooperate because "the very governmental institutions and the individuals responsible for the most egregious acts of violence in El Salvador remained in power" (Buergenthal 1995, p. 301). Buergenthal has also explained that Salvadorans were reluctant to trust the commission because previous investigative bodies had been shams. In the case of military personnel in particular, Buergenthal found, "All of them ... seemed to have great faith in the ability of the system to cover up, to protect them, and to punish those who talked." Furthermore, officers—especially lower-ranking officers—made it clear to the commission that their lives and/or careers would be endangered if they told the truth (Buergenthal 1995, pp. 302–3).[6]

Authoritarian forces used the continuing climate of impunity to reinforce these fears through threats and violence. The death squads continued to publish threats in the form of paid ads during this period. One squad, the Civic Movement for a Free El Salvador, repeatedly bought newspaper space in which to denounce the Truth Commission and the Ad Hoc Commission as attempts to destroy the Armed Forces (Human Rights Watch/Americas 1993, p. 11). In February 1993, unidentified subjects stopped and summarily executed Juan Carlos García and Manuel de Jesús Panameño while they were driving a vehicle associated with the Committee of Mothers and Family Members of Prisoners, the Disappeared and the Politically Assassinated (COMADRES). Emelina Panameño de García—a founding member of COMADRES, as well as Juan Carlos's mother and Manuel's aunt—has stated that her son was helping to prepare the information for the Truth Commission (ONUSAL Human Rights Division 1993a, 98–103; de García 1999).

Yet several thousand Salvadorans did come forward to tell their stories to the commission despite such acts of intimidation. Human Rights Watch has credited local NGOs with helping to mobilize these witnesses, especially in the department of Chalatenango. The Truth Commission received almost one third of the testimonies from residents of this area (Human Rights Watch/Americas 1993, p. 10). The Armed Forces had hit the residents of this department very hard during the war because they lived in the FMLN's rearguard. The residents of this department therefore witnessed—indeed, experienced—some of the worst atrocities committed during the war. Many of the strongest liberation theology and campesino groups had also emerged in this area (see Pearce 1986).

Buergenthal credited the Ad Hoc Commission with helping to convince Salvadorans that providing information to the Truth Commission would be worthwhile. By taking on powerful military officers, including the High Command, the Ad Hoc Commission provided what Buergenthal referred to as "the first clear indication ... that the days of 'business as usual,' of military impunity and cover-ups, might be over." As a result, Salvadorans became more confident in the integrity of the Truth Commission. Buergenthal also reported that the Ad Hoc Commission had helped to undermine the belief of some human rights violators that they would continue to be protected. As a result, many of those Salvadorans who participated in wartime abuses became interested in telling their side of the story to the Truth Commission (Buergenthal 1995, p. 304).

The Truth Commission Report

In the fall of 1992, the Central American University (UCA) warned that the Truth Commission was already facing pressure to omit the names of the human rights violators it identified from its report (UCA 1992c, p. 959). The government and its allies increased this pressure as the official release of the report grew closer. In early March, President Cristiani informed the UN Secretary General that his government could not guarantee the safety of the Truth Commission's sources if the report contained the names of the individuals found responsible for abuses (DH, 3 Mar. 1993). When this came out in the media, Bishop Rosa Chávez responded that the Truth Commission had not intended to name witnesses. He therefore insisted that the president was really motivated by a desire to protect the human rights violators identified by the Truth Commission (El Noticiero 1993e). The FMLN responded by labeling Cristiani's statement a veiled threat (Radio Farabundo Martí 1993). Cristiani and his allies were once again using the climate of impunity to impose silence about human rights abuses.

Following the passage of the 1992 amnesty law, human rights abusers had a very powerful incentive to prevent the commission from naming those individuals it found responsible for human rights abuses. Under this law, they enjoyed impunity for the crimes they committed during the war as long as they were not mentioned in the Truth Commission Report. The inclusion of names would therefore exclude those identified in the report from benefiting from the amnesty law (Cassel 1995, p. 327). The inclusion of this exception within the 1992 amnesty law also implied that the Truth Commission would identify human rights violators. By passing this law, the Salvadoran government gave its consent to name names. As the president who oversaw the intentionally botched investigation of the UCA massacre, Cristiani obviously had a personal motive for attempting to block the identification of human rights violators. Naming abusers could also remove the 1992 amnesty law's protection of ARENA members involved in death squad activities. Buergenthal has explained that Cristiani was also "under great pressure, including thinly veiled threats" from powerful military figures seeking to preserve their impunity (Buergenthal 1995, p. 306).

Cristiani revealed another part of his motives for blocking the names by asking Secretary General Boutros-Ghali to at least prevent the publication of names until after the 1994 elections (DH, 3 Mar. 1993). There was no explanation, however, as to how delaying the publication of this information for a little over a year would contribute to the safety of witnesses. Nor did Cristiani explain why extremists would cause violence if the violators were identified prior to the elections, but would not do so if the report were released afterwards. What is clear, however, is that the elections gave ARENA a clear interest in continuing to conceal the identification of Roberto D'Aubuisson as the intellectual author of the assassination of Archbishop Romero, as well as other ARENA leaders involved in grave violations. Cristiani clearly feared that the truth would cost his party at the ballot box.

The Truth Commission resisted these pressures and included the names of human rights violators in the report it formally presented on March 15, 1993. According to Buergenthal, the Cristiani Administration and the military leadership had initially told the commission that they wanted it to identify individuals guilty of human rights violations in order to protect institutions by demonstrating that "rotten apples" were to blame. They changed their position, however, once they realized that the Commission would not limit itself to naming low-ranking officials. Buergenthal further justified the commission's decision by citing the Truth Commission's mandate that "the complete truth be made known" and emphasizing that the identity of the abusers was an important part of this truth (Buergenthal 1995, p. 306). He has also pointed out that the dire warnings regarding the consequences of naming human rights violators never came true (Buergenthal 1995, p. 309). In other words, the Truth Commission's decision to follow the ethics of conviction was not as irresponsible as Zalaquett and other advocates of the realpolitik approach would suggest (see Zalaquett 1995, p. 205).

Many of the Truth Commission's findings have already been discussed in Chapter Two. The commission blamed the state and its allies for eighty-five percent of the human rights violations that were reported to it. It found the FMLN responsible for five percent of these abuses. The commission identified high-ranking officers as the intellectual authors of crimes such as the massacre at the UCA. Although the investigative body did indicate that ARENA founder Roberto D'Aubuisson was the intellectual author of the assassination of Archbishop Romero, it did not provide the names of civilians who organized and supported the death squads. It did, however, establish that there had been a close relationship between the death squads and the military security forces. The commission also clearly stated that the Armed Forces had carried out such massacres of civilians as El Mozote and Sumpul and contradicted the state's claims that these had been military confrontations. The commissioners blamed the FMLN for abuses such as the assassination of mayors and the indiscriminate use of land mines.

As indicated above, the government and the FMLN had empowered the Truth Commission to make recommendations that would be binding upon the Salvadoran government and the FMLN. The commissioners called for the following measures to help prevent similar abuses in the future:

• Remove all military officers and civil servants identified as violators in the report
• Ban all individuals identified as violators in the report from holding public office for ten years
• Ban all individuals identified as violators in the report from military service for life
• Implement the judicial provisions of the peace accords
• Remove the current members of the Supreme Court of Justice
• Bring legislation in line with the new military doctrine contained in the peace accords
• Provide military training in human rights
• Eliminate military connections with paramilitary forces
• Demilitarize the police force
• Continue the investigation of wartime death squads
• Strengthen the Office of the Human Rights Counsel (PDDH)
• Ratify additional human rights instruments
• Provide human rights victims and their relatives with material compensation
• Provide moral compensation by restoring the good names of the victims, establishing a monument to their memory, and creating a national holiday for remembrance.

In the same section, the Truth Commission claimed that it would be impossible to have fair trials for human rights violators because of the corrupt judicial system (Commission on the Truth for El Salvador 1995, pp. 380–5).

The Backlash Against the Truth Commission Report

The ARENA government and its allies responded to the report by attempting to justify—indeed, to glorify—the crimes examined by the commission and the right-wing figures it listed as responsible for said crimes. *La Prensa Gráfica*, for example, published the following quote from Colonel Francisco Helena Fuentes, whom the commission had identified as one of the intellectual authors of the massacre at the Central American University (UCA): "The only thing that I have done is to defend my people" from the November 1989 FMLN offensive (PG, 2 Apr. 1993). The newspaper failed to question this assertion or provide any opposing viewpoints. The reporter did not ask, for example, how killing the Jesuits or bombing poor neighborhoods contributed to defending the population. Nor did he or she provide the readers with any opposing viewpoints. In a similar vein, ARENA issued a statement declaring, "The major crime of Roberto D'Aubuisson was to awaken the Salvadoran people and to prevent the triumph of international communism in our beloved homeland" (ARENA 1993, p. 491). While preventing "the triumph of international communism" is certainly not a crime, organizing death squads—as D'Aubuisson had done—clearly violated international law.

The Truth Commission's critics also accused the commissioners of violating the due process rights of those they had named as violators. ARENA, for example, complained about "the rash accusations leveled against our founder and highest leader, Major Roberto D'Aubuisson" without "conclusive and irrefutable evidence " (ARENA 1993, p. 491). *El Diario de Hoy* wrote that unspecified "jurists and analysts" had established that the Commission violated Article 11 of the constitution by punishing "individuals who have not been heard and convicted in trial" (DH, 16 Mar. 1993). General Ponce—who was also identified as an intellectual author in the UCA massacre—told the press that the second amnesty law (discussed below) would not have been necessary if the officers had had the chance to defend themselves (DH, 26 Mar. 1993). *El Diario de Hoy* failed to point out, however, that an additional amnesty law for those named in the report would actually prevent these officers from defending themselves in court by preventing trials.

This article should have also challenged Ponce's assertions that the military leaders did not have a chance to defend themselves before the commission. The government and the FMLN had made it very clear in the peace accords that they never intended the Truth Commission to be a judicial body (Government of El Salvador and FMLN 1995a, p. 174). Given the history of retaliation against witnesses during the war, witnesses could not have openly confronted those they accused without serious risk to their lives. Indeed, this is one of the main reasons why a truth commission was necessary. Nonetheless, the Truth Commission took other measures to protect the rights of the accused and to ensure the accuracy of the information it published. The commissioners invited all those it accused of serious crimes to come before them and present their own defense. They also allowed the accused to bring along their lawyers (Buergenthal 1995, pp. 299, 301). The Truth Commission outlined additional measures that the commissioners took to address this issue in its report:

> The Commission insisted on verifying, substantiating and reviewing all statements as to facts, checking them against a large number of sources whose veracity had already been established. It was decided that no single source or witness would be considered sufficiently reliable to establish the truth on any issue of fact needed for the Commission to arrive at a finding [Commission on the Truth for El Salvador 1995, p. 300].

The government and its allies also sought to discredit the Truth Commission by complaining of international conspiracies and violations of the nation's sovereignty. *La Prensa Gráfica,* for example, reported, "The representatives of these sectors"—the reporter did not specify which sectors—call on Salvadorans to unite "in defense of patriotic values, rejecting foreign impositions and intervention" (PG, 19 Apr. 1993). In a similar manner, *El Diario de Hoy* cited unidentified "jurists and analysts" who asserted that the members of the Truth Commission were foreigners and therefore not allowed to take part in the nation's internal affairs (DH, 16 Mar. 1993). The reporter failed to mention that the Salvadoran government approved the creation of this body and gave it the power to make binding recommendations. Nor did he or she point out that Cristiani had also approved the UN Secretary General's choice of commissioners.

The Salvadoran right also accused the Truth Commission of being biased toward the FMLN. One *El Diario de Hoy* editorialist, for example, argued that the single purpose of the Commission was "to wipe out the army and ... to justify the abuses of the FMLN" (Zeldón 1993). Another columnist claimed the commission sought to minimize the FMLN's crimes and to suggest that there are "good crimes" and "bad crimes" (López-

Geissmann 1993). *El Diario de Hoy* itself complained about the space devoted to the massacre of six Jesuit priests while "there is not any mention that in these very same days hundreds of individuals perished when the terrorist [FMLN] death squads took over entire neighborhoods and held thousands of families hostage (DH, 19 Mar. 1993). The paper did not mention, however, that international NGOs and foreign governments had condemned the Salvadoran Air Force for bombing poor neighborhoods while sparing elite areas such as Escalón (see Americas Watch 1991, p. 62).

If the Truth Commission had been biased, there is evidence suggesting that it was actually biased against the FMLN. According to Buerganthal, the three commissioners "had assumed and hoped that we would find a more or less equal number of serious acts of violence attributable to each side in the conflict." "We soon found out," he continued, "that our hope for a quantitatively balanced report could not be realized" because "the government side had committed a substantially larger number of egregious acts than the FMLN" (Buergenthal 1995, p. 313).

Buergenthal has also addressed the alleged evidence that the Salvadoran government had presented against the FMLN. As indicated above, the commission found the government documents to be worthless. He further stated that most officers lied when responding to the commissioners' questions (Buergenthal 1995, pp. 302–3).[7]

For unclear reasons, the Truth Commission placed the assassination of Herbert Anaya, the president of the (nongovernmental) Human Rights Commission of El Salvador (CDHES), in the section devoted to violations by the FMLN. While the commission mentioned the confession of FMLN member Jorge Alberto Miranda that he had acted as a lookout during the crime, it also clearly indicated that said guerrilla had withdrawn this confession. The investigative body then acknowledged that it "did not have sufficient time to resolve" conflicting evidence pointing to military security forces and the FMLN as responsible for this murder (Commission on the Truth for El Salvador 1995, p. 370). It also found that the state violated Miranda's physical and mental integrity during the investigation and trial. It suggested that Miranda may have been paid for his original confession. Furthermore, it reported that Anaya had previously had difficulties with the Treasury Police—a force which the Truth Commission itself identified as heavily involved in the death squads. Anaya's wife told the commission that National Police troops had been seen roughly two hundred meters from their house on the day of the murder. The Truth Commission ended its discussion of this case by stating, "The State failed in its duty under international law to protect human rights, properly investigate the murder of Herbert Anaya and bring to trial and punish the culprits" (Commission on the Truth for El

Salvador 1995, pp. 370–2).[8] Anaya's widow publicly reaffirmed her belief that the military had killed her husband and reported that she had suffered persecution by the Armed Forces following his death (Al Día 1993d).

Why, then, did the commissioners include this case under the heading of violations committed by the FMLN? More specifically, why did they include this case at all if they were unable to resolve the conflicting evidence? The Truth Commission also placed the murder of former Supreme Court of Justice President Francisco José Guerrero in the section devoted to violations by the FMLN. Once again, however, it had not been able to establish whether the FMLN had actually killed him. It also found countervailing evidence that Guerrero had been killed because he had found important information about the UCA massacre (Commission on the Truth for El Salvador 1995, pp. 373–5). Given that the Truth Commission was unable to find the truth in cases such as these, it should have either omitted them from the report or included them in a section specifically identified as unresolved cases.

El Diario de Hoy reported that the military had complained that the Truth Commission did not mention the FMLN's use of land mines (DH, 3 Mar.1993). This would have been a very serious omission, given that the guerrillas had used these mines indiscriminately, thus frequently injuring civilians. The Truth Commission clearly stated, however, that the FMLN began making widespread use of mines in 1985. "As a result of this practice," the commission continued, "a great many civilians were killed or maimed." (Commission on the Truth for El Salvador 1995, p. 307). Yet the reporter did not question the military's assertion even once.

One faction of the FMLN joined the Salvadoran right in complaining that the Truth Commission did not identify FMLN violators other than Popular Revolutionary Army (ERP) leaders such as Joaquín Villalobos. Villalobos argued that he had been made a scapegoat in order to create a sense of balance with the military officers who were named (DH, 16 Mar. 1993). On the other side, General Bustillo complained that the commissioners had not identified the rest of the FMLN's General Command (DH, 18 Mar. 1993). In reality, however, the Truth Commission clearly stated, "There is full evidence that the FMLN General Command approved and adopted a policy of murdering mayors" (Commission on the Truth for El Salvador 1995, p. 307). The fact that the commission did not explicitly name the members of the General Command should not have prevented Salvadorans from easily identifying the five individuals who made up this body.

The dominant media failed to recall an important piece of information during its coverage of these complaints directed against the Truth Commission: the very same people who were denouncing the commissioners had made laudatory statements about their character when the commission was installed in July 1992. General Ponce, for example, had announced that the military was confident that the three commissioners were going to be impartial (DH, 15 Jul. 1992). Armando Calderón Sol— who was then serving as the president of ARENA and would become the president of El Salvador in 1994—remarked on their professionalism and said that their work should not be doubted (Al Día 1992e).

The ARENA government and its allies have further undermined their criticism of the Truth Commission through their willingness to cite the commission as an authority—when it has been in their own interest, of course. In late 1993, the *New York Times* published a report on recently declassified U.S. documents about wartime death squads in El Salvador. Calderón Sol attempted to discredit these documents by reminding the press that his name was not mentioned in the Truth Commission Report (PG, 10 Nov. 1993). This was a very weak defense, however, given that the Truth Commission argued that there should be further investigation of the death squads precisely because "the links of some private businessmen and moneyed families to the funding and use of death squads must be clarified" (Commission on the Truth for El Salvador 1995, p. 361).

The international credibility of the Truth Commission and its findings have also contradicted these complaints. A 1996 ruling by the Inter-American Commission on Human rights (IACHR), for example, stated that this OAS body "agrees with the conclusions of the Truth Commission," that the Salvadoran government failed to investigate the October 31, 1989 bombing of the Committee of Mothers and Family Members of Prisoners, the Disappeared and the Politically Assassinated (COMADRES) office (Inter-American Commission on Human Rights 1996).

The IACHR has also given the ARENA government repeated opportunities to refute the Truth Commission's findings. In its ruling on the UCA massacre, the IACHR emphasized, "the State has not presented any allegations or evidence that would cast doubt on the conclusions of the Truth Commission" (Inter-American Commission on Human Rights 1999d). The IACHR's ruling on the assassination of Archbishop Romero stated,

> The IACHR more than once alerted the Salvadoran State that, in view of its procedural silence, it could apply the presumption that the facts alleged are true. The State, duly notified, did not respond to those communications. Bearing in mind the foregoing, and the expressions of approbation by the State of the Truth Commission's report, the IACHR considers as proven the facts regarding this case that are described below" [Inter-American Commission on Human Rights 2000].

If the ARENA government truly had evidence demonstrating that D'Aubuisson was not behind the Romero assassination, why did it not jump on this chance to prove his innocence?

The Second Amnesty Law

The 1992 amnesty law specifically stated that those human rights violators identified in the Truth Commission Report would not benefit from its protection. Even before the Truth Commission presented its report on March 15, 1993, President Cristiani went on the airwaves and called for an immediate, unconditional amnesty for those individuals to be named as violators by the Truth Commission. He justified this by arguing, "the Truth Commission Report does not respond to the majority of Salvadorans' desire, which is [for] forgiving and forgetting all of this so-painful past" (Cristiani 1993, p. 483). Yet the Cristiani Administration had signed the peace accords, which clearly directed the Truth Commission to investigate "serious acts of violence that have occurred since 1980" (Government of El Salvador and FMLN 1995a, p. 174). Cristiani failed to explain how this mandate could be compatible with the desire to forgive and forget.

Cristiani also called for fairness, asserting, "it is not just to apply certain measures … to some, when others, for the simple fact that they have not been included in the sample that was analyzed by the Truth Commission report, have to be discriminated against" (Cristiani 1993, p. 483). Yet his very own government had approved the first amnesty law, including the exemption for those individuals identified as violators in the Truth Commission Report. Cristiani did not explain why he thought this provision was fair or acceptable in 1992. Nor did he mention what factors had changed his mind. The logical conclusion is that he had not anticipated how many of his powerful allies would be named as violators in the report. Once the commission named them, however, he realized that the costs associated with the exemption were higher than he had anticipated.

Furthermore, Cristiani used spurious reasoning in this argument by suggesting that human rights violators were unable to benefit from the 1992 amnesty law simply because they were "included in the sample" (Cristiani 1993, p. 483). This statement suggests that the Truth Commission used a random or arbitrary method to chose which crimes and/or which cases to investigate. The three commissioners did not, however, draw lots to determine whom and what to investigate. Rather, they chose to include precisely the worst human rights violations committed by both sides during the war. In other words, the Truth Commission followed the mandate established by the government and the FMLN. Cristiani therefore had no reason to complain.

The FMLN, other opposition parties, and civil society groups attempted to condition the passage of a second amnesty on the government's implementation of the Truth Commission's recommendations. Rubén Zamora—one of the authors of the 1992 amnesty law—explained that this was necessary because the Truth Commission recommendations constituted "a fundamental step in the struggle against impunity" (DH, 16 Mar. 1993). The Christian Democrats, the National Unity of Salvadoran Workers (UNTS) and Bishop Gregorio Rosa Chávez also called for the government to implement the Truth Commission's recommendations before passing another amnesty law (DH, 19 Mar. 1993).

Some opposition groups opposed any further amnesty by arguing that it would violate international law. Felix Ulloa of the Salvadoran Institute for Legal Studies, for example, pointed out that President Cristiani himself had signed treaties which established certain crimes which could not be subject to amnesties (Megavisión 1993e).

Some Salvadorans argued in favor of pardons—forgiveness after the violators have been tried and found guilty—instead of a blanket amnesty law. Christian Democratic Party deputy Arturo Magaña, for example, stated that justice must be done prior to forgiveness. The UNTS similarly announced that it would not oppose indulgences after human rights violators had been tried and sentenced (YSU 1993b). This would have been similar to the situation in South Africa, where human rights abusers were granted pardons only after they confessed to their crimes and provided relevant information.

The Assembly passed the amnesty law March 20, 1993 with a total of forty seven votes from ARENA and two smaller right-wing parties. Nine Democratic Convergence deputies voted against the bill, while thirteen Christian Democratic Party deputies abstained (PG, 22 Mar. 1993; DH, 22 Mar. 1993).

As a result of media bias, the opposition was unable to use freedom of expression to prevent the passage of the bill less than a week after the Truth Commission issued its report. *El Diario de Hoy* was quite explicit about its position. In an editorial, the paper reacted to Cristiani's initial call for a second amnesty law by announcing that this was "something that we, since the first moment, have considered to be one of the keys to the success of this stage" (PG 22 Mar. 1993).

The dominant media helped undermine opposition to the amnesty law through misrepresentation and the omission of certain truths. *El Diario de Hoy* reported, for example, "The extreme left conditions its votes on first putting into effect the recommendations made" by the Truth Commission (DH, 16 Mar. 1993). This is a major distortion of the truth, given that the Democratic Convergence was center-left and the Christian Democratic Party was center-right. Nor was David Escobar Galindo—who represented the government during the negotiations and was also a well-known friend of President Cristiani—an "extreme" leftist. Nonetheless, he had also indicated that the amnesty should wait until after the Truth Commission's recommendations were implemented (Montalvo 1993, pp. 44–5).

The dominant media also asserted that ARENA and its allies in the Assembly had the moral authority to pass the amnesty because they represented the majority of Salvadorans (DH, 23 Mar. 1993). This was not the case, however, because the 1991 elections had taken place in a climate of fear and impunity that hindered the Democratic Convergence's campaign efforts (as discussed in Chapter Two). Indeed, the FMLN did not even take part in the 1991 elections.

In June 1993, the University Public Opinion Institute (IUDOP) also contradicted ARENA's claim to represent the Salvadoran people's desires. A total of 55.5% of respondents said that they disagreed with the amnesty law, while only 30.4% stated that they agreed with it.[9] Surprisingly, 49.2% of ARENA supporters opposed the amnesty, while only 39.8% of them expressed support for the measure (IUDOP 1993, p. 719).

The dominant media also told some blatant lies regarding the second amnesty. *La Prensa Gráfica*, for example, reported that the Christian Democratic Party "had given its support to the amnesty" and then backed out by abstaining. Interestingly enough, the paper printed the truth—that the Christian Democrats had conditioned their support on the implementation of the Truth Commission's recommendations—in a separate article buried on page 66 of the same edition (PG, 22 Mar. 1993).

The pro-government media also undermined the calls for justice before pardons. Megavisión reported that the amnesty law could free "the murderers of the Jesuits and Monseñor Romero" (Megavisión 1993c). Yet no one had ever been convicted of killing Romero. While it is true that two military officers were indeed convicted of the massacre at the Central American University (UCA), this news report makes no mention of the intellectual authors of the crime who were identified by the Truth Commission. These military leaders had never even stood trial for the crime. The news program therefore created the false impression that justice had already been done in these cases. In reality, however, the government was promoting the second amnesty law in order to ensure that there would never be justice for these killings.

El Diario de Hoy also helped right-wing legislative deputies Ernesto Velásquez and Moisés Daboub distort the purpose of the new amnesty. The paper quoted the deputies claiming that the new measure was not meant to protect only those mentioned by the Truth Commission report. The paper did not question their assertions, however, nor did it note that the first amnesty law had already granted amnesty to everyone except those identified as human rights violators in the Truth Commission Report. Even worse, the paper did not challenge the deputies' assertion that the second amnesty would benefit Rubén Zamora, whom they accused of being "co-responsible for the crimes and destruction committed by the FMLN" (quoted in DH, 23 Mar. 1993). First of all, Zamora had been a leader in the Democratic Revolutionary Front, a coalition of social democratic parties that formed an alliance with the FMLN when repression increased during the early 1980s. He had never been involved in the FMLN's military affairs. Even if Zamora had been involved in the guerrillas' military actions, however, he would not have needed the second amnesty law because he would have already been covered by the 1992 amnesty law. The Truth Commission never identified Rubén Zamora as a human rights violator. Indeed, it mentioned him as a victim regarding the attack against his home in October 1989 (Commission on the Truth for El Salvador 1995, p. 405).

El Diario de Hoy went so far as to claim that the amnesty law benefited deceased human rights victims. The paper listed, for example, UCA Rector Ignacio Ellacuría and the four U.S. churchwomen who were raped and murdered by National Guard as beneficiaries of the measure (DH, 26 Mar. 1993). This paper also explained that the Jesuits and other priests who were killed needed the amnesty because they "greatly contributed in sowing discord in the Salvadoran family" (DH, 26 Mar. 1993). As discussed in Chapter Two, however, the government and its allies murdered these victims in order to prevent them from exercising their rights, including the right to freedom of expression. Indeed, speaking out about human rights violations is probably what the paper meant by "sowing discord." These victims could not benefit from an amnesty law precisely because the supposed crimes which they committed were actually protected under international law.

Media Suppression of the Truth Commission's Findings

The impact of a report such as that of the Truth Commission obviously depends on how much citizens know about its contents. UN Secretary General Boutros-Ghali urged, "All efforts must be deployed to make sure that the Commission's report attains the farthest reaches of the nation. All Salvadorians must know of it" (Boutros-Ghali 1995a, p. 38). This has not happened, however. Lack of knowledge regarding the

Truth Commission, its findings, and its recommendations has therefore lessened the report's impact on Salvadoran society.

YSUCA Director Carlos Ayala Ramírez, for example, has argued that the media have not given the report the attention it deserves. He attributed this problem to the connections between the media and the powerful groups identified as human rights violators in the report (Ayala Ramírez 2000). One UN expert similarly complained about "poor dissemination of the report's findings. What most people know about the report comes from the media which, at the least, initially were dominated by negative reactions from the military" (Johnstone 1995, p. 39).

The media have indeed misrepresented the contents of the report. *El Diario de Hoy*, for example, quoted Generals Ponce and Zepeda's complaints that the Truth Commission had downplayed the FMLN's "crimes" and overemphasized the "accusations" against the Armed Forces (DH, 26 Mar. 1993). Through such biased language, the paper was implying that these "accusations" had not been proven in the report. It is easy to understand why military officers identified as war criminals would want to distort press coverage in this manner. The real problem, however, was that the paper never questioned this statement.

In another example, Telecorporación Salvadoreña (TCS) *Noticias* reported that the Truth Commission had said that the FMLN or the National Union Federation of Salvadoran Workers (FENASTRAS) itself may have planted the bomb that blew up the labor federation's headquarters on October 31, 1989 (TCS Noticias 1993). In reality, however, the Truth Commission had found that the government had "failed in its duty to guarantee the human rights" of the union's members. It further reported, "There is no countervailing evidence that the FMLN or FENASTRAS members might have carried out the attack" (Commission on the Truth for El Salvador 1995, p. 338).

The poor quality of the Salvadoran education system has also limited the report's impact. Assistant Human Rights Counsel Marcos Valladares Melgar argued most Salvadorans have not had access to the report because of widespread illiteracy (Valladares Melgar 1999). The commission reinforced this barrier through its reliance upon formal, legalistic language. According to one observer, even well-educated Salvadorans have needed to use dictionaries while reading the report (Holiday 1995, p. 103). I must confess that even I found it to be boring, despite my strong interest in the subject matter.

Some groups have tried to increase awareness of the report's contents. Equipo Maíz, an organization that promotes adult literacy programs, has published a comic book version of the report. The Peace Center (CEPAZ) has also begun working with school teachers in order to increase their knowledge of the report so that they can then pass this information on to their students. Some teachers have also sent their students to CEPAZ's archives in order to conduct short research assignments on the Truth Commission and related topics.

The Implementation of the Truth Commission's Recommendations

The rapid passage of the second amnesty law took away one of the opposition's main sources of leverage to coerce the ARENA government into complying with the recommendations in the Truth Commission report. By the time that the Truth Commission issued its report, the FMLN had already dismantled its military structures. As a result, it could no longer postpone the demobilization of its forces in order to pressure the government into fulfilling its obligations, as it had done when the government failed to remove all of the officers whom the Ad Hoc Commission identified as human rights violators. The FMLN, the Democratic Convergence, and the Christian Democrats wanted to use the issue of a second, broader amnesty law as a new source of leverage by conditioning their support for such a measure on the government's compliance with the Truth Commission's recommendations. They could no longer do so, of course, once the government and its allies passed the legislation.

Many of the Truth Commission's recommendations simply repeated and emphasized provisions of the 1992 peace accords. It called upon the government to implement the judicial reform agreed to in the accords, to implement the new military doctrine, to demilitarize public security, and to strengthen the Office of the Human Rights Counsel (PDDH). The Commission increased the moral force behind these provisions of the peace accords by restating them. It also helped bring these issues back to the agenda—especially for the international community—and highlighted the fact that the government had not yet complied with key elements of the peace accords.

As mentioned above, the Truth Commission increased the pressure for compliance with another key element of the peace accords—the purification of the military—through its identification of high-ranking officers as human rights violators. This, in turn, demonstrated that civilian control of the military was possible, and it removed dangerous individuals from positions in which they could do great harm. Observers have credited the report with "a crucial role in the large effort to limit the power and the role of the military" (Popkin 2000, p. 159; Cassel 1995, pp. 326–7).[10]

The Truth Commission went beyond the peace accords by calling for the removal of civilian officials named in the report, as well as a ten-year ban against anyone it had identified as a human rights violator holding a public office. I have found no evidence that the government dismissed civilians for this reason. The FMLN stated that it would voluntarily respect the ban on holding public office only if ARENA pledged to do the same (CL, 14 Apr. 1993). The government did not agree and the UN Secretary General ruled that the implementation of this recommendation would violate the rights of those affected (Boutros-Ghali 1995f, p. 448).

The Truth Commission's recommendations also went beyond the original provisions in the peace accords relating to judicial reform by calling for the immediate removal of the Supreme Court of Justice (CSJ), including its president, Dr. Mauricio Gutiérrez Castro. Gutiérrez Castro replied, "The only one who can remove us is God, by taking our lives." He justified his position by claiming that the recommendations were only binding upon the executive branch (PG, 19 Mar. 1993). Cristiani informed the Secretary General that he would comply with only those recommendations which fell within his constitutional powers as president (Cristiani 1995). The Secretary General then accepted that Cristiani did not have the authority to remove the members of the court (Boutros-Ghali 1995n, p. 483). As a result, Gutiérrez Castro and the other CSJ magistrates continued to serve until their term expired in June 1994.

This does not mean, however, that the Truth Commission had no impact on the composition of the CSJ. Gutiérrez Castro ran for reelection in 1994. According to Supreme Court Magistrate Anita Calderón de Buitrago, the Truth Commission's negative evaluation of the CSJ under Gutiérrez Castro had an impact on both the lawyers and the legislative deputies who participated in the selection of the next court. No one from the previous court won reelection (Calderón de Buitrago 2000). Popkin has also credited the report for this complete break with the past (Popkin 2000, p. 201). Given the evidence that the Truth Commission presented against the members of this court—especially Gutiérrez Castro—this was a very important step forward which increased the likelihood that the judiciary would fulfill its obligation to protect human rights.

Among the most important of the Truth Commission's recommendations was its call for further investigation of the wartime death squads. Given the ARENA administration's displeasure with the Truth Commissions findings, it was no surprise that Cristiani attempted to avoid another investigation. Chapter Seven will discuss how Salvadorans used expression about postwar murders to help force the government to at least partially comply with the spirit of this recommendation through the creation of the Joint Group for the Investigation of Politically Motivated Illegal Armed Groups.

In contrast, the PDDH was very receptive to the Truth Commission's recommendations aimed at strengthening the new agency (Boutros-Ghali 1995n, p. 489). These measures included an evaluation of the PDDH's priorities and needs, the extension of the agency's offices throughout all fourteen of the nation's departments, greater use of its authority to inspect sites (Commission on the Truth for El Salvador 1995, p. 383). It has faced great difficulty in doing so, however, because of insufficient budgets from the state.[11]

The Salvadoran government has never attempted to offer material compensation to the victims or their families. Nor has the it done anything to comply with the Truth Commission's call for a national memorial dedicated to the victims of the war. San Salvador Mayor Héctor Silva (FMLN/United Democratic Center) has, however, worked with human rights organizations to create such a monument in Cuscatlán Park (PG, 1 Feb. 1998). He also commemorated the twentieth anniversary of the assassination of Archbishop Romero by naming a street after the archbishop and placing a monument in front of El Salvador del Mundo.[12]

The Truth Commission's impact was not limited to its recommendations. Human Rights Watch, for example, has referred to the publication of the names of human rights violators as "chiseling a crack in the wall of impunity" in El Salvador (Human Rights Watch/Americas 1993, p. 24). Another observer remarked, "the blow to personal reputation and to institutional prestige ... has opened another breach in the wall of impunity" (Ensalaco 1994, p. 655). One concrete example of this impact took place when the government released Colonel Benavides and Lieutenant Mendoza from their sentences for the massacre at the Central American University (UCA). Both convicts made it very clear that they wanted to avoid any contact with the media, a powerful indication of the shame they felt for having committed acts that they had been told were heroic (El Noticiero 1993d). They literally could no longer show their faces in public.

As mentioned above, the Truth Commission has also had an impact on the Inter-American Commission on Human Rights (IACHR). This intergovernmental organization has cited the report as part of the evidence which led it to establish that the Salvadoran state had violated COMADRES members' right to judicial protection through its inadequate investigation of the bombing of their office in October 1989. It therefore called on the government to launch a thorough investigation of this incident and to punish those responsible for the attack (Inter-American Commission on Human Rights 1996). The IACHR also cited the Truth Commission Report in its rulings on the assassination of Archbishop Romero and the UCA massacre (Inter-American Commission on Human Rights 2000, 1999d).

Human Rights Advocates
Challenge the Amnesties

Human rights advocates in El Salvador began legal proceedings against the second amnesty law almost immediately after the government rushed it through the legislature. In April 1993, an employee of the (nongovernmental) Human Rights Commission of El Salvador (CDHES) filed a petition to the CSJ. The plaintiff argued that the amnesty law violated Article 244 of the constitution, which establishes,

> The violation, infraction or alteration of constitutional dispositions will be especially punished by the law, and the civil or criminal responsibilities in which civilian or military public officials incur, whatever the motive, will not allow amnesty, commutation, or pardon, during the presidential period in which they are committed [quoted in Cáceres Hernández 1993, p. 2].

This would mean that any crimes committed since Cristiani took office in June 1989 could not be covered by an amnesty granted during his term as president. The UCA massacre and other human rights violations that took place during the November 1989 FMLN offensive fell within this period.

The same petition argued that the amnesty law violated Article 144 of the constitution, which establishes that international treaties take precedence over secondary laws. The litigant further argued that the amnesty violated the peace accords, which called for exemplary justice to be applied to the authors of grave human rights violations (Cáceres Hernández 1993, pp. 4–6).

The CSJ upheld the amnesty law. The obvious explanation for this outcome was that the very Supreme Court that the Truth Commission had criticized—including its president, Gutiérrez Castro—was still in place. It would be unrealistic to expect that these individuals would rule to overturn amnesty laws from which they themselves benefited. The CSJ therefore held that it did not have the authority to overturn political agreements such as this law (DH, 21 May 1993). This assertion was rather puzzling, given that all laws are essentially political agreements. If this were true, how could the CSJ overturn any law?

The court also attempted to justify its position by citing international law. It referred to the Additional Protocol II to the 1949 Geneva Convention, which it argued justified the declaration of broad amnesties at the end of military conflicts (Popkin, Spence, and Vickers 1994, p. 12). The IACHR has rejected this interpretation of the protocol. According to the commission, such amnesty laws cannot be applied to human rights violations (Inter-American Commission on Human Rights 1995). The

IACHR has since declared the 1993 amnesty law to be a violation of international law and has called for the Salvadoran government to repeal it (see Inter-American Commission on Human Rights 1999c, 1999d, 2000).

The FMLN's opposition to the amnesty has been spotty, at best. Former General Command member Nidia Díaz, for example, told *La Prensa Gráfica* that FMLN leaders would be willing to face the consequences of overturning the amnesty laws as long as they were not the only ones prosecuted (PG, 16 June 1998). When I asked another FMLN deputy about accusations that the former guerrillas had not done enough to oppose the amnesty,[13] he responded that the party had done all that it could given that it was not represented in the Assembly until after the 1994 elections (Melgar Henríquez 2000).

Once the FMLN obtained seats in the Assembly, however, the party indicated that it was willing to bargain over the issue. ARENA wanted to block former Ad Hoc Commission member Abraham Rodríguez from being appointed as the head of the CSJ for fear that he might overturn the 1993 amnesty law. The FMLN assured ARENA, however, that the former guerrillas would support passage of a revised amnesty law if this happened. (Popkin 2000, p. 157).

The Foundation for the Study of the Application of the Law (FESPAD) and several other Salvadoran NGOs presented another constitutional challenge against the amnesty before the CSJ in December 1998. The court did not issue a ruling until October 2000. While the CSJ did not strike down the amnesty law itself, it did rule that judges should have the discretion to prosecute state officials who violated human rights during Cristiani's term in office (Amnesty International 2001c; Urquilla Bonilla 2000c, p. 6).

The NGOs' next challenge, then, was to get the courts to use this discretion by trying state officials accused of committing human rights abuses between Cristiani's inauguration in June 1989 and the end of the war in January 1992. In December 2000, a judge ruled that the UCA massacre case could not be reopened because the ten-year statute of limitations had already expired. An appeals court upheld this decision in January 2001 (Amnesty International 2001c).

The human rights groups then appealed this decision. They have put forward the argument that the time limit for prosecuting cases cannot count the years in which the amnesty law blocked investigation. In other words, the clock had stopped running until the court ruled that judges could reopen the cases (Urquilla Bonilla 2000b, pp. 7–8). With regard to the Jesuit case, this would mean that only about two years (November 16, 1989 to January 2, 1992) counted toward the statute of limitations.

The Achievements of the Ad Hoc Commission and the Truth Commission

Clearly, the Salvadoran government's implementation of the provisions of the peace accords dealing with wartime abuses was very problematic. The Cristiani Administration and the Armed Forces did not provide sufficient information for the Ad Hoc Commission and the Truth Commission to perform their duties. Moreover, the government and the military resisted their obligations to remove officers indicated by the Ad Hoc Commission and to implement some Truth Commission recommendations, such as the further investigation of wartime death squads. It is easy to understand why some observers have come to the conclusion that Salvadorans did not have much success in expressing themselves because the government was simply unwilling to listen to them.

Yet these commissions did achieve important results, especially when considered in the context of Salvadoran history. Never before had civilians been allowed to scrutinize the Armed Forces and call for the removal of human rights violators. Nor had so many soldiers ever been removed for such reasons. Perhaps most importantly, this was the first time that generals had been removed for human rights abuses. The Truth Commission Report clearly established that the state's propaganda denying and/or justifying human rights violations had been nothing more than lies. The same applied to the dominant media's biased coverage during the war. The Truth Commission's recommendations reinforced the moral authority of existing provisions of the peace accords while it helped undermine the legitimacy of military officers and judges who violated human rights.

These have been partial victories. The government did not remove the military officers on schedule and they continued to enjoy privileges such as paid leave and full pensions. The ARENA government, the military, and their media allies have continued to deny the Truth Commission's findings, even though the government has been unable to present the IACHR with any evidence against the Commission's conclusions. The corrupt Supreme Court of Justice continued to serve the remainder of its term ending in June 1994. The Salvadoran government never continued the investigation into wartime death squads.

Even these partial victories would not have been possible if Salvadorans had not exercised their right to freedom of expression. Civil society organizations and private individuals helped both commissions gather vital information during the brief time allotted for their investigations. While pressure from the international community was clearly needed to prod the reluctant Cristiani Administration into dismissing the officers indicated by the Ad Hoc Commission, international groups and diplomats would not have pressured the government so strongly if Salvadorans had not used their voices to mobilize them. The FMLN's allies successfully used public criticism of the group's leaders to prevent them from backing down on the removal of these officers. The Truth Commission and those Salvadorans who provided it with information have had an important impact on the IACHR's rulings against the Salvadoran government's inaction regarding wartime human rights violations. These contributions are evidence that freedom of expression fits Shue's definition of a basic right as a right without which all other rights remain insecure.

There has been very little progress, however, with regard to punishing the violators identified by these two commissions. ARENA and its allies were unaffected by denunciations against the 1992 and 1993 amnesty laws because the cost of not passing these law would have been so great for them. Furthermore, the dominant media helped to reduce potential electoral costs associated with passing these laws through biased coverage and misrepresentation.

The fact that so many Salvadorans helped the Ad Hoc Commission and the Truth Commission through exercising their right to expression is especially impressive when viewed in light of the forces that hampered expression on these issues. The military and the civilian far right reacted to calls for compliance with much the same threatening rhetoric that had preceded human rights violations during the war. The Cristiani Administration's inability or unwillingness to remove the officers called for by the Ad Hoc Commission sent a message that military remained above the law. The government sent the same message through the 1992 and 1993 amnesty laws. President Cristiani even went so far as to announce that his government would not fulfill its obligation to protect Salvadorans who cooperated with the Truth Commission. The mainstream Salvadoran media clearly showed its bias against both commissions. They distorted the commissions' findings—when they discussed them at all. Nonetheless, Salvadorans were able to use expression to bring about changes that had seemed impossible during the war.

The next two chapters will discuss two issues which are closely related to the Truth Commission's recommendations. Chapter Six will examine the impact of public expression on the demilitarization of public security called for in the peace accords. Chapter Seven will look at the partial fulfillment of the commission's call for further investigation of wartime death squads through the formation of a commission to investigate postwar extrajudicial executions.

6

The Demilitarization
and Remilitarization of
Public Security[1]

The government and the Farabundo Martí National Liberation Front (FMLN) made the dissolution of the repressive military security forces and the establishment of a new civilian police force central elements of the 1992 peace accords. Like the Ad Hoc Commission and the removal of human rights abusers from military service, the public security provisions addressed the issue of how to deal with the individuals and institutions responsible for widespread and systematic human rights violations prior to the beginning of the democratic transition. The public security elements of the peace accords were very different from those discussed in the previous chapter, however, in that the government and the FMLN promised to create a new institution which would protect the rights of all citizens. The old military security forces were trained for national security purposes, especially fighting the FMLN and alleged guerrilla collaborators. This led them to treat citizens as (at least potential) enemies. In contrast, the new civilian force was intended to provide public security, which involves protecting citizens from criminals.

The outcome of this process would have a major impact on the issues covered in the remaining chapters of this project, including postwar political death squad activity, the murder of medical student Adriano Vilanova by National Civilian Police (PNC) agents, and the emergence of vigilante death squads. Once again, the National Republican Alliance (ARENA) government which oversaw the resurgence of repression in the later 1980s assumed ultimate responsibility for implementing these provisions of the peace accords. It is therefore necessary to examine the degree to which opposition forces in El Salvador have been able to use their right to expression as a means of pressuring the government to live up to its end of the agreements.

Opposition forces have encountered great difficulty in their attempts to use freedom of expression to advance the demilitarization of public security through the creation of a new National Civilian Police force. The government and its allies have been unwilling to keep their end of the agreement. Instead, they have fostered structural impunity. The ARENA administration and the military engaged in sleight-of-hand tricks that created the illusion of compliance, such as changing the names of military security forces and transferring soldiers into the "civilian" police force through the back door of the National Police. The dominant media have generally supported these policies of structural impunity through coverage that reinforced the government's deceptive claims of compliance. In the context of very severe postwar crime—especially prior to the full deployment of the PNC—the major media outlets also created the false impression that the government's measures to maintain and restore military involvement in public security were both necessary and effective steps toward establishing law and order.

It is easy to understand why some observers have mistakenly argued that any progress toward overcoming these policies of impunity has been the result of international pressure. While international actors have played a very important role in exposing the Salvadoran state's deception, such forces have also had their limits. Although Salvadoran opposition groups have not been able to use public expression to force the government to comply with all of its obligations, they have nonetheless helped to prevent the situation from becoming much worse.

The development of civilian control over public security functions has thus followed Stepan's dialectical model of democratization as a process of regime concessions and societal conquests (see Stepan 1988, p. 245). As Stepan's theory would predict, authoritarian forces within the regime have attempted to take back the concessions that they made regarding the police and public security. Salvadoran opposition groups have faced great difficulty in their attempts to transform the public security provisions of the peace accords into societal conquests. They have succeeded, however, when powerful economic elites— especially those within the usually pro-government media—have helped them resist the authoritarian forces' attempts to undermine the peace accords.

Efforts to Preserve the National Guard and Treasury Police

The government clearly promised in the peace accords that it would dismantle the National Guard and the Treasury Police. It also agreed that the new PNC would be the only police force with national jurisdiction. The old National Police was the only military security force that was not scheduled to be disbanded immediately. Instead, it would continue to function until the new civilian police force was gradually able to replace it (Government of El Salvador and FMLN 1995c, pp. 196, 198, 203).

The Cristiani Administration, however, put forward its own interpretation of the accords. The president claimed that the accords only required the government to remove the National Guard and the Treasury Police from public security, not to completely dismantle them. The government changed the forces' names to the Border Guard and the Military Police on March 2, 1992. It then transferred these structures into the army. Cristiani had promised in the accords, however, that "their members shall be incorporated into the army," not that the institutions themselves would become part of the army. These forces remained in the same locations where the National Guard and the Treasury Police had been stationed, despite the requirement that all Armed Forces troops be concentrated within zones specified in the peace accords (PG, 28 Apr. 1992; Government of El Salvador and FMLN 1995c, p. 196; Costa 1999, p. 138).[2]

The major media outlets had helped to lay the groundwork for this violation of the peace accords through their coverage of the security forces in January and February 1992. *La Prensa Gráfica*, for example, mentioned the dissolution of the National Guard and the Treasury Police in a January article. The paper failed to report, however, that these forces were being disbanded because of their involvement in human rights violations (PG, 18 Jan. 1992). In another article, the paper quoted Colonel Juan Carlos Carrillo Schlenker, who stated that the National Guard would continue to exist and would be involved in "fighting rural crime" (PG, 4 Feb. 1992). *La Prensa Gráfica* failed to point out, however, that such activity would violate the government's agreements to disband this force and to establish the PNC as the only national police force.

The major media outlets also undermined efforts to demilitarize public security by falsely portraying the National Guard and the Treasury Police as competent, effective against crime, and necessary for citizen security. In February, *El Diario de Hoy* reported that unspecified mayors told the paper that the National Guard and the Treasury Police should simply be purged of bad elements instead of being disbanded.

The mayors also warned that society would be left at the mercy of criminals because there was no transitional phase between the dissolution of these units and the deployment of the new force (DH, 10 Feb. 1992). These unidentified mayors were clearly misrepresenting the peace accords, which stipulated that the National Police would continue to function while the PNC gradually replaced it. Yet the paper failed to question their assertion. *La Prensa Gráfica* praised the Treasury Police's performance during the war as "brave, heroic, and brilliant" (PG, 29 Feb. 1992). As Chapter Two makes clear, this institution was heavily involved in human rights violations during the war. Killing civilians rather than confronting enemy soldiers is more accurately described as cowardly.

The dominant media continued to support the government after it preserved these institutions under different names. *La Prensa Gráfica* portrayed the military security forces as defenders of democracy and failed to mention their role in human rights violations throughout the war. Nor did the paper point out that the government's failure to dissolve this institution was a violation of the peace accords (PG, 3 Mar. 1992).

The large media outlets also helped to divert attention away from the government's violation of the public security provisions of peace accords. One article in *El Diario de Hoy*, for example, quoted several government officials, including President Cristiani, complaining that the FMLN's decision to suspend the demobilization of its military forces was a violation of accords. *El Diario de Hoy* did not, however, indicate that the FMLN took this action to pressure the government in fulfilling its promise to disband the military security forces. Nor did the paper provide quotes from any opposition figures or international observers indicating that the government had also violated the accords by failing to dismantle the security forces (DH, 3 Mar. 1992).

The large media outlets began to change their attitude, however, when the Military Police's actions began to threaten the interests of the business sector. On April 7, 1992, the public became aware that Major José Alfredo Jiménez Moreno had escaped from the Military Police's facilities under suspicious circumstances. He disappeared just before he was sentenced to thirty years for the abduction and ransom of wealthy businessmen in the 1980s. The two Military Police agents guarding him had also disappeared (ONUSAL Human Rights Division 1992, 2; PG, 1 May 1992; CDHES 1992, p. 53). The Distributors' Association of El Salvador placed a paid ad labeling the incident a national embarrassment and demanding immediate action (PG, 1 May 1992; ADES 1992, p. 58).

This was a case where the government's policies of impunity threatened Salvadoran elites. According to Stanley, the role of military security forces personnel in the kidnapping of powerful economic figures for ransom during the war contributed to friction between business elites and the military. They had nonetheless continued to oppose the demilitarization of public security because of their fear that the FMLN would secretly control the "civilian" force (Stanley 1996a, pp. 18, 240). Given this uneasy situation, it is not surprising that the dominant media reacted strongly. *La Prensa Gráfica*, for example, complained in an editorial that the prisoner had escaped from the Military Police "calmly, and without incident." The paper recognized that "impunity, of any kind, is one of the gravest and most dangerous sicknesses that a nation can suffer" (PG, 24 Apr. 1992).

On April 24, 1992—the day of the *La Prensa Gráfica* editorial on Jiménez—the Assembly approved a reform of the enabling legislation for the National Guard and the Treasury Police. This legislative body officially removed the two forces from public security functions, but did not dissolve them. The UN Secretary General later complained that this action "created further misgivings" because it did not comply with the peace accords (Boutros-Ghali 1995m, p. 240). Interestingly, on April 25, 1992 *La Prensa Gráfica* provided ample space for quotes criticizing the legal maneuver from opposition party leaders in its coverage of this change (PG, 25 Apr. 1992). By preserving impunity even for those criminals who had harmed elite interests, the Military Police (former Treasury Police) inadvertently opened political space for debate over the future of the military security forces.

The next major development came on June 17, 1992. The government and the FMLN agreed to overturn the enabling legislation for the National Guard and the Treasury Police. The government would then transfer two thousand troops from these forces into a new Special Brigade of Military Security, which would have no role in public security. The Assembly approved these changes on June 24, 1992 (PG, 25 June 1992). While the FMLN and the United Nations were satisfied with this solution, it did not result in the actual dismantling of the Military Police and the Border Guard. Indeed, the United Nations Observer Mission in El Salvador (ONUSAL) Human Rights Division received testimony from a witness who identified an active duty soldier from the Military Police as one of the two men who killed a local FMLN official in 1993 (ONUSAL Human Rights Division 1994b, 44). The Military Police and the Border Guard also resumed participation in public security at the international airport following the September 11, 2001 terrorist attacks on New York and Washington DC (DH, 12 Oct. 2001).

Clearly, international forces—especially the United Nations—played an important role in pressuring the Salvadoran government to remove these forces from the field of public security. The government remained unwilling to make these changes, however, until after those in control of the mainstream media changed their attitude toward the forces they had been presenting as heroes. This outcome demonstrates the dominant media's ability to ignore opposition voices and thus support authoritarian forces, as well as their potential to bring about positive change—when the owners and managers believe it is in their own interests.

The mainstream media did not, however, continue to press for further changes. As discussed below, they supported the government's efforts to retain the National Police and militarize the new supposedly civilian police force.

Efforts to Retain the National Police

While the peace accords called for the immediate dissolution of the National Guard and the Treasury Police—a provision the Cristiani Administration refused to fulfill—the parties agreed that the government would gradually phase out the final military security force while creating and deploying the new PNC. The government and the FMLN also established in the accords that the majority of PNC agents should be civilians who had never taken part in the military conflict. The parties provided, moreover, for equal portions of guerrillas and National Police agents to enter the new force. The government and the FMLN later agreed to allocate twenty percent of the PNC positions to the former guerrillas and another twenty percent to National Police troops. The two sides therefore agreed that civilians would make up sixty percent of the new force.

With the war over, the National Police quickly became the leading source of human rights violations. ONUSAL reported that 35.2% of complaints that it received for the period of January to October, 1993 were filed against the force. Upon investigation, ONUSAL's Human Rights Division established that almost all of these complaints were true (ONUSAL Human Rights Division 1994b, table no. 6). The Office of the Human Rights Counsel (PDDH) found the National Police to be responsible for 46.2% of the violations it investigated between September, 1993 and January, 1994 (PDDH 1994, p. 11).

The National Police committed violations such as summary executions, arbitrary arrests, and frequent threats against citizens. ONUSAL further reported that the National Police troops it had identified as having executed Héctor David Segovia Verillos on July 9, 1993 had not been disciplined by the end of that year (ONUSAL Human Rights Division 1994b, 90, 95–6). On May 20, 1993, the National Police riot squad fired toward a crowded demonstration of former combatants from both sides of the war, killing a former guerrilla. In 1994, the U.S. State Department criticized the National Police for its refusal to turn the police agent accused of this killing over to the courts (U.S. Department of State 1994). The Salvadoran government also transferred the supposedly demobilized Belloso Battalion into the National Police. It then used these troops to dislodge rural squatters (Cardenal 1992, p. 968).

Despite these problems, the mainstream media threw their support behind the continued existence of the force. Gino Costa came to El Salvador in December 1990 to serve as "the eyes and ears of [UN negotiator and peace accords liaison] Alvaro De Soto." He also worked as a political aide to three ONUSAL directors before returning to Peru in September of 1994 (Costa 1999, pp. 15–6, 18).[3] He found that the pro-government media began using the issue of crime to block the dismantling of the security forces even before the government had demobilized any troops. Costa has also stated that the media sought to create an impression that the implementation of the peace accords would make the crime situation even worse (Costa 1999, p. 144). In April 1992, a columnist for *La Prensa Gráfica* wrote an op-ed piece in which he blamed a postwar crime wave on the dissolution of the National Guard and the Treasury Police. He complained, "the citizenry does not know whom to turn to for aid." The columnist then described the situation as the "law of the jungle" and argued, "only God protects us" (Lazo de Quiñónez 1992, p. 6). In September 1992, a columnist writing for *El Diario de Hoy* complained that the six thousand remaining National Police troops were not enough to protect the population of six million. The author then went on to suggest that this was part of an elaborate FMLN conspiracy to generate chaos. He also objected to ONUSAL's monitoring of National Police activities, which he blamed for protecting criminals at the expense of honest citizens (Jones 1992, p. 6).

While the dominant media were exploiting this situation for political purposes, it was very true that El Salvador has remained a dangerous, violent nation during the postwar period. In 1995, the Pan American Health Organization reported that El Salvador had the second highest rate of male deaths through homicides, accidents, and suicide in the western hemisphere. Only Colombia had a higher rate (IUDOP 1996, p. 241). In its 1996 annual report, the Human Rights Institute of the Central American University (IDHUCA) cited a study by the Inter-American Development Bank which found El Salvador to have more violence and crime than either Colombia or Brazil (IDHUCA 1997b, p. 5). Using data from the Office of the Attorney General of the Republic, José Miguel Cruz and Luis Armando González calculated the annual intentional homicide rate in El Salvador for 1994, 1995, and 1996:

Year	Intentional Homicides per 100,000 Inhabitants[4]
1994	138.2
1995	138.9
1996	117.4

In contrast, there were only 8.5 intentional homicides per 100,000 inhabitants in the United States in 1995 (IUDOP 1996, p. 242). Cruz and González have also estimated the intentional homicide rate during the twelve years of civil war. Without solid evidence of exactly how many homicides were committed during this period, they rely upon the widely used estimate of 75,000. This produces an average annual rate of over 130 per 100,000 (Cruz and González 1997, p. 961). It is particularly alarming that the rates for 1994 and 1995 actually surpass the average annual wartime rates.[5] Factors such as the lack of economic opportunities for former combatants and the ready availability of powerful weapons contributed to the crime problem (Stanley and Loosle 1998).

The dominant media responded to this situation by supporting government actions which strengthened the old, discredited military security forces and undermined the public security provisions of the peace accords. For example, they helped justify the Cristiani Administration's efforts to transfer more troops and resources into the National Police. In February 1992, *La Prensa Gráfica* argued, "The National Police has to be duly reinforced" (PG, 11 Feb. 1992). During an April 1992 broadcast of *Al Día*, Colonel Inocente Orlando Montano called for the transfer of more National Guard and Treasury Police troops into the National Police. Yet the news program failed to point out that this would be a violation of the peace accords (Al Día 1992d). In a December 1992 article, *El Diario de Hoy* presented favorable reactions among Nahuizalco residents to the establishment of a new National Police post in the area. The paper made no suggestion in the article, however, that the government should have prioritized the creation and deployment of the new civilian force (DH, 4 Dec. 1992).

The problem was not simply that the major media organizations were presenting inaccurate information about the peace accords. Through their coverage, media argued that these violations of the peace accords were both necessary and effective for the fight against crime. In reality, however, the National Police and other military institutions had done very little to counter crime prior to the signing of the peace accords in 1992. Given their focus on fighting guerrillas and civilian opposition forces, they did not spend very much time doing mundane police work. Even when they did investigate common crimes, their efforts seldom resulted in the conviction of the perpetrators. A very large part of the problem was that most Salvadorans did not trust the security forces enough to cooperate and supply them with information (Stanley 1993, pp. 2, 14).

The most important omission from the mainstream media's portrayal of the National Police and the other military security forces was their failure to discuss the connections between these corrupt institutions and organized crime. As discussed in Chapter Two, the investigative unit of the National Police (the Commission for the Investigation of Criminal Acts, CIHD) helped protect human rights violators instead of bringing them to justice. Furthermore, officers from the security forces had taken advantage of the impunity that they enjoyed during the war to engage in organized crime activities, such as kidnapping and car theft rings (Stanley and Loosle 1998). Costa has stated that "many sources" (including a former guerrilla serving on the National Public Security Council) believed that military personnel helped create the increase in crime in order to maintain their role in public security (Costa 1999, p. 150).

The dominant media also used the strategy of discrediting the new PNC in order to support the National Police. In December 1992, for example, *El Diario de Hoy* published an op-ed piece referring to the new force as the "FMLN Civilian Police." The columnist supported this assertion by claiming that members of FMLN "front" groups would fill the sixty percent of the PNC set aside for civilians (Jones 1992, p. 17). The author of a March 1993 news article in the same paper referred to PNC Deputy Commissioner Carlos López of Chalatenango as "a 33 year-old former terrorist [who] is responsible for the police forces in the region" (DH, 15 Mar. 1993). The paper did not, however, make similar accusations against PNC officials who had served in the National Police or other institutions known to have been heavily involved in death squad activity during the war.

The Cristiani Administration took advantage of this climate. In June 1992, the government transferred more than three thousand National Guard and Treasury Police troops into the Army and then into the National Police. The Cristiani Administration then transferred entire units from the Belloso Battalion—one of the elite counterinsurgency units known for violating human rights—into the National Police (Costa 1999, p. 147). In May 1993, the UN Secretary General complained, "The National Police was meant to be phased out gradually as the [PNC] was deployed. Instead, it has increased significantly." As evidence of this problem, Boutros-Ghali reported that the government was producing up to one hundred new National Police agents each month (Boutros-Ghali 1995i, p. 432). The following November, he complained that these government actions were "difficult to reconcile with the peace accords" (Boutros-Ghali 1995h, p. 501).

The government also favored the National Police in terms of material resources. Between 1992 and 1994, the National Police received $77 million, more than the PNC ($45 million) and the National Public Security Academy (ANSP) ($22 million) combined (Costa 1999, p. 171). According to the Washington Office on Latin America, the government provided the ANSP with "training centers [which were] in deplorable conditions" (Spence, Lanchin, and Thale 2001, p. 19).

In the fall of 1993, the Cristiani government proposed retaining seventy-five percent of National Police troops until the next administration would take power in June 1994. ARENA's presidential candidate, Armando Calderón Sol, was privately against dismantling the National Police. Costa has argued that Cristiani's proposal was therefore intended to stall until a new ARENA government not subject to international verification could claim that it was not obligated by the peace accords. The international community—including the UN Secretary General and the U.S. Ambassador to El Salvador—rejected this maneuver and pressured the government to expedite the demobilization of the National Police (Costa 1999, pp. 158–9).

The dominant media continued supporting the old police force until Salvadoran journalists witnessed and videotaped an armored car robbery in June 1994. Several of the assailants had been waiting for the vehicle as it approached the bank. Intense gunfire erupted, and more criminals arrived. Twelve of the fifteen robbers were in National Police uniforms. The attackers killed six people and wounded five others. The journalists continued filming the robbery, despite the fact that a reporter from *El Noticiero* was among those injured. They captured footage—which was also broadcast on other stations and reproduced in the papers—which led to the identification of the head of the Criminal Investigation Division of the National Police, Colonel José Rafael Coreas Orellana, as the leader of the operation. The assailants' use of National Police uniforms reflected their confidence in the continuing climate of impunity. Some of them even returned to the scene of the crime in order to retrieve one of their rifles. A court provided further evidence of the impunity enjoyed by military criminals when it released Coreas Orellana. The judge based the ruling on an alibi provided by the head of the National Police (Costa 1999, pp. 167–8; DH, 23 June 1994).

The mainstream media dramatically changed their attitude toward the National Police in the face of such overwhelming evidence of corruption and abuse of authority within the force. *La Prensa Gráfica* published an editorial shortly after the arrest of Coreas Orellana warning the government, "The citizenry is not content with what it is told, that these are personal, isolated incidents." The paper connected the bank robbery scandal to the National Police's role during the war, which it identified as "political control of the citizenry." The paper argued that this had led to corruption instead of genuine security (PG, 28 June 1994). A few weeks later, *La Prensa Gráfica* clearly stated that it had been a mistake not to immediately dismantle all three of the military security forces and replace them with a transitional organization composed of the best agents from each organization. It then warned, "Any concession from the authorities to the protectors [of the corrupt police] and those who conceal the past will be immediately repudiated by public opinion" (PG, 15 July 1994).

While criminal activity such as this robbery is certainly a serious problem, it is important to consider why the dominant media became so outraged by this particular incident, while they had been willing to overlook, downplay, and misrepresent other problems with the force. Most of the National Police's victims were poor Salvadorans. As economic elites, the owners and directors of the large media outlets were apparently more persuaded to oppose impunity by the theft of roughly $227,000 than they had been by the continuing illegal detentions and summary executions of common citizens. The assailants demonstrated that they understood the potential impact of television footage of this incident by firing upon the journalists as they were covering the assault. They made a serious mistake, however; by attacking the journalists, the assailants gave the media even more reason to turn against the National Police.

The Salvadoran government quickly reacted to the publicity surrounding this event. Vice Minister of Security Hugo Barrera announced that the National Police should be dismantled as soon as possible. He also called the force "criminals dressed as police" (Walter 1997, p. 54; CDHES 1995, p. 168). Following this incident, the government launched further investigations of organized crime involving National Police agents and former soldiers (Stanley 1996b, p. 10; Spence, Lanchin, and Thale 2001, p. 19).

A few weeks prior to the robbery, President Cristiani had claimed that the unit led by Coreas Orellana was made up of well-qualified agents. He argued that it should therefore be incorporated into the PNC as an entire unit, rather than as individuals who would each be evaluated before being allowed to join the new force. The leadership of the United Nations Observer Mission in El Salvador (ONUSAL) did not have the necessary information to react to Cristiani's statements, however. According to Costa, the ONUSAL Police Division's decision to conduct its own separate patrols rather than joint patrols with the National Police prevented it from detecting crime networks as large as the one led by Coreas Orellana (Costa 1999, pp. 325–6). The local media therefore had an important impact on the international community's attitude toward the National Police and the government's handling of the institution. The new Calderón Sol Administration reacted to the international pressure and the public outcry within El Salvador following this event by dismantling the division led by Coreas Orellana and ordering the evaluation of its former members (Boutros-Ghali 1995k, p. 578; Costa 1999, p. 326; Stanley 1996b, p. 10).

Most observers have generally agreed the pressure resulting from this incident led to the final demobilization of the National Police in early 1995. Costa, for example, stated, "Without a doubt, these events accelerated the total collapse of the National Police and put an end to the efforts of those who were still resisting dissolution" (Costa 1999, p. 168). The (nongovernmental) Human Rights Commission of El Salvador (CDHES) stated, "The silver lining to this black cloud was public pressure to accelerate the complete demobilization of the National Police" (CDHES 1995, p. 19). Even the usually pro-government *La Prensa Gráfica* referred to the incident as "the coup de grace to the institution" which demonstrated "the levels of rot inside the now extinct force" (PG, 13 Jan. 1995).[6] These events would not have made any difference, however, if the local media had not brought them to the attention of Salvadoran society and the international community.

The Salvadoran justice system, however, did not convict Coreas Orellana despite the video recording of the crime. In a major demonstration of continuing impunity in 1995, the Second Penal Court and the Second Penal Chamber ruled that the tape was not sufficient evidence against him (PG, 22 Feb. 1998). The press mocked the ruling, given that the image in the video matched the defendant's distinctive features (Stanley 1996b, p. 33n).

Efforts to Militarize the New "Civilian" Police Force

Human rights advocates initially had high hopes for the National Civilian Police (PNC). In early 1992, for example, the Human Rights Institute of the Central American University (IDHUCA) called the creation of the new force "the most novel achievement" of the peace talks and "a genuine revolution in public security matters" (IDHUCA 1992, p. 59). In a 1993 report for Hemisphere Initiatives, William Stanley judged the new force to be "extremely successful." He pointed to the new institution's integration of former guerrillas and National Police troops and the population's growing trust in the force as particularly important achievements (Stanley 1993, pp. ii, 3, 14).[7]

As discussed above, the Salvadoran government deprived the PNC of the resources that it needed and prolonged the existence of the National Police. According to Costa, the government also maintained a bloated defense budget at the expense of the new police force. He argued that these maneuvers were aimed precisely at preventing the creation of the new force. Costa has even claimed that the ANSP would not ever have begun training PNC agents if the FMLN had not refused to demobilize any more of its troops until this happened (Costa 1999, pp. 173, 186–7, 215).

This was not, however, the government's only strategy. If there had to be a new "civilian" police force, the government could at least make it less civilian. In 1994, Hemisphere Initiatives warned, "Civilian control over the new PNC ... may be shrinking before the inertia of traditional forces within the military" (Spence, Vickers et al. 1994, p. 35). Stanley, who had reported on the public's initial optimism toward the new force, found that it was common to hear Salvadorans comparing the PNC to the National Police in 1995 (Stanley 1996b, p. 2).

The most basic element of the remilitarization of public security was the violation of the quotas established by the government and the FMLN. By 1995, the United Nations reported the former National Police made up "considerably" more than the twenty percent of the PNC that had been agreed upon (Boutros-Ghali 1995g, p. 552). They were able to do so, in part, because the FMLN had been willing to compromise on this issue. In December 1992, the FMLN agreed to allow intact National Police units into the PNC in exchange for the removal of the officers named by the Ad Hoc Commission (Costa 1999, pp. 228–9).

By agreeing to these revisions of the peace accords, the FMLN's leadership was engaging in the elite pact-making process that scholars such as Huntington and Przeworski have argued is necessary for democratization (see Huntington 1993, p. 169; Przeworski 1991, p. 122). In this instance, pro-human rights forces were unable to generate enough public criticism against the FMLN to force it to demand full compliance with the provisions of the peace accords. Furthermore, the government proved unwilling to keep its end of agreement once it got what it wanted. This outcome is consistent with Stepan's argument that a regime may take back its concessions toward democratization unless democratic forces can transform these promises into societal conquests (Stepan 1988, p. 45).

Some Salvadorans have also suggested that these quotas became irrelevant after the transitional period, which ended with the final demobilization of the National Police in January 1995. A military source insisted to me that former guerrillas, National police agents, or former combatants from any branch of the Armed forces were eligible to join the new force after this initial period (Military Source 2000). United

Nations insider Gino Costa, however, has made the exact opposite argument. According to him, the PNC was supposed to admit former guerrillas and National Police only during the transitional phase. He has further stated that the UN had always maintained that only civilians would be allowed in once the force was up and running normally (Costa 1999, pp. 196, 238).

The government also violated the accords by reassigning troops from the National Guard, the Treasury Police, and other military units to the PNC. In March of 1992, President Cristiani used the crime wave as an excuse to transfer troops from the National Guard and the Treasury Police into the National Police. The Cristiani Administration then transferred the entire Belloso Battalion—one of the counterinsurgency battalions scheduled to be disbanded—into the National Police as a unit. The United Nations condemned these moves as simply putting soldiers into police uniforms (Costa 1999, pp. 146–8). Secretary General Boutros-Ghali labeled these moves "directly counter to the Agreements" (Boutros-Ghali 1995m, p. 242).

The Cristiani Administration made the situation even worse, however, by failing to demobilize these troops along with the National Police. In November 1992 and October 1993, Boutros-Ghali complained that the ANSP was admitting National Police officers who had been transferred from other sectors of the military in violation of the peace accords. The Salvadoran government also undermined ONUSAL's ability to challenge this policy of impunity through its failure to provide accurate and complete lists of those who served in the military units. This prevented the UN mission from identifying these individuals so that it could prevent them from entering the PNC. (Boutros-Ghali 1995l, p. 269; 1995f, p. 489; 1995h, p. 499).

The government promoted structural impunity even further by transferring corrupt National Police units into the PNC without evaluation of individual troops and proper training. In December 1992, the FMLN agreed to allow the government to transfer the Commission for the Investigation of Criminal Acts (CIHD) and the Executive Anti-Narcotics Unity (UEA) into the new force as units rather than individuals. The CIHD became the Criminal Investigation Division (DIC) of the new "civilian" police force. The UEA became the Anti-Narcotics Division (DAN) (IDHUCA 1996, p. 11). The PNC did not follow ONUSAL's recommendation that it investigate forty-six UEA agents whom the FMLN accused of human rights abuses (WOLA 1994, p. 3). Secretary General Boutros-Ghali complained that both units were operating "with excessive autonomy" (Boutros-Ghali 1995k, p. 579).

The Cristiani Administration transferred over one hundred troops into UEA after the FMLN agreed to allow the government to transfer the unit into the PNC. By doing so, it violated its agreement with the FMLN (WOLA 1994, p. 3). In 1995, Public Defense Minister Hugo Barrera ordered the PNC to remove seventy-one of the DAN agents who entered the PNC through this irregular procedure. The entire DAN and DIC responded by going on strike and threatening to burn police files. Many of those who were not directly expelled from the PNC resigned because they refused to take courses at the ANSP. Those agents who left were rewarded with substantial separation packages (Costa 1999, pp. 274–7).

The government also fostered impunity through its policy of reclassifying soldiers as civilians. These new civilians would then join the PNC without consideration of the twenty percent quota or the fact that they may have come from units outside of the National Police. In May 1995, Secretary General Boutros Ghali reported that the government was arguing that demobilized troops from the National Guard and the Treasury Police should be counted as civilians. He condemned this maneuver as "contrary to the Agreement's concept of a completely new civilian police force" (Boutros-Ghali 1995m, p. 242). The government also attempted to count military officers, such as former UEA head Oscar Peña Durán, as civilians. Peña Durán had resigned from the National Police shortly before he entered the PNC as the first head of the DAN. The United Nations rejected the government's assertion that he became a civilian as soon as he resigned (Costa 1999, pp. 237–9).

In June 1993, the government promoted Peña Durán to Deputy Director of Operations. He then assigned himself the rank of Commissioner. He used this position to assign former UEA personnel to leadership positions outside of the DAN, a violation of the government's December 1992 pact with the FMLN. He appointed one of these military figures to head the PNC delegation at San Miguel. Peña Durán also promoted his friends and allies to new ranks, including two to Commissioner and nineteen to Deputy Commissioner. These military figures who had not gone through training at the ANSP now outranked all of the PNC agents who had actually graduated from the ANSP. As a result of these changes, former military figures came to control fifty-two percent of the leadership positions within the "civilian" force (Costa 1999, pp. 157, 241, 258; Boutros-Ghali 1995h, p. 500; 1995g, pp. 551–2).[8]

During his tenure as Deputy Director of Operations, Peña Durán's behavior clearly demonstrated the dangers associated with government's policies of individual and structural impunity. He ordered former National Police within the PNC to spy on agents who had been guerrillas. He also instructed PNC agents to forget the pro-human rights training that they had received at the new academy (Stanley 1996b, pp. 16, 32). The Deputy Director of Operations broke off relations with the ONUSAL Police Division, a move that was followed by a sharp increase in human rights violations by the PNC (Costa 1999, pp. 247–8; WOLA 1994).

In 1999, incoming President Francisco Flores named Mauricio Sandoval as the new director of the PNC. Sandoval's previous position—the head of the State Intelligence Organization (OIE)—raised questions about his status as a civilian. The Central American University (UCA) referred to him as "an expert in psychological warfare and political intelligence" (Editorial 1999, p. 703). Once in office, Sandoval came under criticism for trying to concentrate control of public security in his own hands (Spence, Lanchin, and Thale 2001, p. 21).

The ANSP also became militarized. Hemisphere Initiatives reported complaints from cadets about "arbitrary enforcement of internal regulations without due process guarantees" and military-style discipline (Spence, Vickers et al. 1994, p. 11). Secretary General Boutros-Ghali complained that those in charge of discipline at the academy were predominantly former National Police. He also warned that this endangered the civilian nature of the PNC (Boutros-Ghali 1995g, p. 550).

Public security officials further undermined the civilian character of the new force by creating clandestine parallel police structures. These units were composed of so-called advisors who worked outside the official chain of command. Most of the personnel making up these structures had not graduated from the ANSP. Nonetheless, they sometimes wore police uniforms and used official police vehicles. Following the DAN strike, many of the agents who left the official PNC went to work in irregular institutions such as the Analysis Unit (Costa 1999, pp. 220, 277). Units such as these are very dangerous precisely because they are unaccountable and difficult to monitor. Human rights violators used similar structures to cover up their crimes during the war. These structures also have the danger of turning into another category of clandestine organizations—death squads.

While irregular public security structures prospered, authoritarian forces within the PNC attacked the police unit created specifically for fighting death squads and organized crime. The PNC created the Division for the Investigation of Organized Crime (DICO) in response to the Joint Group's 1994 recommendations (see Chapter Seven). UN Secretary General Kofi Annan called the unit "one of the most promising initiatives in the efforts of the National Civil Police to combat impunity" (Annan 1997, 10). The government placed the DICO under the Criminal Investigation Division (DIC), which was the renamed Commission for the Investigation of Criminal Acts (CIHD). DIC agents harassed and stalked their colleagues in the DICO. They also interfered in the DICO's investigations. Members of the DIC accused DICO agents of being Communists or FMLN members despite the fact that all of them came from the civilian sector (Stanley 1996b, pp. 17–8). In this manner, structural impunity allowed corrupt public security officials to prevent the consolidation of new institutions specifically created for the purpose of ending impunity.

Structural Impunity, Militarization, and Abuses by the PNC

Despite the high hopes of many Salvadorans and international observers, the PNC replaced the National Police not only as the national public security force, but also as the leading source of human rights violations in the nation. The Office of the Human Rights Counsel (PDDH) found that over forty percent of 4,696 complaints that it admitted in 1995 were directed against the new police force (Velásquez de Avilés 1996d, p. 23). The same office found that 55.7% of the complaints that it received in 1996 were directed against the PNC (Velásquez de Avilés 1997a, p. 17).

Many of these problems can be traced back to the government's success in remilitarizing the PNC. At the end of 1993, most human rights violations attributed to the new police force were committed by former National Police troops (IDHUCA 1998b, pp. 1087–8). In 1994, ONUSAL reported that "the transfer to the National Civil Police of members of the former State security forces and armed forces" was one of the leading causes of human rights violations by the PNC (ONUSAL Human Rights Division 1994c, 130). Agents from the Executive Anti Narcotics Unit/Anti-Narcotics Division (UEA/DAN) in particular stood out for their frequent human rights violations (Holiday and Stanley 2000, p. 46). The (nongovernmental) Human Rights Commission of El Salvador (CDHES) blamed former military personnel for bringing techniques such as torture into the new force. This NGO also blamed ex–National Police troops for many of the summary executions committed by police agents (CDHES 1995, pp. 8, 11).

The PDDH's 1994–1995 report provided an example of the connection between the perversion of the PNC's civilian character and human rights violations by the new force. This document includes a resolution regarding abuses committed by PNC agent Cornejo Quiños, whom the PDDH identified as a former member of the military security forces. The agency described how Cornejo Quiños and other police agents abducted several victims and tortured them with beatings, cigarette burns, asphyxiation, and mock executions.[9] The PDDH identified these techniques as "practices, that in periods we hope are already past, used to constitute the prelude to forced disappearances." The human rights office found no indication that Cornejo Quiños was punished for this incident (PDDH 1995a, pp. 452–5).[10]

The inadequate training of PNC leaders has been another important source of police abuse. In 1997, the force's own Inspector General's Office reported that only twenty-one percent of police chiefs knew that unjustified beatings are human rights violations. The same report found that only four percent of these chiefs understood that they should not arbitrarily arrest an individual, beat him, and fabricate evidence because of his resemblance to a suspect (Costa 1999, p. 349).

This does not mean, however, that the efforts to create a new police force have failed completely. In a March 1995 survey, 28.5% of Salvadorans identified the PNC as one of the two institutions that defended human rights the best. This evaluation can be explained in part by the fact that 39.9% of the same respondents identified criminals as the main source of human rights violations (IUDOP 1995b, pp. 356, 363); it was logical for those who considered criminals to be the main source of human rights violations to see the institution which fights crime as the best protector of human rights. Later that year, 48.6% of Salvadorans surveyed said that the PNC was better than the National Police (IDHUCA 1997b, p. 12).[11] Some members of the new force have even been willing to take great personal risks in order to protect the lives of others (as discussed in Chapters Eight and Nine).

Pressure to Clean Up the PNC

Many observers have argued that domestic expression had little impact on the implementation of the peace accords and that the progress that was achieved resulted from international pressure. Human Rights Institute of the Central American University (IDHUCA) Director Benjamín Cuéllar, for example, responded to my question about the impact of Salvadorans exercising their right to expression by saying, "No, that was done above and outside of the nation. Within and below, the people did not get involved" (Cuéllar 2000).

While the international community certainly played an important role, it is necessary to recognize its limits. When the National Public Security Academy (ANSP) refused to admit sixty-nine agents from the National Police Anti-Crime Battalion, for example, Hugo Barrera nonetheless allowed many of them to join the PNC. He also hired five officers from the military unit as his own unofficial "aides." He then refused UN demands that he fire these individuals (Costa 1999, p. 169). According to Central American University (UCA) Rector José María Tojeira, foreign governments have been willing to press for improvements in the PNC, but they have not been willing to back up the carrot of their aid with the stick of threatening to cut it off. Tojeira said that the idea behind this strategy is that cutting aid would worsen the situation. This rationale, he explained, is "similar to the flawed argument that the U.S. government used during the war: 'If we did not aid the military, we would have less control over it'" (Tojeira 2000). As discussed in Chapter Two, this strategy encouraged further human rights abuses during the war.

There have also been cases where diplomacy has done more harm than good. The United States government supported counter-productive measures such as the appointment of Peña Durán as the PNC Deputy Director of Operations, as well as the incorporation of the Executive Anti Narcotic Unit (UEA) and the Commission for the Investigation of Criminal Acts (CIHD) into the new force. According to Costa, the U.S. government did so in order to maintain the influence that it had developed through the institutions it had helped create during the war. The U.S. Embassy even withheld evidence of Peña Durán's involvement in a car theft ring in 1987 (Costa 1999, pp. 190, 225, 261). The U.S. government was therefore contributing to both individual and structural impunity.

United Nations officials have recognized the importance of Salvadorans' expression about public security issues. Pedro Nikken, for example, served as the United Nations Independent Expert for El Salvador, a position created by the Secretary General at the request of the UN Human Rights Commission. In his 1995, Nikken reported that NGOs and the political opposition had "repeatedly expressed" their concerns about the growing military influence in the PNC to him during his visits to El Salvador (Nikken 1995, 2, 76).[12] Perhaps the importance of Nikken's reports—as well as his working relationship with human rights organizations—was best illustrated by the Salvadoran government's efforts to hinder his contact with Salvadoran groups. In his 1994 report, Nikken explained how the government refused to respond to his requests to schedule a visit in January. The government then tried to blame Nikken for canceling the trip (Nikken 1994, 24, 26–7). *El Diario de Hoy* helped the government undermine Nikken's credibility by running (without comment) Minister of the Presidency Oscar Santamaría's assertion that Nikken wrote the report "by remote control"(DH, 8 Feb. 1994).

Figures from the U.S. government have also acknowledged the important role of expression from the Salvadoran opposition. I asked Congressman James McGovern about the respondents who said that Salvadorans who expressed themselves in favor of implementing the peace accords did not have a significant impact. "I'm international pressure," he replied. "I know what to pressure," he continued, "because I've got professors, unionists and human rights workers coming into my office.

Or I visit them. They ask me to take action." McGovern explained that the international community had a general perception that "everything was great" until Salvadorans increasingly denounced violations of the peace accords. "Then," he stated, "people like us in Washington said, 'OK. Let's put pressure on our State Department. Let's put pressure on the Salvadoran government [and] let them know that we are watching.'" Once they were motivated, international actors such as McGovern were able to obtain results on some, though not all, issues (McGovern 2001).

I also had the opportunity to speak with Congressman Moakley and his assistant Stephen Larose. Moakley compared his work on El Salvador since 1992 to that of the Fire Department. "When something really bad down there happens," he explained, "somebody gets in touch with us" (Moakley 2001). According to Larose, Moakley took action when he heard about human rights problems through Salvadoran NGOs, such as the IDHUCA and Tutela Legal. Larose further explained that human rights violators took Moakley's interest quite seriously given his history in the investigation of the Jesuit massacre and his continuing commitment to El Salvador (Larose 2001).[13] In April 1994, Moakley wrote Secretary of State Warren Christopher regarding the negative impact of Peña Durán and the former UEA and CIHD on the PNC (Moakley 1994b). A few weeks later, Peña Durán resigned citing health reasons. According to Hemisphere Initiatives, however, he actually resigned in response to pressure from the United States and the United Nations (Stanley 1996b, p. iii). Later that year, Representative Moakley led an international campaign to force the PNC to either dismiss the seventy-one Anti-Narcotics Division (DAN) agents who had not taken classes at the new academy or to force them to take the required courses. Public Security Minister Barrera responded by dismissing the agents in early 1995, the catalyst that brought on the DAN strike and the resignation of the agents in question, along with many of their colleagues (Spence, Lanchin, and Thale 2001, p. 20). If Salvadoran human rights advocates had not exercised their right to communicate with Moakley, he probably would not have taken action on this issue. If Moakley had not taken this action, Peña Durán would have been able to continue undermining the civilian character of the PNC even longer.

In general terms, NGOs and the media have used their oversight function to help limit excesses by the PNC and other public security officials. According to National Public Security Commission member David Escobar Galindo, civil society groups have used their watchdog role to force "the police and the authorities in general to be much more careful and to exercise better control over their members." While some authorities have continued to commit illegal actions, "they come to light, and this helps prevent these actions from being repeated" (Escobar

Galindo 2000). A television reporter expressed similar views, arguing, "as the media, we are watching their every movement, so they worry a bit more about the things that they do." "This," he explained, "has already made things better" (Two TCS reporters 2000).

A concrete example of the importance of the oversight exercised by the media and NGOs occurred in November 1995. The Unit for Maintaining Order—the riot police—responded to a demonstration by former FMLN and Armed Forces troops in front of the office of the fund for wounded veterans. Agent Tomás Antonio Coronado Valles killed a protester by shooting him with a rubber bullet at close range. The Salvadoran media aired and printed images of this incident. According to Carlos Rafael Urquilla Bonilla of the Foundation for the Study of the Application of Law (FESPAD), "no action would have been taken if this [media coverage] had not happened." The court convicted Coronado Valles of manslaughter, placed him on probation, ordered him to pay compensation to the victim's family, and removed him from the police force. The PNC agreed to work with the Office of the Human Rights Counsel (PDDH) to improve police training on how to handle such situations. The U.S. State Department reported that the PNC's conduct toward similar situations improved after this incident (Urquilla Bonilla 2000a; U.S. Department of State 1996, 1998). The UCA remarked, "It is regrettable that in order to adopt these ... measures it has been necessary to kill a Salvadoran before the television cameras" (Editorial 1995, p. 1079).

The dominant media have limited civil society's oversight of the police, however, through their tolerance and/or support of some of the PNC's actions, as well as their attitude toward some of the victims. As discussed in Chapter Nine, the media has generally played a negative role with regard to the rights of the accused through sensationalistic reporting and the message that human rights favor criminals (see, for example, Velásquez de Avilés 1997a, p. 47).

In order to remove human rights abusers and corrupt agents from the PNC, it is necessary to investigate their conduct. The government has not routinely conducted such investigation, however. According to Channel 12 News Director Mauricio Funes, investigations have gone forward "only in the degree to which there has been a citizen's denunciation that has been spread through the media" (Funes 2000). Another journalist explained, "the media's role in denouncing such situations has made the Office of the Inspector General pay attention and investigate more thoroughly" (Arguda 2000). NGOs and human rights victims have also had an indirect impact on the Inspector General by denouncing police abuses to the PDDH (see Velásquez de Avilés 1997a, p. 47).

While the removal of corrupt and abusive individuals from the police force is certainly important, the major media outlets have not devoted consistent attention to systematic problems within the force. As a result, they have generally brought about only slow change through the removal and/or punishment of individual police agents. In May 2000, the public became aware of police participation in two kidnappings and the robbery of a Holiday Inn near the U.S. Embassy. This provoked public outcry, not only about these incidents, but also regarding neighborhood-level police abuses. This led PNC Director Mauricio Sandoval to request special powers to root out criminals from the police force. *El Diario de Hoy* reported that Sandoval's request was also motivated by a PDDH report on police crime that came out the day before. Given that PDDH investigations have relied heavily on public expression for information, this meant that the Salvadorans who provided the information contained in the report had an indirect impact on Sandoval's actions. In July, *El Diario de Hoy* credited itself for motivating Sandoval's decision through evidence it printed on police involved in criminal acts (DH, 8 Oct 2000; DH, 27 May 2000; Two U.S. Government Sources 2001; Spence, Lanchin, and Thale 2001, pp. 18). The authorities investigated PNC agents for crimes such as murder, robbery, abduction, and extortion "thanks to citizens' denunciations" during the unusually extensive evaluation process (DH, 7 July 2000). By the end of the year, the PNC had removed over fifteen hundred agents (Spence, Lanchin, and Thale 2001, p. 18). These important changes would not have happened without the media's coverage of the Holiday Inn robbery and the abductions committed by PNC agents. Even with this coverage, however, common Salvadoran citizens needed to denounce the routine human rights abuses and other offenses committed by police agents in order to broaden the focus of this inquiry.

It is important to point out, however, that there were serious problems with this cleansing of the PNC's ranks. The courts reinstated some of the purged agents on the basis of due process violations. Sandoval responded by getting the Assembly to pass legislation suspending civil service protections for one hundred twenty days (Spence, Lanchin, and Thale 2001, p. 18). The media and opposition politicians also complained that the authorities were not investigating high-ranking police officers (U.S. Department of State 2001).

While opposition groups and the media have brought about some positive changes in the PNC, much more remains to be done. According to FMLN leader Shafick Handal, "We currently worry more about the authoritarian distortion that ARENA ministers want to impose on the National Civilian Police, than about what happens in the Armed Forces" (Handal 1997, p. 168). Fellow FMLN member and President of the Public Security Committee in the Assembly José Manuel Melgar Henríquez predicted that if problems within the PNC were not solved, "we will have a police [force] that is civilian in name only" and "very similar to the [National] Guard" (Melgar Henríquez 2000). This outcome would effectively prevent the consolidation of democracy and point the way to a return to overt authoritarianism.

The Armed Forces Reclaim Their Role in Public Security

The ARENA administrations have not limited the remilitarization of public security to compromising the PNC's civilian character. They have also provided the military with a direct role in the war on crime. Within a year of signing the peace accords, the Salvadoran government had already deployed regular Armed Forces troops for anti-crime patrols.

President Cristiani first used regular Armed Forces troops for public security duties in late 1992 and early 1993. He justified this action by the need to protect the annual coffee harvest from rural bandits. According to Costa, the FMLN and other opposition groups helped limit the scope and duration of this particular deployment through their criticism of the measure (Costa 1999, p. 213). By 1995, however, there were at least as many soldiers performing public security functions as there were National Civilian Police (PNC) agents (Spence, Vickers, and Dye 1995, p. 30). Since then, military troops have continued to function as part of Joint Work Groups officially led by civilian police agents. Military participation in public security is therefore no longer the exception to the rule that the Armed Forces would stay out of internal security. Rather, it has become the unofficial rule.

Sources within the U.S. government have told me that the Salvadoran military was actually ambivalent about the prospect of getting involved in public security functions. According to these respondents, the military no longer had sufficient troops to do so because of postwar cutbacks. They also argued that military officers viewed anti-crime measures as "secondary" to their main mission, defending national sovereignty. These sources attributed this new professional outlook to the fact that the officers "had the new [military] doctrine drummed into" their heads (Two U.S. Government Sources 2001).

Military leaders have themselves provided evidence against this argument. General Ponce continued to serve as the Defense Minister until shortly after the publication of the Truth Commission Report. In 1999, he told *Tendencias* magazine that the Armed Forces had the constitutional duty "to be prepared to reestablish internal peace when the public forces are overcome by any subversive or violent act and the internal order is broken" (quoted in Ruballo 1999, p. 16). Colonel Humberto Corado Figueroa succeeded Ponce as Defense Minister and served in the position until the end of 1995. In 1997, he wrote that the crime problem demonstrated the harmful effects of restricting the Armed Forces' role in internal security. "A state that weakens its military instrument," he argued, "is attacking its own interests." He also referred to the restrictions on the military as "a political concession that will continue to have negative repercussions on Salvadorans' quality of life" (Corado Figueroa 1997, pp. 100–1).

The military leadership had additional incentives to participate in public security functions. According to Costa, the military suffered from a profound identity crisis because there were no longer any external enemies threatening national sovereignty and the integrity of Salvadoran territory (Costa 1999, p. 216). Criminals provided the military with an internal threat. Military leaders and their allies also used the Armed Forces' role in public security functions to justify maintaining a relatively high Armed Forces budget at the expense of resources which could have gone to the new police force (FESPAD 1998, p. 17).

Key UN figures have argued that the ARENA administrations' use of military troops has violated both the peace accords and the constitution. In 1994, for example, UN Independent Expert Pedro Nikken stated the he was "unaware that such a decision [to deploy the military to fight crime] is based on any legal act that meets the requirements of form and of substance laid down in the Constitution" (Nikken 1994, 101). In 1995, the Human Rights Division of ONUSAL reported,

> although this measure [of using the military for public security] is, in theory, based on the Constitution, the spirit of the peace agreements requires that it be subject to legal rules which establish expressly and restrictively the requirements and conditions which must be met before domestic peace, tranquility, order or public safety can be considered to be endangered, in exceptional cases, and before the normal means for their preservation can be considered to have been exhausted [ONUSAL Human Rights Division 1995, 37].

The UN Secretary General further complained, "ONUSAL has pressed the Government, so far without success, to make such a report" of the exceptional circumstances justifying these deployments "in order to respect this constitutional prevision" (Boutros-Ghali 1995h, p. 497). The fact that the Salvadoran government has nonetheless continued relying upon Armed Forces troops for public security provisions therefore offers further evidence of the limits of international pressure.

Salvadoran NGOs have argued that the ARENA governments' frequent use of the military in public security matters has contradicted the constitutional provision which allows the president to do so only under exceptional circumstances. The Human Rights Institute of the Central

American University (IDHUCA), for example, complained that one such "exception" lasted through almost all of 1995 (IDHUCA 1996, p. 12). FES-PAD specifically pointed to the extended duration of the Joint Task Force patrols in 1997 as a violation of the constitution (FESPAD 1998, p. 16).

One of the most important—though not necessarily successful—arguments against using the Armed Forces for public security has been that military troops have been involved in serious human rights abuses while performing this function. In November 1994, for example, some authority—which authority has not been clearly established—called for military troops to support forty-five PNC agents during a confrontation with bus owners and drivers blocking access to San Miguel City. The crowd became further agitated when seventy soldiers arrived. While it is not clear which side fired the first gunshot, two protesters and one Army sergeant died during the confrontation. Twenty other individuals were wounded. Many observers doubted President Calderón Sol's assertion that he had called in the military troops as part of his constitutional authority. PNC Deputy Commissioner César Flores Murillo had earlier claimed that he had called for military reinforcements (PG, 16 Nov. 1994; DH, 15 Nov. 1994). ONUSAL Human Rights Division Director Dr. García Sayán complained that the authorities had not exhausted all other options before calling in the military, as was required in the constitution (PG, 16 Nov. 1994).

Soldiers also committed less visible human rights violations in the course of public security duties. In June 1995, for example, the Office of the Human Rights Counsel (PDDH) opened an investigation in response to an article in *La Prensa Gráfica* about a "criminal" who had been killed during a confrontation with a mixed PNC/Armed Forces patrol (PG, 1 June 1995). The PDDH found a witness who told the investigators that a soldier had silently approached the supposed criminal from behind. He then shot the victim five times without any warning. The witness also reported that PNC agents had tried to coerce her into signing a statement they had prepared indicating that the soldier fired in self defense (Velásquez de Avilés 1997b, p. 210). The autopsy supported the witness's account. The PDDH therefore concluded, "the victim was in a defenseless state" (Velásquez de Avilés 1997b, p. 211). The facts established by the PDDH suggest that this execution may have been connected to "social cleansing" death squads similar to Sombra Negra.[14]

The opposition has had little, if any, positive impact through its criticism of the military's participation in public security functions. One important reason for this is that the major media outlets have supported military intervention. According to Costa, for example, the press provided a long campaign prior to military patrols in July 1993 (Costa 1999, pp. 213–4). Even the article which brought the June 1995 summary execution discussed above to the PDDH's attention was biased in favor of the mixed PNC/Armed Forces patrol. *La Prensa Gráfica* reported, "A criminal died yesterday morning upon confronting a police and military patrol." By using the word "criminal," the author indicated a clear presumption of guilt—a serious violation of journalism ethics. The reporter also implied that the victim did something to deserve retaliation from the police and soldiers by using the word "confronting." The article further indicated that "military sources" used this incident to justify their decision to increase the mixed civilian/military patrols in the area (PG, 1 June 1995). The paper did not, however, question the military's authority to make such a decision.

The opposition has not been able to use expression against military involvement in public security to turn public opinion against the practice. In a 1997 poll, for example, the University Public Opinion Institute (IUDOP), found that almost eighty percent of respondents believed that the use of the military against crime was necessary (Cruz 1997, p. 981). Hemisphere Initiatives found that the high level of popular support for using the Armed Forces in public security caused the FMLN to drop its objections to this measure (Spence, Vickers, and Dye 1995, p. 9). U.S. government sources have also indicated that the FMLN has not seriously opposed the military's role in public security because doing so would be "political suicide" (Two U.S. Government Sources 2001).

Recently, the U.S. government has supported the further militarization of public security in El Salvador. Following the return of the Panama Canal zone to Panama, the U.S. military has sought to establish new bases in the region, including one at the San Salvador Airport. In June of 2000, a U.S. Embassy spokesman stated, "We're trying to help [Salvadorans] decide what role the military should have" in public security. The Salvadoran government has already established in both the peace accords and the Salvadoran constitution, however, that the military should not play any role in these activities except under exceptional circumstances. When the FMLN objected to the base, the party's opponents accused it of being connected to Colombian guerrillas and drug traffickers (Brackley 2000, p. 21).

The Mixed Results of Efforts to Demilitarize Public Security

In terms of protecting civil and political rights, the demilitarization of public security was one of the most important components of the peace accords. It is therefore not surprising to find that the military and the ARENA administrations have promoted structural impunity by violating the public security provisions in the accords. In many cases, the dominant media have helped the government do so by ignoring and/or actively opposing the opposition groups' calls for the government to comply with its obligation to truly demilitarize public security. In the context of an extremely severe crime wave, the large media outlets have preyed upon the population's understandable fear and anxiety to justify government actions—and inaction—which have contributed to the problem rather than resolving it. Without accurate historical background, the government's and the press's argument that the military security forces were needed to fight crime sounds quite reasonable. The government and the dominant media misrepresented the situation, however, by portraying the members of the former security forces as heroic, competent, and effective against crime. The large media outlets have also undermined restrictions on the incorporation of National Police members into the PNC and the ban on the transfer of other military troops into the new force. They have supported the ARENA administrations' frequent use of active duty soldiers as part of anticrime patrols. In this context of a serious crime wave and media and ARENA advocacy of militarized solutions, it was very difficult for human rights advocates to inform the population that the government's policies of retaining these corrupt institutions actually aggravate the crime problem.

When the large media outlets did change their positions, however, the government finally took such crucial steps as overturning the enabling legislation for the National Guard and Treasury Police, as well as the complete demobilization of the National Police. The dominant media only did so, however, once they realized that these state agents who enjoyed impunity threatened elite interests.

The next three chapters further explore the consequences of the militarization of public security. They also evaluate the efforts of Salvadorans who have attempted to use their right to expression in response to specific cases of postwar human rights abuses.

7

Death Squads Seek to Destabilize the Transition

As discussed in Chapter Three, authoritarian forces in El Salvador have continued to use violence to hamper freedom of expression and the enjoyment of other human rights during the postwar era. The Truth Commission had warned that this would happen as long as the powerful figures behind the wartime death squads were not exposed by further investigations. It therefore called upon the Cristiani Administration to conduct such an inquiry. As part of the peace accords, the Salvadoran government had promised that it would implement all of the Truth Commission's recommendations. The Cristiani Administration had reason to fear such investigations, however, because of the ruling party's historic ties to the death squads. As long as the government did not investigate these clandestine groups, however, they would be able to continue threatening the stability of both the peace process and the transition to democracy.

This chapter examines the difficulties involved in uprooting clandestine structures which the government prefers to not confront. President Cristiani tried to avoid a serious, independent inquiry into postwar death squad activity by asserting that the murder of Farabundo Martí National Liberation Front (FMLN) leaders was simply the result of common crime and coincidence. The government also alleged that the FMLN had itself committed these killings, just as it had claimed that the guerrillas killed Archbishop Romero and the Jesuits at the Central American University (UCA) during the war. Cristiani eventually announced that institutions historically linked to cover-ups such as the Commission for the Investigation of Criminal Acts (CIHD) would investigate the murders.

The dominant media generally supported Cristiani's strategies. Eventually, however, Salvadoran dissidents succeeded in using public expression to motivate the Office of the Human Rights Counsel (PDDH) and the international community to pressure the government to launch a serious investigation of these killings. Only then did Cristiani agree to do so.

In contrast to the Ad Hoc Commission and the Truth Commission, the ad hoc body formed to investigate postwar political violence—the Joint Group for the Investigation of Politically Motivated Illegal Armed Groups—was not directly mentioned in the 1992 peace accords. It was connected to the accords, however, through the Truth Commission's binding recommendation that the government establish another commission to continue its investigation of wartime death squads. Once the government finally agreed to create such a body, it limited the Joint Group's powers by giving it a much narrower mandate than those of the Ad Hoc Commission and Truth Commission. In fact, this mandate was so narrow that it failed to meet the standards called for by the Truth Commission because it restricted the body's investigation to postwar killings.

The Joint Group relied upon information it obtained directly and indirectly through public expression, just as the Ad Hoc Commission and the Truth Commission had done. Despite its limited mandate, the Joint Group established that the wartime death squads continued to operate and explained how they had adapted themselves to the new environment. These findings demonstrate the weakness of arguments in favor of amnesty laws by showing that the government fostered further instability by accommodating human rights violators with impunity. The investigative body also offered specific recommendations for preventing further political violence.

The government has made very little progress in most of the cases examined by the Joint Group. The October 1993 murder of FMLN leader Francisco Velis has become one of the rare exceptions in which the judicial system has identified and punished at least some of the individuals responsible for the crime. Salvadorans who exercised their right to expression as witnesses have provided much of the information that has led to progress in this case. The attempts to silence these individuals demonstrate that some police agents continue to view anyone who attempts to challenge them as enemies of the state (in accordance with the National Security Doctrine).

Unfinished Business: The Investigation of the Death Squads

We have already examined the partial implementation of peace accords provisions aimed at eliminating impunity, including the removal of human rights violators from the Armed Forces, the Truth Commission investigation, and the dissolution of particularly repressive military structures such as the National Guard. It would be reasonable to assume that these measures indirectly affected the death squads. The peace accords did not, however, include any provisions directly aimed at uprooting and dismantling the death squads. While the accords did contain a section devoted to paramilitary forces, it only addressed the civil defenses, reserves, and private security forces. The two sides did not even acknowledge the existence of the death squads in the peace accords (Government of El Salvador and FMLN 1995c, pp. 197–8). This is consistent with the state's purpose for sponsoring death squads in the first place: creating deniability to conceal its involvement in human rights abuses. Clearly, the FMLN had a very strong stake in stopping death squad violence because its own members would be vulnerable to the clandestine groups. Nonetheless, the FMLN could not add a section on the death squads to the peace accords without the government's approval.

The government and the FMLN did clearly state in the accords, however, that both sides would be required to implement the Truth Commission's recommendations. The commission recommended that "a thorough investigation of this issue [death squads] be undertaken immediately" (Commission on the Truth for El Salvador 1995, p. 382). Specifically, it called for the government to "make serious efforts to investigate the structural connection that has been found to exist between the death squads and State bodies" (Commission on the Truth for El Salvador 1995, p. 360). The commission justified this order on its belief that the death squads would remain a latent threat to democracy unless the government took decisive action against them. Furthermore, the Truth Commission warned the government that the death squads could expand their involvement in organized crime in order to finance their political murders (Commission on the Truth for El Salvador 1995, pp. 360–1).

Once again, the very president who had served during the resurgence of repression in 1989 and the early 1990s was ultimately responsible for the implementation of this recommendation. Predictably, President Cristiani made it clear that he had no intention of doing so. "We do not agree," he told the media, "with continuing to spend energy on the past" because "it will not accomplish anything" following the 1993 amnesty. Instead, he argued, "The important thing is to prevent new clandestine groups from forming" (Megavisión 1993d).

Preventing the formation of new death squads was certainly a valid goal. Nonetheless, Cristiani overlooked the Truth Commission's warning that the wartime death squads still existed and could therefore resume their acts of terror. In his statement, the president failed to consider that increased knowledge of past death squad participants and practices could be very useful in efforts to prevent new squads from forming. The problem for Cristiani, of course, was that the Truth Commission Report had already injured the interests of his party by linking the National Republican Alliance (ARENA) and its founder to the death squads. He would therefore risk further problems for his party if he ordered *genuine* investigations of past paramilitary groups. He would also risk harming the interests of other powerful military and economic figures through such investigations.

Cristiani's refusal to follow the Truth Commission's recommendation is consistent with the first part of Stepan's dialectic of regime concessions and societal conquests (see Stepan 1988, p. 45). As Stepan's theory suggests, the government took back its earlier concession—that it would comply with the binding recommendations of the Truth Commission. The theory also suggests that the Salvadoran opposition would have to apply political pressure on Cristiani in order to force Cristiani to uphold even part of his original agreement.

The Truth Commission's Warnings Were Accurate

The death squads were continuing to kill dissidents even before the Truth Commission formally began its investigation. In May 1992, for example, the FMLN temporarily suspended its participation in the National Commission for the Consolidation of Peace (COPAZ) to protest an attack on Vladimir Flores Ramos, who worked as a driver and bodyguard for the Front. While the government and the media argued that this incident was merely a case of common crime, the victim's relatives and the FMLN maintained that it was an attempt on his life. The FMLN also expressed concern that this attack could be the start of a "dirty war" (DH, 20 May 1992).

The FMLN's fears appeared to be justified as attacks and threats against its members escalated. In early 1993, the United Nations Observer Mission in El Salvador (ONUSAL) reported that the terror campaign "reached its peak" on October 22, 1992 when a group calling itself the Maximiliano Hernández Martínez Brigade issued a threat to kill sixteen high-level FMLN leaders, along with figures from ONUSAL and the foreign press. Several radio stations read the threat on the air, just as media outlets had carried death squad announcements throughout the war (ONUSAL Human Rights Division 1993b, 84). The same group later warned Dr. José María Méndez that it would harm his family unless he persuaded Dr. Francisco Lima to end his run for Vice President on the FMLN ticket (PG, 26 Oct. 1993). The government's policy of closing its eyes and ignoring the death squads obviously did nothing to stop the violence.

In the fall of 1993, however, death squads engaged in "more frequent, brazen, and selective" attacks (Human Rights Watch/Americas 1994, p. 1). The killings reached an unprecedented level when gunmen assassinated FMLN leader Francisco Velis on October 25, 1993. They shot the victim in his head while he was taking his daughter to daycare. This modus operandi resembled that used in the 1987 murder of (nongovernmental) Human Rights Commission of El Salvador (CDHES) President Herbert Anaya. FMLN commander Roberto Roca told the media that Velis's killers used an explosive bullet (Teleprensa 1993). The ONUSAL Human Rights Division reported that pieces of Velis's brain and skull were found up to eight meters from his corpse, evidence which supports Roca's version of events (ONUSAL Human Rights Division 1994b, ¶ 35). Two National Police agents who were one hundred meters from the crime scene claimed to have not heard anything (DH, 26 Oct. 1993). According to Megavisión's news broadcast, Velis became the twentieth FMLN member to have been killed since the beginning of 1993 (Megavisión 1993a). He would not be the last, however.

The Velis case drew a great deal of attention because he was a member of the FMLN's National Council and an alternate candidate for the Assembly. This made him the highest level FMLN official to be killed up to this point. While the murder of national figures such as Velis helped bring international attention to political violence in El Salvador, the focus on elites did not raise awareness of the killing of lower-level FMLN officials. According to Human Rights Watch, clandestine groups continued committing such murders "largely unnoticed and underreported" (Human Rights Watch/Americas 1994, pp. 8–9).

The Motives Behind the Murders of Opposition Figures

The ARENA administration rejected any suggestion that the crimes were politically motivated. In August 1993, for example, the government argued that the left was complaining that the killings were politically motivated solely for the purpose of misinforming the international community, blocking economic aid, and preventing the consolidation of democracy (LPG, 13 Aug. 1993). In November 1993, President Cristiani asserted that the FMLN was trying to "politicize" the murders in order to "win popular sympathy" (quoted in DH, 4 Nov. 1993). These accusations are similar to Carlos Nino's complaints that criticism from Argentine human rights groups only served to undermine the legitimacy of the

Alfonsín government (see Nino 1995, p. 429). They treat citizens who exercise their democratic right to criticize the government as threats to democracy, despite the fact that the government was clearly not fulfilling its obligation to protect the rights of its citizens.

Having ruled out political motivations a *priori*, the ARENA government and its allies offered two main explanations for the attacks. In one approach, they argued that these FMLN members had been victims of common crime. In August 1992, for example, National Communications Secretary Ernesto Altschul told the media that Vladimir Flores had been attacked because of a conflict over his wife having an affair (Buenos Días 1992a). The Cristiani Administration also quickly ruled out the possibility of political motivation in the October 30, 1993 killing of FMLN commander Eleno Hernán Castro. The ONUSAL Human Rights Division responded that the government should not claim to have established such a conclusion before the outcome of an investigation (ONUSAL Human Rights Division 1994b, 11). Indeed, why bother investigating if the answers were already known?

The government stuck to its story, however, and concluded in the initial investigation that Hernán Castro had been shot during a traffic dispute while he was driving to Usulután. According to this version, landowner Juan Arnoldo García argued with the FMLN leader after the victim's car collided with the one being driven by the landowner's sister, Marina Isabel García. The man then shot the victim and fled. Authorities have been unable to apprehend him. His sister, however, insisted that two unknown men had commandeered her vehicle and collided with Hernán Castro's car on purpose. They then got out and shot him. This story was consistent with the FMLN's claim that several unknown subjects emerged from the car and shot the victim. A witness also reported seeing several men in the car, one of whom told Hernán Castro that his time was up before shooting him. The victim had also received phone threats—some of them up to fifteen minutes long—prior to the murder. His wife reported that Hernán Castro had told her he was being followed for several months before his death (PG, 1 Nov. 1993; DH, 1 Nov. 1993; Human Rights Watch/Americas 1994, p. 7; ONUSAL Human Rights Division 1994b, 37; DH, 4 Nov. 1993: 43; Al Día 1993b). This evidence pointed to a premeditated—and politically motivated—murder.

Two further attacks also cast doubt upon the official explanation of the Hernán Castro murder. On November 8, 1993—little more than a week after Hernán Castro's death—unidentified assailants fired high caliber machine guns at a vehicle carrying FMLN members who were working on land transfers near San Vicente. One of the men on board the FMLN vehicle had worked with Hernán Castro on the land commission (Megavisión 1993b). Furthermore, the department of San Vicente is next to Usulután—the department that Hernán Castro had been driving toward when he was stopped and killed. The connections between these two attacks suggest that powerful economic interests in the region were using death squad violence to derail the modest agrarian reform called for in the peace accords.

The second incident which undermines the official explanation of the Hernán Castro killing took place on November 10, 1994. Gunmen shot FMLN leader David Faustino Merino Ramírez while he was having lunch with two colleagues in a San Salvador restaurant. Like Hernán Castor, Merino Ramírez had been working on the FMLN's commission dealing with the land transfers promised in the peace accords. Furthermore, he had received death threats related to land transfers in Usulután—the very issue that Hernán Castro was working on when he was killed. ONUSAL characterized the government's investigation of the Merino Ramírez murder as having "an almost inexplicable degree of inefficiency" (ONUSAL Human Rights Division 1994b, 37; 1995, 68; CDHES 1995, p. 7). These two incidents suggest that the government's failure to identify and punish those responsible for crimes such as the Hernán Castro murder permitted—and even encouraged—further violence.

ARENA was quick, however, to label attacks against its own members as politically motivated. Several of the party's legislative deputies blamed the FMLN for a February 1994 attack on René Alfonso Tenorio, the son of an ARENA mayor. ONUSAL concluded, however, that four of Tenorio's own relatives had killed him. ARENA also claimed that an attack on one of its alternate deputy candidates was politically motivated. The victim, however, stated that it was not. The media asserted that another ARENA militant had been killed as the result of political violence, but the victim's family blamed rival merchants who had made death threats against him. The same ONUSAL report did, however, find that the stabbing of San Marcos ARENA candidate Rubén Osvaldo Escalante may have been politically motivated (ONUSAL Human Rights Division 1994c, 41, 44–5, 47–8).

The government and its allies had another strategy for responding to claims that the murders of FMLN members were politically motivated. They asserted that other FMLN members had killed the victims as the result of conflicts within the organization. In May 1992, *El Diario de Hoy* cited unidentified "other sources" who recalled, "the communists have an old history of fabricating martyrs, which is why some security officials are investigating the possible participation of the subversives in this attack" (DH, 21 May 1992). Vice President Merino also suggested that the assault against Vladimir Flores had been an internal hit. He then charged the FMLN with taking advantage of the attack to justify not complying with the peace accords (PG, 22 May 1992). Following the Velis murder, ARENA Deputy René Figueroa went so far as to accuse the Catholic Church of conspiring with the FMLN in order to discredit the Salvadoran government and the peace process. Instead of acknowledging the possibility that the murders were part of a dirty war, Figueroa labeled the Church's expression against the killings as a part of a "dirty war" against the government (DH, 3 Nov. 1993). Those who made such claims were rehashing the same argument that human rights abusers had put forward to explain crimes such as the assassination of Archbishop Romero and the Central American University (UCA) massacre. It is important to remember that the government, the dominant media, and the death squads had used such arguments to justify repression against those who called for justice in cases such as the Romero assassination during the war.

The explanations pointing toward political motivations were much more plausible. The first postwar elections were scheduled to take place in March 1994. Many Salvadorans referred to this event as the "elections of the century." The fact that this was the first time that the FMLN would participate in elections was not the only reason for this phrase. Salvadorans would have the opportunity to vote for the President, the Assembly, and local government in 1994—a combination which occurs only once every fifteen years. Left-wing presidential candidate Rubén Zamora argued that the death squads were killing FMLN members in order to "prevent an electoral process because [the death squads] are afraid of the state of the popular will" (YSU 1993a). According to the UCA, the Armed Forces were even worried about the possibility that the FMLN/Democratic Convergence coalition could lose the election and yet still become the second leading political force. This would then mean that the ruling party would have to negotiate with the left on issues such as civilian control over the military (Editorial 1994, p. 618).

Some observers also argued that the murders were intended to demobilize the population. In the fall of 1993, Zamora asserted that such killings would not succeed in frightening the political leaders of the FMLN and the Democratic Convergence. Instead, he stated that the forces behind the killings intended to intimidate the people (YSU 1993a). Velis himself had made similar statements in August 1992 (YSU 1992a). Hemisphere Initiatives later echoed these remarks, writing, "The FMLN is not going to drop out of politics as a result of these killings, but local level activists from all parties, or others thinking of becoming active will surely shrink away from political participation" (Spence and Vickers 1994, p. 14).

Perhaps the most troubling explanation was that the murders were directed at the peace process itself. ONUSAL argued that death squads were not interested in eliminating groups or individuals, but rather directed their violence "against the democratic political system which has been worked out by the Government and the FMLN" (ONUSAL Human Rights Division 1994b, 16). The leadership of the FMLN indicated that it believed this explanation through its declarations that the organization would not be provoked (DH, 2 Nov. 1993). If the FMLN had responded to these murders in kind, the situation could have resembled something similar to the vicious circle of violence that we have seen recently in Israel and the occupied territories. Indeed, U.S. State Department officials warned in 1993 that El Salvador could become "another Haiti, Bosnia, [or] Somalia" (Los GAIMOP ... 1994, p. V). This explanation of the death squad activity supports McSherry's argument that attempting to appease human rights abusers by providing them with impunity for past crimes actually contributes to instability (McSherry 1997, pp. 227–8, 286).

The FMLN Chooses the Pen Over the Sword

There were in fact signs that such a strategy could have destroyed the peace process. Following the May 1992 murder attempt against Vladimir Flores, FMLN leaders told the media that a resumption of the dirty war would be a violation of the cease-fire (Al Día 1992a). In August 1992, the FMLN warned of possible "actions against certain soldiers and right-wing extremists" unless the Cristiani Administration launched a thorough investigation of postwar death squad killings (PG, 13 Aug. 1992). Following the deaths of Velis and Hernán Castro in the fall of 1993, someone claiming to be a mid-level FMLN commander called the media and threatened to launch military attacks against businesses associated with the death squads. He claimed, however, that the group's leaders had not given approval for his actions (DH, 3 Nov. 1993).

The FMLN had in fact left open the possible resumption of violence by secretly retaining many of its best weapons. In May 1993, an arsenal belonging to the former guerrillas exploded in Managua, Nicaragua. The United Nations later reported that the cache had contained approximately twenty percent of the FMLN's total weapons. This discovery also forced the former guerrillas to turn in an additional one hundred fourteen weapons deposits, accounting for another ten percent of the group's total arms. FMLN leader Shafick Handal told the United Nations that the former guerrillas had kept the weapons in case they needed another bargaining chip to ensure that the government kept its side of the accords (DH, 25 May 1993; Boutros-Ghali 1995j, pp. 473–4; 1995e, p. 458).

Part of the reason why the peace process did not collapse was that

FMLN members used freedom of expression as an alternative to violence. In May 1993, FMLN leader Salvador Sánchez Cerén told the UN Secretary General that the weapons "had become an onerous and unnecessary burden" precisely because the group's "chances for expression were increasing" (Boutros-Ghali 1995e, p. 459).[1] In other words, the former guerrilla leaders understood that the increasing political space had created the opportunity to defend themselves with words rather than bullets.

A few years later, *El Diario de Hoy*'s Executive Director stated, "The media are the escape valve that prevents people from taking justice into their own hands, starting revolutions and seeking change through violence" (Altamirano 1996, p. 13). The truth of Altamirano's words was demonstrated by an example of what happens when people become frustrated because they lack adequate freedom of expression. Following the murder of Hernán Castro, FMLN leader Joaquín Villalobos and union leader Humberto Centeno launched verbal attacks against *El Diario de Hoy* for its historic links to death squads and its biased coverage of the ongoing attacks against the opposition. The paper blamed the remarks for inciting a riot against its headquarters, which it referred to as "Terror on East 11th Street" (DH, 2 Nov. 1993).[2]

The fact that the government's main opponents were willing to forgo violence in favor of freedom of expression undermines Carlos Nino's argument against criticizing the civilian government during a transition to democracy. According to Nino, doing so undermines the legitimacy of the democratic regime and thus strengthens authoritarian forces (Nino 1995, p. 429). The FMLN's denunciations of death squad activity did undermine the Cristiani Administration's image by demonstrating that it had not reigned in political violence. Cristiani's legitimacy as the president who brought peace would have fallen much further, however, if the FMLN had broken the cease-fire. Such a response would also have strengthened the military's position in relation to that of the civilian government. This, in turn, would probably have undone all of the pro-human rights measures implemented under the peace accords.

Calls for Further Investigations of the Death Squads

Opposition figures argued that the Salvadoran government was responsible for the killings, even if members of the Cristiani Administration were not directly involved. Following the Velis murder, Rubén Zamora complained that the government should have complied with the Truth Commission's recommendation to continue the investigation of wartime death squads. He also called on the government to investigate the current attacks and to punish those responsible (YSU 1993a). The Popular Forces of Liberation (FPL)—one of the two largest FMLN factions—stated, "The political responsibility for this act falls completely upon the Cristiani Administration, because of its refusal to comply with the recommendations of the Truth Commission" (FPL 1993, p. 1067). These arguments are consistent with international law, which holds governments responsible for human rights violations when they fail to take measures to ensure human rights.[3]

The opposition further accused the government of conducting biased investigations of the postwar killings. Francisco Velis, for example, had criticized the Commission for the Investigation of Criminal Acts (CIHD) investigation of an attack on a municipal FMLN leader in August 1992. He warned that serious investigations were needed in order to prevent the far right from using common crime as a cover for political violence. Velis cited the fact that victims had been bound and tortured as evidence of political motivation (YSU 1992a). A little over a year later, a death squad killed Velis himself. Perhaps he would still be alive today if the government had responded positively to his calls for serious investigations of postwar violence.

Rather than setting a precedent that death squad activity would be punished in the postwar era, the Cristiani Administration continued to use the same methods and institutions which had blocked the investigation of such abuses during the war. According to Costa, the CIHD "served more to cover up the presumed authors of these crimes—as it did before, in the [1989] Jesuit case" (Costa 1999, p. 279). ONUSAL, for example, identified Salvador Guzmán as a suspect in the murder of FMLN leader Oscar Grimaldi and presented the information to the CIHD. Despite the mission's pressure to arrest Guzmán, the CIHD failed to do so before the accused killer was himself found dead. ONUSAL complained of further irregularities concerning the autopsy performed on Guzmán. The authorities also failed to arrest the individual suspected of murdering Guzmán (ONUSAL Human Rights Division 1994b, 29; 1994a, 73). These irregularities offered further evidence that the attacks were indeed politically motivated because state institutions were responsible for blocking the investigation through otherwise inexplicable acts of omission.

As in the Grimaldi case, the Salvadoran government placed the Velis investigation in the hands of the CIHD. Five years after the killing, *La Prensa Gráfica* complained, "The only thing that remains clear in this case is that the investigations were tainted from the beginning" (PG, 4 Oct. 1998). The CIHD put Ramón Astrídez Díaz Ramos, alias "Perico," in charge of the investigation. Díaz Ramos and other CIHD agents would later become suspects in the case (LPG, 4 Oct. 1998; El caso Velis (I)

2001). Given the widespread knowledge of the CIHD's role in protecting human rights violators and covering up politically motivated crimes—especially after Congressman Moakley issued his investigation of the UCA massacre—President Cristiani must have known that this institution could not be trusted to investigate such important and controversial murders.

The government responded to the calls for special investigations of these killings by creating the Interinstitutional Commission. This ad hoc body was led by Minister of the Presidency Oscar Santamaría and included officials from the Attorney General's Office, the Presidential Human Rights Commissioner,[4] the head of the State Intelligence Organization (OIE), the Director of the National Civilian Police (PNC), and the CIHD. The proposed commission did not, however, include anyone from the Office of the Human Rights Counsel (PDDH). The FMLN objected that this body was not independent from the Cristiani Administration (PG, 2 Nov. 1993). ONUSAL also objected, stating that the body "did not meet the United Nations criteria for the investigation of summary executions" (Boutros-Ghali 1995h, p. 497).

In addition to blaming the Salvadoran government for not following the Truth Commission's recommendations, the UCA criticized ONUSAL for not applying more pressure on the Cristiani Administration to investigate postwar death squads (Editorial 1993, p. 944). While the leadership of the Jesuit university was not satisfied with the UN mission's use of the evidence it collected, the ONUSAL Human Rights Division did pay close attention to the denunciations made by Salvadoran non-governmental organizations (NGOs) and churches. In its report covering February to April 1993, ONUSAL listed the names of individuals whom these groups had identified as death squad victims. Although the mission found many of them to have been cases of common crime, it did name six cases which appeared to be politically motivated (ONUSAL Human Rights Division 1993a, 12). According to Costa, however, the professional background of most members of the ONUSAL Police Division made them predisposed to believe that attacks upon FMLN members were the result of internal disputes (Costa 1999, p. 323). In other words, they were predisposed to believing the government's explanation of the attacks without empirical evidence.

Media Coverage of the Killings

For the most part, the dominant media failed to challenge the government's inadequate investigations of these killings during the first few years of the postwar era.[5] Following Cristiani's announcement that he had ordered the CIHD to handle the Velis investigation, neither *La Prensa Gráfica* nor *El Diario de Hoy* mentioned anything about the CIHD's record of conducting biased investigations and protecting human rights abusers (PG, 26 Oct. 1993; DH, 26 Oct. 1993). *El Noticiero* and *Al Día* television news programs also failed to criticize this decision (Al Día 1993a; El Noticiero 1993a). Furthermore, the leading papers failed to object when the government announced the results of the Velis investigation before actually conducting an investigation. *El Diario de Hoy*, for example, failed to provide any opposing views when it quoted ARENA Deputy Kirio Waldo Salgado's assertion that the FMLN itself had killed Velis in a dark conspiracy to take over the government and avoid elections (DH, 31 Oct. 1993).

La Prensa Gráfica did, however, publish an editorial which began to question the government's explanations on November 17, 1993. The paper recognized that these killings "presumably have political motives" and compared them to "the methods of intimidation and levels of insecurity" of the past. It then criticized the use of the phrase "illegal armed groups" as a "convenient euphemism" for death squads. The paper ended the editorial by emphasizing, "the depth of overall democratization of society is what is in question" (PG, 17 Nov. 1993).[6]

The Government Reluctantly Creates the Joint Group

The Cristiani government did not agree to create a truly independent commission to investigate the postwar murders until after high-level FMLN leaders Velis and Hernán Castro had been killed. In September 1993, the PDDH became the first state entity to call for the creation of a credible and independent commission to investigate these killings (Joint Group for the Investigation of Politically Motivated Illegal Armed Groups in El Salvador 1994, p. 8). Former Human Rights Counsel Carlos Molina Fonseca told me that he took this action in response to social forces who denounced the killings and called for such an investigation. He explained that the PDDH "perceived society's sentiment that there should be a thorough investigation of these unexplained crimes." This decision also reflected Molina Fonseca's belief that the PDDH should serve as "a bridge between civil society and public administration" (Molina Fonseca 2000). In other words, the agency should facilitate freedom of expression and make sure that it reaches the relevant government authorities.

Once again, international actors played a key role in pressing the Cristiani Administration to eventually create such a commission. According to the Human Rights Institute of the Central American University

(IDHUCA), the Salvadoran government ignored the PDDH's proposal until it received strong pressure from the UN Secretary General (IDHUCA 1997a, p. 1152). Secretary General Boutros-Ghali put that pressure on the government after Special Representative Marrack Goulding consulted with "all of the interested [parties]" and then formalized Molina Fonseca's proposal (Joint Group for the Investigation of Politically Motivated Illegal Armed Groups in El Salvador 1994, p. 9 n1). In this manner, Salvadorans who expressed themselves in favor of thoroughly investigating these killings had an indirect impact on the reluctant Cristiani Administration through their influence on the PDDH and the United Nations.

Many of the Salvadorans I interviewed also stated that public expression within El Salvador helped force the government to create a truly credible and independent commission to investigate these murders. According to Carlos Rafael Urquilla Bonilla of the Foundation for the Study of the Application of the Law (FESPAD), the social reaction to the killings "forced [the government] to create the Joint Group [for the Investigation of Politically Motivated Illegal Armed Groups in El Salvador]" (Urquilla Bonilla 2000a). David Morales of the PDDH stated that the commission was created "because [these murders] generated a very large shock, which made the formation of the Joint Group possible" despite the Cristiani Administration's objective of "maintaining the impunity" (Morales 2000). Channel 12 News Director Mauricio Funes has attributed the creation of the Joint Group to "a strong pressure from the citizenry to clarify some crimes that took place in the postwar era" (Funes 2000).

Two U.S. government sources have provided an interesting explanation of why President Cristiani responded to this pressure. While many of the attacks on FMLN figures were clearly political, the sources maintained that some of the violence was indeed criminally motivated. The Cristiani Administration therefore had a credibility and image problem. The president needed a credible, independent institution to investigate the murders and to clearly establish which killings were politically motivated and which were indeed cases of common crime (Two U.S. Government Sources 2001).

This outcome provides evidence against Carlos Nino's argument against freedom of expression during democratization. Nino has suggested that opposition forces actually harm transitions to democracy by criticizing civilian governments in this manner. By doing so, he asserts, they undermine the transitional government's legitimacy and thus indirectly support the authoritarian forces (Nino 1995, p. 429). The explanation from these U.S. government sources, however, clearly demonstrates that there are other ways to protect the government's credibility. One of the most important—and perhaps most obvious—approaches is for the government to restore its credibility by acting in a credible manner.

In this case, the opposition used public denunciations of the President Cristaini's actions to force him to fulfill his obligations to protect the rights to life and to due process of law by launching a thorough and independent investigation of the killings.

The Joint Group operated under a much narrower mandate than those of the Ad Hoc Commission and the Truth Commission. The body did not really fulfill the Truth Commission's binding recommendation to investigate wartime death squads because its mandate only authorized the investigation of such groups *after* the signing of the peace accords on January 16, 1992. One positive feature of the mandate was that it empowered the commission to investigate possible links between death squads and state structures. The mandate also addressed concerns that the Interinstitutional Commission would be subject to political control by clearly stating that the Joint Group would be autonomous, impartial, and apolitical. The government was careful to avoid a repeat of the controversy surrounding the Truth Commission Report by establishing that the new body could not release the names of the suspects it identified. The Joint Group would withhold such information from its public report. It would instead pass this data on to the proper authorities in a separate, confidential report. The government also restricted the Joint Group's work by giving it a short mandate which allowed it to operate only from February to May 1994. The Calderón Sol Administration did, however, extend this mandate until July 1994 (Joint Group for the Investigation of Politically Motivated Illegal Armed Groups in El Salvador 1994, pp. 9–12).

The question of who would serve on the Joint Group had been a contentious issue. The government rejected calls that it include non-governmental figures. The eventual compromise allowed the Cristiani Administration to name two of the four individuals who would lead the investigation. The president chose two lawyers, José Leandro Echeverría and Juan Jerónimo Castillo. Human Rights Counsel Carlos Molina Fonseca also served in the Joint Group. Given the fact that the PDDH was created through the peace accords, as well as the growing legitimacy of the new institution, this move helped alleviate doubts about the independence of the commission. The fourth member, ONUSAL Human Rights Division Director Diego García Sayán, also brought legitimacy to the investigation.

Death Squad Activity Decreases But Does Not End

Several observers have claimed that the establishment of the Joint Group caused a significant decrease in the political violence leading up to the March 1994 elections. According to the Inter-American Commission on Human Rights (IACHR), the "investigation of such acts as those reported have an immediate deterrent effect, which helped considerably to generate a climate of peace" (Inter-American Commission on Human Rights 1995). Stanley found that the commission's work "had a chilling impact on remaining assassination squads" (Stanley 1996a, p. 265). ONUSAL also suggested that the Joint Group's investigation helped deter further violence during this period (ONUSAL Human Rights Division 1994a, 16).

This decrease in political violence clearly contradicts the arguments favoring appeasement and impunity. Authors such as Huntington would have us believe that challenging powerful human rights violators such as those behind the death squads would lead them to threaten the stability of the democratic regime and thus create further human rights violations (Huntington 1993, pp. 220–1). Yet exactly the opposite happened, as those causing instability—the death squads—reduced their activity.

As discussed above, Salvadorans who denounced the government's inadequate response to the earlier killings played a key role in forcing the Cristiani Administration to create the Joint Group. The evidence that the Joint Group's work had an immediate impact on the killings therefore suggests that those who denounced these murders and called for a truly independent investigation had a significant—though indirect— impact on the behavior of the death squads.

It is also important to consider other factors which may have contributed to the relative decline in political violence during this period. International actors helped to close the space for death squad activities. Congressman Joseph Moakley had heard about these killings through contacts with Salvadoran groups such as the IDHUCA and Tutela Legal, as well as international NGOs such as Amnesty International. Moakley reacted to threats of further violence by informing Salvadoran officials that his office was watching the situation (Larose 2001). Moakley also addressed the issue when he traveled to El Salvador in February 1994 to accept an honorary degree at the Central American University (UCA):

> When a candidate for the legislature [Velis] is shot to death in broad daylight, outside a preschool and a robbery does not take place ... this is a political crime. To not recognize and energetically condemn the obvious, will not stop the assassins.... The assassins will not stop ... until those who perpetrate these crimes realize that they have to pay a price [Moakley 1994a, p. 352].

In a similar manner, UN Independent Expert Pedro Nikken reported that NGOs had expressed their concern over the continuing paid ads placed by death squads. He then pointed out that the media was legally obligated to determine and divulge the identities of those making threats which endanger the lives of others (Nikken 1993, ¶ 103).

While the death squads may have reduced their activities following the creation of the Joint Group, they did not completely cease using political violence. On the contrary, there were at least fifteen political killings during the official campaign period running from November 20, 1993 to March 16, 1994. Fourteen of the victims were FMLN members (CDHES 1995, p. 6). This means that there were at least 3.75 political killings per month during this period. In contrast, the IDHUCA reported a total of eighty-four death squad murders for all of 1993 (IDHUCA 1994b, p. 46). In other words, the death squads killed an average of seven victims per month during the year.

While the quantity of attacks may have decreased following the creation of the Joint Group, the political value of the targets actually increased. The government officially established the Joint Group on December 8, 1993. The following day, assailants shot FMLN Central Political Commission Member José Mario López to death when he attempted to stop an assault on an elderly woman who had just come out of a bank. Once again, the government argued that this murder was not political. The FMLN and NGOs such as Tutela Legal disagreed. López's bodyguard also insisted that the alleged robbery attempt had been staged in order to set up the true target, López (Human Rights Watch/Americas 1994, p. 8; U.S. Department of State 1994).

There were other aspects of the case that suggested López had indeed been the target. The FMLN leader had received death threats. He went to his grandmother's home everyday (PG, 10 Dec. 1993). Such predictable behavior would have seriously endangered his security by giving potential enemies useful information for the purpose of staging an ambush.

Even the Joint Group has been unable to settle the issue of why López was killed (see Joint Group for the Investigation of Politically Motivated Illegal Armed Groups in El Salvador 1994, p. 87). If the death squads did indeed kill him, he would have been the highest ranking FMLN official they murdered up to this point. López had been one of the FMLN's representatives during the negotiations to end the war. He was serving on the FMLN's Central Political Commission at the time of his death.

The attack on Nidia Díaz in February 1994 raised the stakes even higher. During the war, Díaz had been a high-level commander in the FMLN. She continued to play a major role in the party and was running for a seat in the Assembly. On February 24, 1994, three men opened fire on an SUV used by Díaz outside her home in San Salvador. Her bodyguard/driver fought back. The assailants wounded him during the exchange of gunfire. Although Díaz was not present at the time of the attack, the assailants fired at the rear of the vehicle, where she would have been seated (ONUSAL Human Rights Division 1994c, 46).

The voters elected Díaz to the Legislative Assembly in March 1994. She was then appointed to the Assembly's Human Rights and Justice Committee. In May 1994, assailants again ambushed her vehicle while she was not in it. Her bodyguard/driver once again fought back and was wounded. Díaz blamed the authorities for facilitating this assault through their flawed investigation of the February attack against her. The day after the second attack, a police agent who had been assigned to protect Díaz was killed while guarding the office of a nearby NGO. ONUSAL later reported that the Criminal Investigations Division (DIC)—the renamed Commission for the Investigation of Criminal Acts (CIHD)—appeared to deliberately avoid investigating serious leads in the second attack on Díaz's vehicle (PG, 20 May 1994; ONUSAL Human Rights Division 1994a, p. 27; CDHES 1995, p. 7).

Neither ARENA nor the FMLN obtained enough votes to win the presidency in March 1994. On the day of the runoff election (April 16th), two men with M16s threatened Rubén Zamora's driver and forced him out of his car while he was waiting for the FMLN/Democratic Convergence candidate. The election was further marred by the murder of an FMLN poll watcher just hours after the voting ended. ONUSAL reported that the suspects were identified as "well-known members" of ARENA (ONUSAL Human Rights Division 1994a, 20, 30).[7]

El Diario de Hoy continued to insist that attacks against the FMLN were not politically motivated. In December 1993, the paper cited unidentified "diverse sectors" claiming, "The deaths of former guerrilla commanders Heleno Castro and Mario López at the hands of common criminals has served the leftist groups to justify the escalation in street violence" (DH, 11 Dec. 1993). Once again, the paper failed to examine or criticize Cristiani's decision to rule out political motivation in the López murder prior to a thorough investigation. Nor did *El Diario* criticize the government's attempt to prevent the Joint Group from including the case in its investigations and its decision to place the corrupt CIHD in charge of the case (DH, 11 Dec. 1993).

El Diario de Hoy also attempted to discredit denunciations of the attacks against Nidia Díaz. After the February assault, the paper reported that the FMLN "took advantage of the event to unleash a series of statements in which they assumed the role of victims." This claim is rather odd within the context of ongoing attacks in which FMLN members were in fact the victims. The paper then cited unidentified "political sectors" who argued that the FMLN was the only group to have benefited from "an attack that should have left at least one death" (DH, 25 Feb. 1994). By using this phrasing, *El Diario* suggested that the FMLN had faked the attack because a genuine assault would have ended in the death of Díaz's bodyguard/driver. The language is also troubling because it can be interpreted to mean that the paper wanted Díaz dead (DH, 14 July 1994).

Support for the Joint Group Investigation

As it did with the Ad Hoc Commission and the Truth Commission, the government gave the Joint Group a relatively short period of time in which to investigate many cases. The Joint Group dealt with this problem in much the same way as the previous bodies had—by drawing upon information already gathered by other groups. The body drew upon data from institutions which obtained much of their information from public expression, such as ONUSAL and the Office of the Human Rights Counsel (PDDH).

The Joint Group actively sought out information from Salvadorans committed to exercising their right to freedom of expression. In one of the annexes to its report, the Joint Group lists organizations from which the body specifically requested information, including NGOs such as the (nongovernmental) Human Rights Commission of El Salvador (CDHES) and the IDHUCA. It also listed labor organizations, business associations, and, of course, the FMLN. By providing this information, sources helped the Joint Group decide which cases it would investigate (Joint Group for the Investigation of Politically Motivated Illegal Armed Groups in El Salvador 1994, pp. 31, 68).

As in the cases of the Ad Hoc Commission and the Truth Commission, authoritarian forces used the impunity they enjoyed to hinder the expression that the Joint Group depended on for its investigation. As the Joint Group reported, "Fear, mistrust of institutions charged with conducting investigations, and impunity have a decisive impact on the will of the citizens, causing them to hold back from behavior that might bring subsequent reprisals" (Joint Group for the Investigation of Politically Motivated Illegal Armed Groups in El Salvador 1994, p. 56). The UCA further argued that the amnesty following the publication of the Truth Commission Report discouraged cooperation with the Joint Group by demonstrating "these investigations are not worth the trouble" (Editorial 1994, p. 625).

Human rights abusers hampered cooperation with the Joint Group through highly visible threats made against those expressing themselves to the investigative body. A death squad threatened Archbishop Rivera y Damas and Bishop Rosa Chávez. The same group even threatened Joint Group members Carlos Molina Fonseca and Juan Castillo (PG, 8 June 1994; PG, 13 Jun. 1999).

The Results of the Joint Group Investigation

The Joint Group issued its report on July 28, 1994. While the investigative body had not been able to resolve every case it examined, it did find strong evidence connecting many of the postwar killings to the individuals and institutions that participated in death squad activity during the war. These included former members of the Armed Forces, the security forces, and the civil patrols. It reported that current high-ranking military officers, National Police agents, public officials, judges, and powerful economic figures continued to be involved in political violence. The investigative body emphasized that continued military involvement in domestic intelligence activities—a violation of the peace accords—posed a great danger. The body also established that former FMLN troops were taking part in some rural groups associated with crime and death squad activities (Joint Group for the Investigation of Politically Motivated Illegal Armed Groups in El Salvador 1994, pp. 14, 26–7, 39, 56).

The Joint Group reported that the postwar death squads had similar objectives to those of their wartime predecessors. It found that rural groups sought to protect local economic elites and intimidate anyone who might oppose them. Their urban counterparts were more selective in terms of their targets, focusing on leaders of opposition organizations and figures who took part in the armed conflict. The Joint Group also confirmed the hypothesis that postwar death squad killings were intended to destabilize the peace process. On a related note, it stated that the death squads served to undermine the legitimacy of state institutions (Joint Group for the Investigation of Politically Motivated Illegal Armed Groups in El Salvador 1994, pp. 27–8, 59).

These findings clearly contradict the theory that providing authoritarian forces and repressive institutions with impunity for the past crimes fosters stability during democratization. Human rights abusers took advantage of such impunity to commit further crimes and undermine the government. The Salvadoran government permitted the existence of a major source of instability through its failure to promptly uncover and dismantle these clandestine structures. Rather than being content with not being brought to justice for past crimes, those forces behind the death squads saw their postwar impunity as an opportunity to gain further advantages by working to bring about the collapse of the peace process.

One of the Joint Group's most important findings was that postwar death squads had indeed been using common crime as a cover for political murders. Furthermore, the report established that these groups had adapted to the postwar era by expanding their involvement in organized criminal activities such as money laundering, drug trafficking, and kidnappings for ransom. This diversification provided the paramilitary organizations with funding which allowed them to engage in political violence. It also provided the death squad organizers with a pool of criminals from which they could recruit assassins for political murders (Joint Group for the Investigation of Politically Motivated Illegal Armed Groups in El Salvador 1994, pp. 23–4, 31). Taken together, these findings clearly undermined the government's and the dominant media's repeated assertions that the FMLN had been misrepresenting the killing of its own members for political gain.

This diversification into crime for profit did not, however, mean that the death squads had severed all of their connections to state actors and institutions. As mentioned above, the Joint Group found that high-ranking military officers and public officials continued to be involved in death squad activities. Furthermore, the report cited the May 1994 armored car robbery by National Police (discussed in Chapter Six) as evidence of its belief that organized crime could not exist on the scale seen in postwar El Salvador without protection from leaders of the public security forces. Echoing complaints from the FMLN, NGOs, and churches, the Joint Group criticized the government's "faintheartedness in the investigation and sanctioning of those state agents presumed to be involved in politically motivated crimes or in organized crime." It also singled out the courts in particular for their role in the maintenance of impunity for these crimes (Joint Group for the Investigation of Politically Motivated Illegal Armed Groups in El Salvador 1994, pp. 24, 27).[8]

The Joint Group was not able to resolve many of the cases it investigated, however. It was able to identify the groups behind only five of the eight illustrative cases it analyzed in the main section of its report. The Joint Group determined, for example, that Armed Forces troops were responsible for the December 1993 massacre of six inhabitants of Primavera Canton. It also established that local authorities were involved in death squad structures in Usulután and Morazán. In another illustrative case, the Joint Group expressed its certainty that an August 1992 summary execution of a member of the Military Intelligence Battalion had been a politically motivated murder. It could not, however, establish whether the FMLN had killed the victim in revenge for his role as a government spy during the war or if right wing forces had targeted him because of sensitive information he had uncovered during his unconstitutional postwar espionage activities (Joint Group for the Investigation of Politically Motivated Illegal Armed Groups in El Salvador 1994, pp. 33–55).

The Joint Group also summarized the existing evidence in sixty-one cases in which it had been unable to uncover new evidence. It ended the short paragraph of its report on the December 1993 murder of FMLN leader José Mario López, for example, by simply noting, "A number of assessments of this case have been presented, based on the investigations carried out by various institutions." Upon reviewing the available data, the Joint Group found that there was sufficient evidence of political motivation in at least thirteen of these cases. It recommended further investigations to determine the motivation behind the remaining cases (Joint Group for the Investigation of Politically Motivated Illegal Armed Groups in El Salvador 1994, pp. 73–93).[9]

The Joint Group's mandate did not give it the authority to make binding recommendations. Nonetheless, the Joint Group did propose a number of reforms that it argued would help overcome the problems of both politically motivated violence and organized crime. It called for improvements in the investigative capacities of the National Civilian Police (PNC), including the creation of a special police division to deal with these issues. The investigative body emphasized the need for judicial reform in order to counteract impunity and corruption. It proposed allowing authorities to trade sentence reductions in exchange for cooperation and information facilitating the identification and trial of those responsible for planning these crimes. The Joint Group called for better control of the military to prevent abuses, as well as increased oversight of intelligence activities. The body also addressed an important barrier to freedom of expression through its recommendation to provide better security for victims, their families, and witnesses (Joint Group for the Investigation of Politically Motivated Illegal Armed Groups in El Salvador 1994, pp. 59–62). These recommendations were consistent with those made by the Truth Commission—many of which the government had refused to follow.

The Government and Its Allies Attack the Joint Group Report

The government and its allies reacted to the Joint Group Report in a manner similar to their responses to the Truth Commission Report. Given that the peace accords had officially established military subordination to civilian authority, it was clearly not the military's place to announce the government's policy regarding the report, especially before having read it. Nonetheless, Defense Minister General Humberto Corado Figueroa told the media, "If we consider that [the Joint Group's] conclusions are not valid, then we will have to ignore it" (Al Día 1994). He also asserted that the military's Honor Tribunal should have jurisdiction in the investigation and punishment of corrupt military figures (YSU 1994). In a genuine democracy, an active duty military officer would not be allowed to dictate the government's actions in this manner. The

Defense Minister clearly demonstrated that the Salvadoran military retained many of its anti-democratic prerogatives.

While the Joint Group did not have the authority to publicly name individuals as suspects in the cases it had examined, it did present a confidential report containing this information to President Calderón Sol and Attorney General Romeo Melera Granillo. According to the Office of the Human Rights Counsel (PDDH), this document included "valuable clues with names and addresses for definitively eradicating this social stain" of death squad activity (PDDH 1995a, p. 28).[10] Nonetheless, the government failed to investigate most of these cases further and to punish those responsible for the political violence (Molina Fonseca 2000; Morales 2000).[11] Nor did government officials implement the Joint Group's recommendations, except for the creation of the short-lived Division for the Investigation of Organized Crime (DICO) within the PNC (Annan 1997, 19; Montenegro 2000). As discussed in Chapter Six, the Criminal Investigation Division (DIC) harassed members of this unit and interfered in its investigations. The government eventually disbanded the DICO, despite praise for it from figures such as UN General Secretary Kofi Annan.

It is also important to note that clandestine groups have continued to engage in sporadic political violence after the Joint Group published its findings.[12] In November 1995, for example, three unidentified assailants dressed in black uniforms and hoods intercepted a vehicle carrying FMLN Deputy Humberto Centeno along with a bodyguard and three members of the Salvadoran Foundation for Democracy and Development. The attackers opened fire with automatic weapons, but the victims managed to escape (Velásquez de Avilés 1996d, pp. 29–30). The FMLN claimed that the death squads were behind a machine gun and grenade attack on a group of its activists in the town of Nejapa shortly before the 1997 elections in which two of the victims died. The party further stated that its offices in Mejicanos and Ayutuxtepeque had also been attacked the same night (CL, 21 Feb. 1997). In 2000, the National Action Party blamed local ARENA officials for the murder of two of its activists in Metapán (CL, 2 Feb. 2000).[13]

This does not mean, however, that Joint Group's investigation had been completely useless. As discussed above, some observers have claimed that the mere existence of the investigative body led to a significant decline of political violence during the 1994 electoral campaign. According to PDDH researcher David Morales, the report has become "an essential tool in the protection of human rights" because it provides important insights into the operation of death squads and organized crime (Morales 2000).

The dominant media greatly diminished the impact of the Joint Group report, however, through their attacks on the document. Shortly before it was released to the public, *El Diario de Hoy* published an article entitled "Joint Group hands in report without evidence." This headline was extremely misleading, given that the article quoted the Joint Group's claim that it found sufficient evidence to warrant further investigations (DH, 29 July 1994). Another article in the same paper reported that the Joint Group established that the postwar killings had been "eminently criminal," a clear misrepresentation of the investigative body's findings (DH, 30 July 1994).

Given the media's reaction to the report, it is not surprising that few Salvadorans are familiar with the Joint Group's findings. As Rubén Zamora explained, "What happened? Nothing. There was very little knowledge [of the report]" (Zamora 2001). One might assume that this applies mainly to common Salvadorans, while elite Salvadorans might be more familiar with the investigation. In 2000, however, I interviewed the leader of a Salvadoran NGO concerned primarily with historical documentation. When I brought up the subject of the Joint Group, he asked, "What Joint Group?" When I explained that I was referring to the Joint Group for the Investigation of Politically Motivated Illegal Armed Groups, the respondent replied, "I don't know what you are referring to. Are you talking about the Truth Commission?"[14]

Calls for Justice Lead to Further Action on the Velis Case

As discussed above, the Salvadoran government has demonstrated very little political will toward resolving the cases analyzed in the Joint Group Report. Within this context, the 1993 murder of Francisco Velis has become one of the rare cases in which the authorities have at least identified and convicted the material authors. Holiday and Stanley have argued that ONUSAL's investigation was the only reason for progress in this case (Holiday and Stanley 2000, p. 51). While the UN mission certainly contributed to the resolution of this case, Salvadorans also exercised their right to expression, thereby maintaining pressure to keep the investigation open. An FMLN deputy on the Human Rights and Justice Committee in the Assembly, credited the media for continuing the investigation of this case and for preventing it from being abandoned (Coto de Cuéllar 2000). The press's long-term interest in this story should be seen in the context of the improvements within the media that took place in the mid 1990s (discussed in Chapter Four). The media had an important incentive to cover the Velis investigation. Some of those individuals accused of killing the FMLN leader had also been implicated in another case which received extensive attention from the media, the June 1994 murder of architect Ramón Mauricio García Prieto. The news organizations paid special attention to the García Prieto case because the victim's middle-class parents have accused retired General Mauricio Vargas—the Armed Forces representative during the peace talks—of ordering the killing in response to long-standing land dispute with the family (see Velásquez de Avilés 1996c). The Central American University (UCA) has identified Velis's mother's calls for justice as a crucial factor in keeping the FMLN leader's case open. The Jesuit university also credited its own human rights institute—the IDHUCA—for helping her during the long and difficult process of the investigation (El caso Velis (II) 2001).

Witnesses provided crucial information in this case by exercising their right to expression. The government and its allies had portrayed the murder as a common crime. Velis's widow, however, told the media that the family had suffered harassment and surveillance during the two months prior to the killing. She further stated that they had heard unusually loud noises outside of their home on the night before Velis's death (Amnesty International 1996b). These activities were consistent with the modus operandi of highly organized death squads that could count on protection from powerful state actors. They were not consistent, however, with the government's assertion that common criminals were responsible for the murder of her husband. The director of the daycare center where Velis was taking his daughter at the time of his death reported that the facility had also been under surveillance and that she was herself followed on a continual basis. By expressing this information, the head of the daycare center prompted ONUSAL to investigate who had been conducting this espionage. The UN mission then identified the person following her as a sergeant in the Armed Forces (Joint Group for the Investigation of Politically Motivated Illegal Armed Groups in El Salvador 1994, p. 77). Once again, expression from a witness provided substantial evidence that political/state forces were behind the murder.

Over a year after the murder, the DICO found a witness who accused Commission for the Investigation of Criminal Acts (CIHD) detectives René Díaz Ortíz and Carlos Romero Alfaro (alias "Zaldaña") of having planned the murder with two other individuals in a cafeteria near her workplace in the Central Market. She identified a third suspect, Arnoldo Martín Martínez,[15] during a lineup. A male witness who had been an informant for the CIHD confirmed her story. He reported hearing Romero Alfaro, José Gonzalo Flores Guardado, Ramón Arístides Díaz Ramos, and Gilberto Antonio Sánchez Sánchez planning the murder at the CIHD building. He further claimed that the National Police agents had invited him to take part in the killing. The witness explained that he had arrived late on the day of the murder and was later reprimanded by the killers when they returned to the CIHD. He also stated that Díaz Ramos later told him that they had indeed carried out the execution (PG, 4 Oct. 1998; El caso Velis (I) 2001).

Authoritarian forces continued to take advantage of their impunity to hamper the witnesses' expression during the investigation. As mentioned previously, President Cristiani had announced that the CIHD would be in charge of the case. This was problematic in and of itself, given this unit's notorious history of covering up human rights violations during the war. Even more alarming, however, was the fact that the police assigned detective Díaz Ramos (alias "Perico")—whom a witness later identified as a suspect—to the case. The Office of the Human Rights Counsel (PDDH) found that Díaz Ramos—who had also served in the Special Military Security Brigade with suspect Flores Guardado—used the opportunity to detain and threaten a witness. The PDDH further reported that the detective attempted to bribe the witness into testifying that the FMLN had killed Velis (PG, 4 Oct. 1998; PG 4 Oct. 1998). In August 1996, several men tried to abduct a witness in the case (Amnesty International 1996b). Another witness agreed to testify only after ONUSAL promised to protect her and eventually help her flee the country (Holiday and Stanley 2000, p. 51).

Given that CIHD personnel became suspects in the Velis murder, it is clear that there would not be any genuine advances in this case as long as the corrupt unit remained in charge. As a result, *La Prensa Gráfica,* the UCA, and UN insider Gino Acosta have argued that the investigation began to move forward only after the police put the DICO—the special unit which had been created at the recommendation of the Joint Group— in charge (PG, 4 Oct. 1998; El caso Velis (I) 2001; Costa 1999). The DICO's success in cases such as this have fueled accusations that the police later disbanded this unit precisely for the purpose of protecting impunity.

The Velis case provides a clear example of the way in which authoritarian forces have created obstacles to human rights and justice through structural impunity—especially in the form of the remilitarization of the National Civilian Police (PNC). Suspects such as Romero Alfaro, Díaz Ramos, and Flores Guardado had been serving in the National Police's CIHD at the time of the murder. They later became "civilian" police agents, as discussed in Chapter Six, when the FMLN made a pact with ARENA to support the government proposal to incorporate this corrupt unit into the new civilian force. The PNC changed the unit's name to the Division for Criminal Investigation (DIC). By agreeing to this pact, the FMLN allowed military elements to further strengthen structural impunity.

It is therefore not surprising that the CIHD, now renamed the DIC, helped to undermine the investigation and prosecution of this case. The division had evidence implicating Romero Alfaro in the Velis murder since April 1994—less than six months after the crime took place. *Primera Plana* later blamed a DIC detective for protecting the suspect since May 1994 (Ayala 1995, p. 5). Following pressure from ONUSAL, the Salvadoran judiciary finally ordered Romero Alfaro's arrest in March 1995. DIC Chief Mendoza Jérez did not comply with the ruling, however. Instead, he provided the suspect with money and allowed him to flee the nation. U.S. authorities eventually located Romero Alfaro in Houston, Texas (PP, 9 June 1995; PG, 4 Oct. 1998; Costa 1999, p. 286 n83). An FMLN leader remarked that these events "[have] made evident the linkage of the death squads to the PNC structures" (quoted in PP, 12 May 1995). At least one other suspect, Díaz Ramos, also fled to the U.S. (Amnesty International 1996b).

The U.S. government extradited Romero Alfaro back to El Salvador in March 1996. Upon his return, one of the eyewitnesses to the murder identified the suspect during a lineup. In 1998, the government charged Ortíz Díaz as another material author in the case. This suspect was already in prison for having taken part in the García Prieto murder in June 1994 (*El caso Velis (I)* 2001; U.S. Department of State 2000).

In February 2000, a lawyer at the Foundation for the Study of the Application of Law (FESPAD) told me that this case had yet to go to trial "despite pressures from the beginning," including actions before United Nations bodies. He cited this as an example that proves that freedom of expression was not one hundred percent effective, given that many other variables were also important. Nonetheless, he explained, "without a doubt, it is an indispensable tool" (Urquilla Bonilla 2000a).

The trial of those accused of murdering Velis began in September 2001—nearly eight years after he had been gunned down. The jury found Romero Alfaro, Martín Martínez, Julio Díaz Ortiz, and Jesús Escobar Peña guilty. The prosecution attributed the convictions to the defense witnesses' lack of credibility. The prosecutors further emphasized that they had demonstrated the testimony of a DIC detective on behalf of the defendants to be false (DH, 11 Sept. 2001; PG, 11 Sept. 2001; PG, 10 Oct. 2001).

While Romero Alfaro, Martín Martínez, and Díaz Ortiz had served in the National Police, *La Prensa Gráfica* identified Escobar Peña as an FMLN member who was also convicted for attacking Nidia Díaz's vehicle (PG, 4 Oct. 1998). Taken as a whole, however, the convictions do not support the government's assertion that forces within the FMLN had killed Velis as part of an internal dispute. The majority of those convicted came from the National Police. Given El Salvador's economic problems during the postwar period, it is certainly not inconceivable that a former guerrilla would join a right-wing death squad if offered sufficient monetary compensation. Witnesses cited above also provided information that the killers planned the murder at the CIHD. Furthermore, the attempts to cover up the crime and to help Romero Alfaro flee the nation were inconsistent with the theory that this was an internal FMLN hit. If the FMLN had been behind the murder, the government would have had very a powerful incentive to resolve the case as soon as possible in order to discredit its main rival.

To my knowledge, however, the government has not made any progress toward identifying the intellectual authors of this crime. Instead, it has been left for FMLN leaders such as Francisco Jovel and Nidia Díaz to call for further investigation to determine who was behind this case. Nidia Díaz has claimed that not doing so would allow the continuing existence of assassins willing to kill anyone in exchange for a few coins (CL, 11 Sept. 2001).

Impunity Fosters Instability and Organized Crime

Democratic forces cannot guarantee human rights by simply ending a military conflict and establishing elections. While the government agreed in the peace accords to many important provisions aimed at protecting human rights and eliminating individual and structural impunity, it did not have the political will to fully implement these measures. As a result, the death squads—one of the most threatening manifestations of political violence—were able to continue operating in the postwar era. The evidence in this chapter has clearly demonstrated that ARENA's policies promoting structural impunity—such as the transfer of the CIHD into the new "civilian" police force and the decision to place this corrupt institution in charge of investigations—have facilitated political violence during the postwar transition. The murders examined here clearly demonstrate how authoritarian forces take advantage of strategies aimed at appeasing human rights violators to commit further abuses and to generate instability.

The government was reluctant to take one of the most important steps toward reducing political violence—acknowledging its existence. Without strong pressure from the domestic opposition—as well as the PDDH and the United Nations—the Cristiani Administration would not have authorized a truly independent investigation of the killings discussed in this chapter. As Stepan's dialectic would predict, pressure from the Salvadoran opposition helped force the government to follow through on at least some of its earlier concessions during the peace process (see Stepan 1988, p. 45). Furthermore, the Joint Group would not have been able to achieve the limited successes that it had without assistance from Salvadoran groups and individuals who exercised their right to express themselves on the issue of death squads. This offers further support to the argument that freedom of expression should be considered one of Shue's basic rights which are necessary for the security of all other human rights.

The opposition has not been able to generate enough pressure, however, to force the subsequent ARENA administrations to follow the Joint Group's recommendations for preventing further political violence and eliminating the structures which facilitate human rights abuses. As a result, the majority of those Salvadorans involved in postwar death squad activity have retained their impunity, despite the fact that the 1992 and 1993 amnesty laws do not cover crimes committed after the cease-fire. Partial justice has been achieved in only a few rare cases such as the Velis murder. Death squads have continued to take advantage of structural impunity by conducting limited operations throughout the 1990s as a result of the government's unwillingness or inability to confront these clandestine groups and the state institutions which have protected them.

8

The Unusually Successful Prosecution of Police Agents in the Vilanova Murder[1]

As discussed in Chapter Six, the new National Civilian Police (PNC) quickly established itself as the leading source of human rights violations in postwar El Salvador. Indeed, abuses by the force have become so common that the media quickly loses interest in the majority of cases, which then remain unresolved. The case of Adriano Vilanova was different, however, because the media maintained their interest up to and beyond the conviction of five PNC agents for the killing. It is essential to understand why this case was an exception and to explore how Salvadorans used their right to freedom of expression to move the investigation forward. Even in such exceptional cases, however, it is important to remember that Salvadorans who speak out in favor of justice and human rights have continued to face almost insurmountable obstacles to expressing themselves.

Salvadorans have used many manifestations of freedom of expression to contribute to the investigation and resolution of the murder of medical student Adriano Vilanova. Journalists published the results of their own investigations, which state authorities have drawn upon to move the case forward. Nongovernmental organizations (NGOs) and the media have also provided oversight of public officials to prevent and remedy problems during the investigation. The Vilanova family has helped keep the case open through the parents' calls for justice. A key witness for the prosecution came forward after hearing the mother's pleas in the media.

The Vilanova case was similar to the Velis case (discussed in Chapter Seven) in that both murders were committed by police agents. This murder was different, however, because the perpetrators killed Vilanova in September 1995—several months after the National Police was finally disbanded. Adriano Vilanova's killers were therefore part of the new "civilian" police force when they committed the crime. Nonetheless, several of the figures involved in the murder and the subsequent cover-up had a history of involvement with some of the most abusive structures of the war, including the military security forces and irregular police structures. Once again, police agents and other figures who benefited from the impunity provided in the 1992 and 1993 amnesty laws threatened and attacked those Salvadorans who called for justice or provided information on this crime. Even after the jury found five PNC agents guilty of killing Vilanova, anti-democratic forces—including public security officials—continued using violence and intimidation against key figures such as the reporter who broke the case, the key witness for the prosecution, and even a member of the jury.

The mainstream media demonstrated that they had made significant progress since the end of the war by providing important leads in this case and monitoring the authorities' actions during the investigation. The behavior of these dominant media have also made it clear, however, that these changes have not become permanent and that news directors and media owners can easily close the political space back up once again. The mainstream media endangered the safety of a whistle blower through its unethical conduct following the trial. *El Diario de Hoy* later fired the reporter who broke this case. The paper also published an exposé of the reporter's alleged ties to organized crime, in which it failed to consider the readily available evidence in her favor.

Adriano Vilanova Is Reported Missing

On September 4, 1995, Lidya Rosa Velver de Vilanova went to the PNC office in Panchimalco to report that her son, medical student Manuel Adriano Vilanova Velver, had not been seen since September 2. Agent Perlera Saravia took her statement, along with a recent photograph of Adriano (DH, 14 Sept. 1995).[2] She would later testify that the police acted suspiciously and attempted to force her to sign a false statement (DH, 11 Oct. 1998).

She had good reason to be suspicious. The Panchimalco PNC office had received a phone call alerting it that a corpse had been found in a five-meter deep ravine on Sunday, September 3, the day before Mrs. Velver de Vilanova went to the police station. The office told the guard who discovered the body to expect the police to arrive shortly. The property owners had to call the police the following day, however, because no one had shown up to collect the body. After several further attempts to get the police to perform their duty, the owners of the property decided to call television reporters from Cuatro Visión. Cuatro Visión, in turn, reported the incident to medical examiners and arrived to film the removal of Adriano Vilanova's corpse on September 5 (DH, 14 Sept. 1995).

Investigative Journalism Begins to Find Answers

Further help came from an unexpected source, *El Diario de Hoy*, the newspaper with the worst reputation for protecting human rights violators and slandering victims during the war. On September 14th— twelve days after Vilanova had disappeared—the paper published what it referred to as "an unprecedented journalistic investigation." The three-page article established that Vilanova had been walking home from a bar with his friend Nino Tinetti on the night of September 2. Both men had been drinking heavily, and Vilanova began to vomit. He told his friend to go ahead and promised that he would soon catch up. A short while later, Tinetti saw several police agents pass by in a white PNC pickup truck without noticing him. He also observed that the police vehicle turned off of the highway and headed toward the area where Vilanova's body would later be found (DH, 14 Sept. 1995).

An unnamed witness provided a similar account and described how Vilanova appeared to be hiding from the police. Despite his efforts, the police intercepted Vilanova as soon as they saw that we was alone. The source said that the agents proceeded to beat the victim to death after a short discussion. They then decided to move the body to the location where it was found. The witness's description of the police vehicle matched that given by Tinetti. *El Diario de Hoy* suggested that this quick interception indicated that the police had known that Vilanova was in the bar and had therefore planned to intercept him (DH, 14 Sept. 1995).

The newspaper also found evidence that Vilanova had recently had problems with the local PNC. The article quoted an unnamed relative of the victim who indicated that the family believed the police had killed Vilanova (DH, 14 Sept. 1995).

The article reported that medical examiners had determined that the victim died of severe multiple traumas to the abdomen three days before they recovered his corpse. He had five broken ribs and serious wounds on other parts of his body. This information was starkly contrasted by one of the photos in the article, a portrait of young Vilanova smiling and dressed in a tuxedo (DH, 14 Sept. 1995).

Human Rights Counsel Velásquez de Avilés credited *El Diario de Hoy*'s coverage of the murder for unleashing "reactions in national public opinion, even among the nation's leading public security officials" (Velásquez de Avilés 1996b, p. 24). Indeed, PNC Director Rodrigo Ávila reacted to the report even before it was published by ordering the detention of all agents assigned to the Panchimalco and Apopa PNC delegations (DH, 14 Sept. 1995).

The Human Rights Counsel Builds Upon the Media Investigation

The newspaper report also had an important impact on the Office of the Human Rights Counsel (PDDH). The government agency depends upon expression by citizens in order to begin its investigations. Most of its cases begin as the result of denunciations filed by human rights victims or their relatives. The PDDH launched its inquiry into Vilanova's death on its own initiative, however, after encountering the September 14th article in *El Diario de Hoy* (Velásquez de Avilés 1996b, p. 3).

The article's impact on the PDDH investigation was not limited to simply calling the matter to the institution's attention. In its report on the Vilanova case, the PDDH credited the newspaper's account with providing important information. Such acknowledgment was very appropriate, given that the PDDH repeated much of the information originally published by the newspaper. While the original article had not credited any reporters, the PDDH revealed that Violeta Rivera had led the newspaper's investigation (Velásquez de Avilés 1996b, p. 24).

The PDDH confirmed that Adriano Vilanova had been having problems with local PNC agents shortly before his death. According to his father, Dr. Adriano Vilanova Córdoba, the victim had encountered these agents on August 23 while they were investigating a traffic accident in which Manuel Mauricio Beltrán Villacorta (a.k.a., "Tarántula") had been run over. Adriano Vilanova panicked and fled because he had been driving without a license. The next day, PNC Corporal Perlera—the same agent who took Mrs. Velver de Vilanova's missing persons report—told Dr. Vilanova that the police were attempting to arrest his son for running over "Tarántula." This led Dr. Vilanova to suspect that Perlera had been involved in his son's death. This account was supported by the victim's girlfriend, who informed the PDDH that Adriano had told her that the police blamed him for the death of some man (Velásquez de Avilés 1996b, pp. 8–9).

The PDDH also confirmed that Vilanova's death had been a homicide. In its original report, the medical examiner's office had stated that Vilanova was killed in a traffic accident. Dr. Velásquez de Avilés argued, however, that it would have been impossible for the impact from such an accident to have thrown his body so far from the highway. If Vilanova had been killed by a vehicle, someone would have had to intentionally move the body to the location where it was discovered. Upon being questioned by PDDH representatives, medical examiner Dr. Aguilar Beltrán admitted that Vilanova's injuries could also have been produced by a fall from a considerable height or a very harsh beating (Velásquez de Avilés 1996b, pp. 6–7, 34).

Public Security Minister Hugo Barrera had put forward another theory. Barrera called the Vilanovas fifteen days after they had buried Adriano to tell them that their son had committed suicide (Currlin 1999, p. 2). He argued that Adriano Vilanova had killed himself as the result of taking drugs and alcohol. The PNC supported this theory with a written report, in which the agents assigned to investigate the case alleged that Nino Tinetti stated that Vilanova had been taking drugs. The PDDH dismissed this report, however, because Tinetti had not authenticated the agents' version of events by signing it. Velásquez de Avilés also found it unlikely that Vilanova would have been able to walk so far from the highway if he were so intoxicated; logically, he would have fallen and killed himself much sooner (Velásquez de Avilés 1996b, pp. 34–6).

One of Barrera's associates, a mysterious foreigner using the pseudonym "Zacarías," offered the parents another version of the suicide theory. According to this figure, Vilanova was so desperate to escape the police that he threw himself to his death (CL, 13 Oct. 1998). This theory also assumes that the fall into the five-meter ravine caused the student's death. The PDDH, however, found that the forensic evidence did not support this assumption. Dr. Nuila, another medical examiner who took part in the autopsy, stated that Vilanova would have had to have fallen several kilometers in order to have sustained a fracture as serious the one found on his arm. Furthermore, she told the PDDH that Vilanova would have been killed by a head injury if this had happened—not by the damage to his abdomen that had actually caused his death. Having rejected the explanations from the police and the government, the PDDH concluded that only remaining explanation was "that of the probable homicide caused by a intentional blow with blunt objects or even the probable intentional running over [with a car].... This possibility is the only one acceptable and consistent with the evidence" (Velásquez de Avilés 1996b, pp. 7, 34–6).[3]

The PDDH also further investigated Violeta Rivera's report that PNC Director Ávila had ordered the detention of all PNC agents who had been assigned to the Panchimalco and Apopa delegations on the night of Vilanova's disappearance. The PNC authorities attempted to justify this procedure by classifying it as a *concentration* of the agents rather than preventive detention. The PDDH, however, found that sequestering these agents was "totally inappropriate for the transparency of investigations" because these potential witnesses to the crime could be coerced, intimidated, or manipulated" (Velásquez de Avilés 1996b, pp. 17–9).[4]

The PDDH determined that the investigation was not being handled by official PNC personnel. Rather, it discovered a clandestine office was running it. Zacarías was effectively directing the investigation. Detectives within this irregular agency told the PDDH that there was no evidence implicating PNC agents in Vilanova's death. They once again claimed that the medical student had fallen to his death because he was drunk. Dr. Velásquez de Avilés concluded that these individuals were probably preparing reports that would then be signed by the PNC agents who were supposed to be conducting the investigation, a pattern of behavior "which had been a systematic practice" in the military security forces. The PDDH also pointed to the historic link between such structures and the death squads (Velásquez de Avilés 1996b, pp. 11–2, 20–2, 41).[5]

The PDDH concluded, "there are serious indications that lead one to presume the participation of Panchimalco National Civilian Police agents, particularly Corporal Hugo ... Perlera, in the homicide of young Vilanova Velver" (Velásquez de Avilés 1996b, pp. 37–8).[6] The agency also established that the retardation of justice during the investigation of Vilanova's death constituted a due process violation. Finally, the PDDH found that the public security authorities had violated the Panchimalco police agents' rights by arbitrarily and illegally detaining them in the police post at the start of the investigation (Velásquez de Avilés 1996b, p. 43).

Public Censure by the Human Rights Counsel

While the PDDH was not able to completely end the practice of maintaining irregular and clandestine public security units, the media did help it pressure the government into dismantling the office headed by Zacarías. In the PDDH's report on the Vilanova murder, Dr. Velásquez de Avilés recommended that this unit and others like it be dismantled (Velásquez de Avilés 1996b, p. 44). Salvadoran law, however, did not give her office any power to enforce such rulings. As a result, the PDDH has relied upon the tool of public exposure and censure, which the former Human Rights Counsel claimed is something that "many officials fear. And therefore they act, in some manner, upon the recommendations." This, in turn, means that the PDDH depends upon the media to spread knowledge of its resolutions and to perform oversight of public institutions (Velásquez de Avilés 2000). The media will only do this, of course, to the degree that they are independent enough to exercise their right to criticize the government.

According to Dr. Velásquez de Avilés, the authorities did indeed dismantle Zacarías's office as the result of public censure through the media (Velásquez de Avilés 2000). Carlos Rafael Urquilla Bonilla, a lawyer from the Foundation for the Study of the Application of Law (FESPAD), confirmed her account. "That is an example," Urquilla Bonilla stated, "of how denunciation becomes a tool in the work of defending human rights" (Urquilla Bonilla 2000a).

David Morales, an investigator for the PDDH, explained in a similar manner that Dr. Velásquez de Avilés's public censure of the judicial system for retardation of justice helped to move the investigation of Vilanova's death along. As discussed above, the PNC had maintained that the young medical student had killed himself. "This denunciation," by the Human Rights Counsel, he claimed, created "a public scandal and the media put the case on the front page. The day after her pronouncement, the President of the Republic ordered that the Vilanova investigation be reopened" (Morales 2000). Mrs. Velver de Vilanova also credited media oversight with ensuring that the judge and prosecutors acted appropriately (Velver de Vilanova 2000). *El Diario de Hoy* credited its own coverage as leading to the February 1997 arrest of seven PNC agents on charges of killing Adriano Vilanova (DH, 21 Feb. 1997).

Violence Against Those Who Spoke Out

In her groundbreaking article from September 1995, Violeta Rivera indicated that Vilanova's relatives had avoided contact with the newspaper because they were afraid for the safety of his parents and his four surviving brothers. One unidentified relative did tell her, however, "We have not gone to the police because we believe that they were the ones who killed Adriano" (DH, 14 Sept. 1995). The family had good reason to be frightened. Mrs. Velver de Vilanova received phone threats at home. Dr. Vilanova was also threatened at his clinic. Armed men—some in police uniforms—came to their house. Suspicious vehicles with dark windows—a trademark of the death squads during the war—watched their home. Even the family's maid was threatened (Currlin 1999; CL, 5 Sept. 1998).

It is important to point out that these intimidating acts took place in the context of a campaign by public security officials to slander and discredit the Vilanovas and their supporters. National Civilian Police (PNC) Director Ávila claimed that the politicization of the case endangered not only the police force, but the very stability of the nation itself. Vice Minister of Public Security Alberto Carranza scolded the Vilanovas and other families for turning to the Human Rights Institute of the Central American University (IDHUCA), the PDDH and Tutela Legal for assistance (Cuéllar 1997, pp. 148–9). Public Security Minister Barrera accused the Communist Party of using the Vilanova murder and other well-known human rights cases as part of a slander campaign against the government. He also accused the media, the IDHUCA, and the victims' families of being part of a conspiracy against the PNC and the Salvadoran population as a whole (CL, 17 Sept. 1998; DH, 18 Sept. 1998; CL, 18 Sept. 1998). These accusations were remarkably similar to the smear campaigns that state officials launched against opposition figures shortly before they were assassinated during the war. They should therefore be considered threats to freedom of expression.

The worst part of these attempts to silence the Vilanova family was that the victims could not turn to the PNC—the state institution that had primary responsibility for protecting them against such harassment. As Mrs. Velver de Vilanova has explained, "Protection by whom? If they assign police to me, I am going to be even more worried" (Currlin 1999, p. 3).

Despite these obstacles, the Vilanovas continued to call for justice. Mrs. Velver de Vilanova in particular "did not rest [while] visiting officials and institutions, media and human rights activists. She struggled so that investigations moved forward and could arrive at the truth." The family also lobbied the Mexican, U.S., Spanish and German embassies in El Salvador (Currlin 1999, pp. 1–2).[7]

Why didn't the Vilanovas keep quiet? Mrs. Velver de Vilanova has answered this question by explaining, "I was not afraid that they would kill me, because since they took my son's life they had killed a part of me." Her husband was initially more cautious because he feared for the safety of his wife and their remaining children. Part of the answer was to send two of their children abroad. Dr. Vilanova eventually gave his wife his total support once he understood her determination. (Currlin 1999, p. 4).

It is important to remember that the Vilanovas were able to count on support from human rights NGOs, including the IDHUCA, Tutela Legal, and the (nongovernmental) Human Rights Commission of El Salvador (CDHES). The IDHUCA in particular helped the Vilanovas with media work. These organizations also monitored attempts to intimidate the Vilanovas and reported this information to state authorities, the media, and international institutions.

The Vilanovas' socioeconomic status also helped them to overcome obstacles to expression. Dr. Vilanova was a successful oncologist. While not rich by U.S. standards, the Vilanovas were far better off economically than the nation's campesinos or maquila workers. As Elmer Mendoza of the Committee of Family Members of Victims of Human Rights Violations in El Salvador (CODEFAM) explained, families such as the Vilanovas had sufficient resources to protect themselves, while most Salvadorans had to rely on inadequate state protection (Mendoza Zamora 1999). Adriano Vilanova was presented in the media as "a sensitive youth who hated violence" (CL, 10 Oct. 1998). It was surely easier for most Salvadorans—including the media—to sympathize with a young medical student pictured in a tuxedo than it would be for them to sympathize with more typical human rights victims, such as accused criminals murdered by vigilante death squads.

Journalist Violeta Rivera also began receiving threats after the publication of her exposé of the Vilanova murder. In July of 1996, shortly after Rivera's judicial testimony had been recorded on video tape, anonymous callers reported her death in a traffic accident to various media organizations, including *El Diario de Hoy* (Velásquez de Avilés 1996b, pp. 29–30). This was especially intimidating in light of the fact that public security officials had originally claimed that a traffic accident had caused the death of Adriano Vilanova. In other words, these callers were telling her to keep quiet unless she wanted to suffer the same fate as Vilanova.

A contingent of PNC agents surrounded the journalist's home on July 31, 1996. The police told her that they did not need a warrant when she asked to see one. The agent who then entered her home informed her that there had been an anonymous call stating that she was holding kidnapped children inside and planned to ship them out of the country. The only child that the police found, however, was Rivera's newborn daughter. The Police Chief of the Soyapango delegation, Deputy Commissioner Mauricio Antonio Arriaza Chicas, told the PDDH that the caller had said that her boss, whom she identified as "Señor Fausto," had told her about the kidnapped children (Velásquez de Avilés 1996b, pp. 28–9). It is important to point out that "Fausto" had been the pseudonym that Rivera had given to an anonymous source inside the PNC. The Journalists' Association of El Salvador (APES) denounced the disproportionate use of force against Rivera and argued that this action was part of a larger pattern threatening the freedom of the press (DH, 3 Aug.1996). Violeta Rivera left El Salvador for several months to protect herself and her family.

Deputy Commissioner Arriaza Chicas contacted Rivera in February of 1997 and offered to give her information. When she arrived at the PNC's Criminal Investigation Division (DIC), he shut the door behind her and threatened that he would not release her until she divulged the names of her sources. She had previously refused to do so in her July 1996 testimony.[8] Arriaza Chicas ordered her to stay out of the investigation and made threats against her mother, husband, and infant daughter. He also revealed his knowledge of details from her personal life. He carried out this attempt to intimidate Rivera a few days before the authorities arrested six PNC agents and charged them with the murder of Adriano Vilanova (PDDH 1999c; Velásquez de Avilés 1996b, p. 27).

It is important to point out that Rivera would have endangered her sources' lives if she had revealed their identities. This is demonstrated by the mysterious Zacarías's surprise visit to the only identified witness in the case, Nino Tinetti. Zacarías got the youth intoxicated shortly after the investigation began and then pressured him not to testify. He succeeded in preventing Tinetti from testifying for several years (PG, 3 Oct. 1998).

The Panchimalco PNC also arrested Tinetti and charged him with stealing less than ten dollars. PNC Director Ávila labeled Tinetti a habitual thief who stole to support his drug habit. Yet the authorities released the youth few days later. The Vilanovas saw this a clear attempt to intimidate the witness (IDHUCA 1998a, p. 46).

Past and Present Impunity for Vilanova's Killers

Once again, these efforts to silence public expression in favor of human rights were connected to the government's policies of impunity. Indeed, at least three central figures in the Vilanova murder and its cover-up had connections to institutions known for facilitating human rights violations and impunity during the war. They also represented the dangers associated with the militarization of the National Civilian Police. The IDHUCA therefore referred to the Vilanova case as "an event that helped to reveal the obstacles that arise at all levels when there is an attempt to end the impunity that certain individuals enjoy" (IDHUCA 1998a, p. 45).

It is reasonable to assume that these acts of intimidation were intended to protect the main suspects in this case. Both the victim's father and Human Rights Counsel Velásquez de Avilés accused Corporal Hugo Orlando Perlera Saravia of taking part in the murder. This particular National Civilian Police (PNC) agent had been a member of all three of the military's security forces—the National Police, the National Guard, and the Treasury Police (DH, 21 Feb. 1997; CL, 10 Oct. 1998; CL, 18 Sept. 1998). It is important to recall that these branches of the Armed Forces were very closely linked to death squad activities and other human rights violations during the war. The amnesty laws passed in 1987, 1992, and 1993 therefore blocked investigations and trials that might have put Perlera into prison instead of a police uniform. The government also promoted structural impunity by transferring Perlera into the PNC despite his connections to the National Guard and the Treasury Police.

At least two other figures who attempted to silence those who spoke out about the Vilanova murder had ties to the repressive structures of the past. Like Perlera, Arriaza Chicas was also a former member of the National Guard (Costa 1999, p. 285 n. 81). His presence in the PNC—especially in a leadership position—was therefore a serious violation of the peace accords. Zacarías—whose real name was Víctor Rivera—was a Venezuelan who had come to El Salvador in order to investigate kidnappings in the 1980s and early 1990s. In other words, he had previous experience heading clandestine parallel investigative offices in El Salvador (PG, 13 Oct. 1998). As Dr. Velásquez de Avilés pointed out in the PDDH's report on the Vilanova murder, such institutions served to protect human rights violators during the war (Velásquez de Avilés 1996b, pp. 21–2). Like Perlera, both of these individuals enjoyed protection against prosecution for any of the human rights abuses and other crimes that they may have committed during the war. Public Security officials' decision to continue relying upon clandestine offices such as the one headed by Zacarías was another example of structural impunity.

Expression Helps Bring About Partial Justice

In order to successfully prosecute the defendants, it was first necessary to bring them to trial. In February 1997, San Marcos Judge Victor Manuel Zelaya ordered the arrest of seven PNC agents accused of killing Adriano Vilanova. During a pre-trial hearing in January 1998, however, the same judge released five of the defendants in response to the defense team's argument that there was insufficient evidence against their clients. Two new witnesses found by *El Diario de Hoy* helped to convince an appeals court to reinstate the charges against three of these police agents in June 1998. As a result, five police agents eventually stood trial (DH, 21 Feb. 1997; DH, 11 June 1998).

The trial in the Vilanova murder case finally took place in October 1998. The authorities moved the trial to the First Court of Instruction in San Salvador in order to ensure a fair hearing (DH, 12 Oct. 1998). Both the Vilanova family and the IDHUCA had maintained a strong presence in the media in the final period leading up to the trial (Flores 2000).

The court had to make special arrangements for media access due to the high level of interest in the case. Over two hundred domestic and foreign journalists were accredited to cover the trial. The sheer number of people covering the trial resulted in problems such as conflicts over which news team would get the best location for filming. The print media described Cuatro Visión as generating "coverage similar to a boxing spectacle" because its journalists used the language of "sports casting" (PG, 10 Oct. 1998; DH, 10 Oct. 1998).[9]

As in the United States, Salvadoran judges and juries are not supposed to be subject to pressure from the state or society. In other words, the fact that the PDDH, numerous NGOs, and the relatives had used the media to call for first the investigation and trial, and then the convictions of the defendants should not influence the final verdict.

It is nonetheless appropriate—even crucial—for citizens to use other forms of freedom of expression in the context of a criminal trial. The media provided the prosecution with important evidence. Reporter Violeta Rivera played an important role in this regard. According to former prosecutor Pedro Cruz, Rivera "contributed a lot to the investigation. She published many reports on the case in *El Diario de Hoy* and gave information to the Office of the Attorney General. That [information] helped the case come out well" (Cruz 2000). While researching the case, the media also turned up new witnesses who had driven by and seen the PNC agents beating Vilanova. One of these witnesses told *El Diario de Hoy*, "I have never spoken about this because I was afraid. But, if you help me, I believe that it is time to testify, to tell the truth" (DH, 21 Feb. 1997). In this manner, the newspaper, family members, human rights advocates, and other Salvadorans who had exercised their right to freedom of expression about this case helped to convince other Salvadorans to do the same.

Violeta Rivera could not be present for the trial, however. The Office of the Attorney General announced that the journalist and her family had left the nation due to increasing threats against them. While *La Prensa Gráfica* carried this explanation, her own newspaper, *El Diario de Hoy* stated that she was "supposedly threatened," thus suggesting that this explanation was untrue (PG, 5 Sept. 1998; DH, 10 Oct. 1998). The prosecution showed the videotaped testimony that Rivera had given in July 1996 to the jury.

Witnesses play an important role in criminal trials by exercising their right to express themselves. Ten witnesses testified on behalf of the accused, while the prosecution put forward nine. The most important witness of all was a policewoman using the pseudonym "Eva." The witness testified that she had been riding in the bed of the PNC pickup with the defendants on the night of murder. They pointed a light at Vilanova, and then pursued him on foot. They began beating the victim and Eva asked if they were going to kill him. Agent Melgar told her to look for a weapon that Vilanova had thrown away, but she knew that he had not done so. Nonetheless, she did walk away. She still "heard him begging them and they were joking" (Currlin 1999, p. 2). She also heard them taunting him, "Cry, I want to hear you cry" (DH, 11 Oct. 1998).

The jury voted unanimously in favor of convicting the five defendants. The two senior agents each received twenty-five year sentences. The court sentenced the remaining three defendants to twenty-three years in prison. In its annual human rights report on El Salvador, the U.S. State Department credited the PDDH and *El Diario de Hoy* investigations for the verdict (U.S. Department of State 1998). Some observers also pointed to the testimony of Violeta Rivera and Nino Tinetti as major factors in the jury's decision (DH, 14 Nov. 1998). Eva received the most credit, however. *La Prensa Gráfica* described her testimony as "the beginning of the end for the police" (PG, 12 Oct. 1998). *El Diario de Hoy* argued, "she practically convicted them with her testimony." The paper also quoted the Attorney General himself praising Eva as a model citizen (DH, 13 Oct. 1998). The dominant media appeared to be celebrating the right to freedom of expression.

Given the impact of Eva's testimony, it is not surprising to learn that she had received threats from those who were attempting to cover up the case. Despite PNC Director Ávila's and Public Security Minister Barrera's claims that she had not reported what she had witnessed, Eva had told the mysterious Zacarías what had happened that night. He responded by threatening her and warned that she should not tell anyone about what she had witnessed (CL, 14 Oct. 1998). Arriaza Chicas may also have been involved in this interrogation (CL, 15 Oct. 1998). Eva was threatened again during the irregular detention of all agents from the Panchimalco delegation—just as Dr. Velásquez de Avilés had suspected. She was particularly warned not to offend Agent Melgar, who was later convicted on the basis of her testimony (Currlin 1999, p. 2). According to the prosecution, these acts of intimidation prevented Eva from testifying for quite some time (DH, 13 Oct. 1998).

Eva remained silent until she contacted the prosecution a few weeks before the trial (CL, 15 Oct. 1998). The prosecutors warned her of the danger that she would be facing, but she felt that she could not keep quiet. She later explained that she was moved to act by seeing the suffering of the victim's mother in the media (Currlin 1999, p. 2; No se conocían 1999, p. 3). Mrs. Velver de Vilanova therefore had a profound impact on the outcome of this trial through her public expression of grief. The media had also contributed to this outcome by reporting her calls for justice.

Why Did PNC Agents Kill Adriano Vilanova?

The case was not completely settled with the conviction of these five police agents, however. One outstanding issue was the question as to whether the they had acted on their own or had received orders from someone else. Violeta Rivera's 1995 exposé and the PDDH's 1996 report on the killing had both suggested that the National Civilian Police (PNC) agents had killed Vilanova because they believed that he was responsible for the death of "Tarántula" in a traffic accident. Some have also suggested that Corporal Perlera wanted revenge because "Tarántula" was his friend (PG, 10 Oct. 1998).

Several weeks before the trial, however, the media revealed that Violeta Rivera had made a much more startling accusation during her videotaped testimony in July 1996. She claimed that one of the accused agents told her that the widow of deceased death squad founder Roberto D'Aubuisson was upset that Adriano Vilanova was romantically involved with her daughter. Mrs. de D'Aubuisson therefore asked Public Security Minister Barrera to have the medical student frightened so that he would stop seeing her.[10] According to this version, Barrera ordered Perlera to take care of this for him and things simply got out of hand (DH, 4 Sept. 1998; LPG 10 Oct. 1998). The case would obviously have much more serious implications if such powerful figures were involved.

Prominent figures called for further investigations into possible intellectual authors after the October 1998 trial. IDHUCA Director Benjamín Cuéllar accompanied the Vilanovas on Channel 12 as they called for an investigation into the identity of those who had ordered the police agents to commit the crime (DH, 13 Oct. 1998). Monseñor Rosa Chávez argued that the killers could not have acted on their own initiative. Attorney General Córdova Castellanos announced that a warrant had been issued against Zacarías as the first step toward investigating this issue (PG, 13 Oct. 1998). He had already ruled out investigating Barrera and D'Aubuisson's widow back in September, however (DH, 8 Sept. 1998).

It appeared that an important break came in November when one of the convicted police agents requested that Judge Zelaya come to the prison so that he and two other prisoners could reveal information about the case. It turned out that these were the three agents who had received twenty three year sentences because they had been following orders from Perlera and Melgar. When the judge arrived, however, the convicted agents announced that they had decided to keep quiet (PG, 10 Nov. 1998). It is important to point out here that the prisoners would not have received any reduction of their sentences if they had cooperated. Furthermore, Salvadoran law would not have admitted their testimony had they given it without any conditions. Prisoners are not able to testify in

El Salvador because they are not considered to be in full possession of their rights.

As of June 1999, the PDDH had found that the Office of the Attorney General had not conducted a sufficient investigation into the possible intellectual authors who may have been behind Vilanova's death. The PDDH also pointed out that nothing had been done to determine whether or not Violeta Rivera's accusations against Barrera and Mrs. de D'Aubuisson were true (PDDH 1999c).

The Killers Try for Another Chance at Impunity

Salvadoran law does not allow defendants to appeal convictions by juries. The convicted agents' lawyers responded to this situation with two different strategies. They appealed the sentence. They also tried, however, to get the courts to declare the original trial invalid on a technicality. A few days after the trial, they announced that one of the five jurors had been unfit to serve because of an outstanding warrant for writing bad checks (PG, 15 Oct. 1998).

The prosecution countered that the defense attorneys had known about this problem all along and had intentionally not challenged the juror's qualifications so that they could request the trial to be thrown out in the event that they lost. Furthermore, they argued, the juror had already paid off his debt. The only reason that he was still facing charges was that the offended business had taken its time to notify the authorities that the matter had been settled (DH, 5 Nov. 1998). Nonetheless, the appeals process lasted until April 23, 1999, when the court finally ruled out the possibility of a second trial (DH, 24 Apr. 1999).

The media later revealed that the juror in question had been abducted, beaten, and threatened shortly after the trial. One prosecutor on the case accused the defense attorneys of leaking the juror's identity (PG, 25 Apr. 1999).

There continued to be a high risk of reprisals against witnesses, especially in light of the fact that the possibility existed that they might be called to testify at a new trial. Given the importance placed on Eva's testimony, she therefore stood out as a key target. Her safety was further endangered by the likelihood that some fellow police agents—especially those she helped to convict—would see her as a traitor. It is therefore very difficult to understand what possible justification *El Diario de Hoy*, *La Prensa Gráfica*, and *El Mundo* could have had for publishing information about her identity. By doing so, they would endanger not only her right to expression as a witness, but also her life, physical integrity, and emotional integrity. Yet that is exactly what the three papers did. Part of the secret witness's real name appeared in at least the following issues:

- PG, Oct. 11 1998
- DH, Oct. 12 1998
- EM, Oct. 12 1998
- PG, Oct, 13 1998
- PG, Oct. 19 1998
- PG, Nov. 15 1998
- PG, Apr. 8 1999
- PG, Apr. 10 1999

The October 13, 1998 article in *La Prensa Gráfica* also revealed the location of the police delegation where Eva was working after the trial (PG, 13 Oct. 1998). The April 10, 1999 article from *La Prensa Gráfica* included part of her mother's name (PG, 10 Apr. 1999). This irresponsible behavior contradicts the dominant media's apparent celebration of freedom of expression by the key witness. To my knowledge, *CoLatino* did not publish any information that would identify the secret witness.

One *La Prensa Gráfica* reporter went even further by discussing Eva's identity with Zacarías. He claimed to not remember her. Nonetheless, he found her name when he "searched in a list that appears in the summary of the Vilanova case that he had in his office" (PG, 19 Oct. 1998). The reporter must have given Zacarías her full name in order for him to conduct this search. Given the PDDH's public censure of Zacarías, as well as the discussion of his role in the cover-up during the trial, how could this reporter—and his or her supervisors—not have known that this action would endanger her life?

The Journalists' Association of El Salvador (APES) had not yet published its ethics code when these articles were written. If it had, all of these examples would have violated Article 27 of said code, which forbids publishing "any information that leads to identifying" the victims of violent acts (APES 1999, p. 8).

There are two possible explanations for the newspapers' behavior. The publication of this information could be the result of extreme negligence on the part of all of the journalists involved in these articles. Or it could be the result of malicious intent against the witness.

This case offers a clear example of why this professional norm should be respected. Eva began receiving death threats after the trial, including one delivered to her at work through a child: "A man said to tell you that you are going to die of a big mouth" (Currlin 1999, p. 3). Strangers began following her and asking neighbors about her routine. Her mother and three children also received death threats. Unidentified subjects even surrounded her home while power was cut off in the neighborhood on December 31, 1998 (PG, 15 Nov. 1998; PG,10 Apr. 1999; DH, 10 Apr. 1999; Currlin 1999, p. 3).

It is not hard to understand how such persecution could cause extreme emotional distress. Eva reported, "Anywhere I go I fear for myself, for my family, for my children." (Currlin 1999, p. 4). She eventually had to be admitted to a psychiatric hospital for two weeks as a result of the extreme pressure that she was under (PG,10 Apr. 1999). This clearly demonstrates that Eva's persecutors violated her right to mental and emotional integrity. Such acts of intimidation therefore constitute a form of psychological torture.

Then the National Civilian Police (PNC) gave a copy of Eva's medical records from this hospitalization to the media. On March 17, 1999, *El Mundo* printed a photocopy of one of these documents. It included Eva's complete name and address, as well information about her medical condition. The caption underneath read, "With this certificate, [the police] are trying to show that the witness who claimed to have seen how her colleagues beat Vilanova had mental problems" (EM, 17 Mar. 1999).

The paper obviously increased Eva's vulnerability by providing her complete identification and exposing her home address when it printed this confidential document. Although the APES ethics code would not be published until September 1999, it is still important to point out that *El Mundo*'s actions would have violated Article 22: "The journalist should respect the right of individuals to their privacy and image in cases or events that generate situations of affliction or pain (APES 1999, p. 7). Of course, it would also have been a further violation of the aforementioned Article 27. While the public security officials who provided this document to the press clearly violated Eva's rights to privacy and security, the editors at *El Mundo* and the reporter who wrote the article are also clearly responsible for the consequences Eva suffered as the result of this article.

An unknown figure made a serious attempt on Eva's life two weeks after *El Mundo* published this information. The witness was about to go to sleep in the women's dormitory at the police station where she worked when a man wearing a PNC uniform and a ski mask climbed on top of her. She fought back as he began choking her. Eva believed that the attacker fled because he had expected her to be sedated. Her commander attempted to downplay the incident and suggested that it was a dream (DH, 10 Apr. 1999; Currlin 1999, p. 4). *La Prensa Gráfica* subtly supported this assertion by referring to the incident as "a supposed murder attempt" (PG, 8 Apr. 1999).

Eva found herself in the same position as the Vilanovas—unable to defend herself from the very institution bearing primary responsibility for protecting her. "How," she asked, "am I going to accept security from the PNC if the guy who wanted to strangle me was a police agent?" (Currlin 1999, pp. 3). Mrs. Velver de Vilanova compared the persecution of Eva with that of Archbishop Oscar Romero, who had been murdered for telling the truth (PG, 25 Apr. 1999).

Later that month, the appeals court ruled that the charges against the juror had been a mere formality because he had already made reparations. It therefore ruled to uphold the conviction of the five PNC agents (DH, 24 Apr. 1999). Eva would not have to testify again. Yet she would have to live in fear of reprisals for her original testimony. Furthermore, the actions taken against Eva were especially troubling with regard to freedom of expression and the rule of law in El Salvador because they served as a warning to discourage any potential whistle blowers in the future.

Further Threats and Slander
Against Journalist Violeta Rivera

Violeta Rivera's former employers surprisingly turned against her several years after the trial. On January 23, 2000, *El Diario de Hoy* published an exposé of Violeta Rivera titled "The journalist who took the bait" [bribe] in its weekly magazine, *Vértice*. The paper downplayed her role in the Vilanova investigation by emphasizing the role of other unnamed journalists and stating that she had worked under the close supervision of Managing Editor Lafitte Fernández. *El Diario de Hoy* also disputed Rivera's claim to have fled El Salvador in 1998 because of persecution. Rather, it said that Fernández had fired her for "grave ethical errors" and that she had fled from her own lies. The paper charged that she had been working on the 1996 massacre of seven members of the Gaytán Lemus family in a drug dispute in Valle Nuevo, Ilopango without authorization.[11] It further claimed that she even refused to stop covering the case when ordered to do so. Furthermore, the paper claimed that she was trying to help Miguel Angel Pozo Aparicio, who was eventually convicted of orchestrating the Valle Nuevo massacre. The paper asserted that she had made calls to Pozo on several occasions while he was a fugitive in Panama. The most serious charge was that the police had found a payment from Pozo in the bank account of her husband, Channel 6 journalist José Luis Magaña. *El Diario de Hoy* also indicated that she had "an unhealthy professional relationship" with Pozo. The paper claimed that it therefore fired her on April 30, 1998 (La periodista que ... 2000, pp. 4–5).

It is important to point out that *El Diario de Hoy*'s accusations had a profound impact on Rivera's reputation. Before I was even aware that this article existed, I asked the *El Noticiero* News Director Julio Rank a question about Rivera being persecuted. "That's totally false," he replied. "If you read last Sunday's *El Diario de Hoy*, the [media] corporation has demonstrated that this girl was paid off by someone interested in the case" (Rank 2000). A reporter at another paper told me that he was certain Rivera "could not find work in another media corporation in this country, precisely because she was accused by such a powerful news organization as *El Diario de Hoy*" (Driotes 2000).

Why did the paper publish this article in January 2000, over a year after Rivera and her family had left the nation? The answer becomes obvious when one looks at the structure of the story. It began by relating a meeting between Lafitte Fernández and retired General Mauricio Vargas. Vargas had been the military representative during the peace talks and later oversaw implementation of the peace accords on behalf of President Cristiani. He has also been accused of being behind two very prominent murders in the postwar era, those of businessman Ramón Mauricio García Prieto Giralt and RCS news announcer Lorena Saravia (see PG, 31 Oct. 1998; CL, 10 Sept. 1998). In the article, Vargas told Lafitte Fernández that Violeta Rivera and Pedro Cruz—a former prosecutor who is "now linked [*vinculado*] to the Human Rights Institute of the Central American University (IDHUCA)"—were conspiring to ruin his reputation by implicating him in the Saravia murder. Fernández responded that the information was "a further confirmation of the chain of lies" from Rivera after she was fired. (La periodista que ... 2000, p. 4). This left me, along with many of the Salvadorans whom I interviewed, with the impression that the main purpose of the article was to protect General Vargas.[12] After all, the paper was well-known for its role in supporting military leaders such as Vargas during the war.

Many of my sources also complained that this article was one-sided. One radio journalist told me that Rivera "was a very good journalist. I would like to personally know Violeta's version so that I can really make my own conclusion" (Arguda 2000). Pedro Cruz, whom the article also mentioned unfavorably, remarked, "For me, this article is written without ethics because it has not provided enough space for those individuals mentioned in it to tell their version of events" (Cruz 1996).

There is yet another strange twist to this story. In June 1999—seven months before *El Diario de Hoy* published "The journalist who took the bait"—the Office of the Human Rights Counsel (PDDH) issued a resolution concerning the persecution of Violeta Rivera. This report contradicts the paper's claim that she played a minor role in the Vilanova investigation by citing photographer José Milton Flores's claim that she was indeed in charge of the investigation. The same photojournalist for *El Diario de Hoy* also told the PDDH that the paper had put Rivera in charge of the Valle Nuevo case (PDDH 1999c). This contradicts Lafitte Fernández's assertion in the *El Diario de Hoy* exposé that Rivera had not been assigned to that story.

An unnamed official from *El Diario de Hoy* told the PDDH that Rivera was fired because the PNC Director had shown him a check made out to her husband from Pozo Aparicio "apparently because they were involved in drug trafficking" (PDDH 1999c). The management at the paper should have seen this as cause for suspicion, given the hostile statements that Rodrigo Ávila and other high-ranking public security officials had made about a conspiracy to destroy the PNC through the manipulation of the Vilanova case.[13]

The reader may also recall that former National Guard member Deputy Commissioner Arriaza Chicas played an important role in the efforts to divert the investigation of the Vilanova murder, including threatening Violeta Rivera. The journalist had crossed paths with him again. He warned her to stop investigating the Valle Nuevo case and once again threatened her children. Arriaza Chicas had also made threats to use evidence he had against Rivera's husband if he did not turn over a videotape implicating the police official in another homicide case. The Chief of Investigations in Soyapango confirmed that there was an investigation of Arriaza Chicas and that Rivera had been pressured for a video. Arriaza Chicas told another journalist that he was going to "fuck" Violeta Rivera with evidence linking her to Pozo. He also claimed that Rivera was part of a conspiracy framing him for planting evidence implicating Nelson Comandari in drug trafficking (PDDH 1999c).

The PDDH reported that this evidence led it to believe Arriaza Chicas and Deputy Inspector Armando Huezo Grande "threatened, intimidated and unjustly investigated" Rivera and her husband "with the aim that they not continue investigating the cases in which [these officials] were presumably involved." Furthermore, the PDDH found it troubling that Arriaza Chicas claimed to have evidence linking Rivera's husband to Pozo despite the fact that such investigations were not under his jurisdiction in the Finance Division. The agency noted, "This practice of inappropriate structures inside the National Civilian Police carrying out inappropriate or illegal investigations with the aim of favoring private interests has been indicated on other occasions by this institution, such as is the case of the death of Adriano Vilanova." The PDDH also found that Arriaza Chicas and Huezo Grande were responsible for violating Rivera's rights to personal safety, privacy, and freedom of expression (PDDH 1999c).

Given that PDDH issued this report in June 1999, why didn't the author(s) of the *El Diario de Hoy* article consider the PDDH's evidence that the criminal accusations made against Rivera and her husband had been fabricated? One explanation would be that the newspaper was negligent, i.e., that it had not conducted serious research before publishing this article. The other possibility would be that the paper intended to slander Rivera.

El Diario de Hoy must have been aware that information coming from Arriaza Chicas was not reliable because he was well-known for fabricating evidence. The authorities had charged him with planting a rifle and drugs in the home of Nelson Comandari in order to implicate Comandari in drug trafficking. Despite his mysterious acquittal, the PNC later cited this incident as grounds for suspending Arriaza Chicas during the summer of 1999—as *El Diario de Hoy* had itself reported (DH, 15 July 1999)! It is also strange that the newspaper would accept evidence concerning the Valle Nuevo case from Arriaza Chicas, given that he was also accused of fabricating evidence in that very case (CL, 18 Sept. 1998). Furthermore, he had been linked to the effort to frame several other police agents for the 1997 murder of journalist Lorena Saravia (DH, 25 Apr. 1998). Pedro Cruz has pointed out that the fact that the police had not arrested Rivera should have raised suspicion about the authenticity of the evidence shown to *El Diario de Hoy* (Cruz 1996).

The PDDH stated, "the fact that these police agents publicly spread this information constitutes an irresponsible act that damages the image and honor of Mrs. Rivera" (PDDH 1999c). The same thing can be said about *El Diario de Hoy*. Article 7 of the APES ethics code—which was already published when *El Diario de Hoy* printed these accusations—states, "The journalist should publish only established information and avoid imprecise and unfounded information that could harm or devalue the dignity of individuals" (APES 1999, p. 5).

The paper did not damage only Violeta Rivera, however. According to Pedro Cruz, the January 23, 2000, article serves as a warning to other journalists who may consider challenging powerful interests: "This is a bad message for journalists. It says, 'Don't investigate, don't mess with the powerful forces'" (Cruz 2000). This is yet another threat to the security of the rule of law and freedom of expression in El Salvador.

Lessons from an Atypical Case

The Vilanova case is certainly not typical. The victim came from a family which was far better off economically than most Salvadorans, although it would not have been considered rich by U.S. standards. The attitude of the media and the general public toward this case was quite different from their attitude toward less sympathetic human rights victims, such as the accused criminals discussed in Chapter Nine.

What really sets this case apart, however, is the high level of public expression about it. Many people would have backed down when faced with the persecution that the Vilanovas suffered. Yet Adriano Vilanova's parents became very vocal and highly visible in the efforts to find justice for their son. Given the risks associated with testifying, very few Salvadorans would have gotten involved if they were in Eva's place.

This case is also different in the sense that there was at least partial justice through the conviction of five of Adriano Vilanova's killers. As we have seen, individuals and institutions played a crucial role in this outcome by exercising their right to freedom of expression. This result, in turn, had serious implications for the development of the new police force. As Human Rights Counsel Velásquez de Avilés argued, "If a police agent violates the law or human rights, the way to strengthen the institution and to defend the PNC is by investigating and punishing. Doing otherwise would be to pervert the PNC's democratic conception" (Velásquez de Avilés 1997a, p. 47). The IDHUCA has also used this case as an example of what citizens can accomplish through active participation in its efforts to inspire Salvadorans to speak out against human rights violations (IDHUCA 1998a, p. 41). This stands in stark contrast to the many human rights abuses which the state has failed to resolve. It also provides further evidence that freedom of expression should be considered one of Shue's basic rights, one which individuals must be able to exercise in order for them to securely exercise other human rights.

The Vilanovas and their supporters have achieved an important victory for the rule of law despite the efforts to silence and intimidate them. This is especially important when the guardians of law themselves—the remilitarized "civilian" police—have often acted outside of the law. While the guilty verdict in this case set important precedent for the rule of law, the fact that authoritarian forces attempted to reverse this outcome through further slander and acts of intimidation demonstrates the precarious nature of human rights in postwar El Salvador.

Given the numerous attempts to silence those calling for justice and providing evidence in this case, it is unlikely that many other families of human rights victims will achieve as much as the Vilanovas unless Salvadoran NGOs, media professionals, public officials, and regular citizens continue the struggle to defend and enlarge the public space available for freedom of expression. Doing so will require a long struggle to overcome individual and structural impunity in order to establish and maintain the rule of law. Only then will human rights abusers not be able to silence their opponents with impunity. As Chapter Nine demonstrates, many Salvadorans have continued to face greater restraints on freedom of expression and have not been able to enjoy the protection of the rule of law.

9

Expression for and against the Vigilante Death Squad *Sombra Negra*[1]

In order to fully understand Salvadorans' potential to use freedom of expression to protect their other human rights, we must also examine cases in which pro-rights forces have been unsuccessful in their efforts to do so. Throughout the world, human rights advocates encounter great difficulty in their efforts to protect the rights of the accused. The public is not likely to be sympathetic to the victims of this category of abuse. This is especially true in cases where the media and other groups create a climate which is hostile to human rights. It is also important to ask whether the media have used their right to freedom of expression appropriately in their coverage of crime issues, or if they have abused this right by violating professional ethics.

This chapter focuses on a series of summary executions of accused criminals by the vigilante death squad known as Sombra Negra (Black Shadow). While Sombra Negra killed many more victims than the single murder of Adriano Vilanova, the media published much less expression from the families of the vigilante death squad's victims than that of the Vilanovas. Furthermore, the police whistle blower in this case had to flee the nation prior to the 1997 trial. The media also played a very different role in the Sombra Negra investigation than it did in the Vilanova case. Instead of creating pressure to punish the vigilantes, the media helped create an environment which was hostile toward the rights of the accused and supportive of authoritarian responses to the crime problem.

During the eventual trial of accused Sombra Negra participants, the authorities failed to set a precedent that vigilantes would be punished for their actions. As a result, it is very difficult to identify any positive results from this case in terms of securing the rule of law, improving police conduct and procedures, or protecting the rights of the accused. While no group has used the name "Sombra Negra" after the trial, social cleansing death squads have continued to operate following the acquittals in this case.

The Sombra Negra Executions

Death squads substantially reduced their activity against political figures—especially assassinations—after the Joint Group issued its report. At the same time, however, "social cleansing" death squads began appearing with the stated goal of killing criminals. The most infamous of these new groups was Sombra Negra, which first emerged in the city of San Miguel in December 1994. The media have attributed a total of twenty-one murders between December 29, 1994 and April 23, 1995 to this death squad (PG, 24 Jan. 1995). Sombra Negra also threatened, but did not execute, several judges whom it labeled corrupt (CL, 8 May 1995).

Apart from their youth, Sombra Negra's victims had little in common with Adriano Vilanova, whom the media presented as a friendly, nonviolent young man dressed in a tuxedo. In contrast, Sombra Negra targeted accused criminals. Furthermore, the death squad claimed that many of its victims belonged to the *maras*, the violent gangs that have terrified the Salvadoran population during the postwar era. Indeed, many victims bore the tattoos associated with gang membership (see DH, 19 Apr. 1995, for example). Naturally, these suspected gang members did not come from the same upper-middle class background as medical student Adriano Vilanova.

The perpetrators followed the same basic modus operandi during all of these executions. The death squad focused on those accused criminals who were released due to lack of evidence (DH, 19 Apr. 1995). This implies that Sombra Negra selected its targets on the basis of the theory that human rights protect criminals. Nonetheless, the group claimed to carry out thorough investigations to ensure that only genuine criminals were killed (PG, 10 May 1995). These alleged investigations could not meet basic due process requirements, of course, because of their clandestine nature and the inability to appeal the decisions. Sombra Negra would carry out its death sentence by shooting the victim in the back of the head at close range. The bullet would pass through the target's skull, destroy his or her face, and thus impede identification of the body (PG, 10 May 1995).

Investigators found strong indications that Sombra Negra's activities were tolerated and supported by powerful forces within both the state and society. In a pattern similar to the 1993 death squad assassination of Farabundo Martí National Liberation Front (FMLN) leader Francisco Velis, nearby police patrols failed to take any action to stop the executions (PG, 24 Jan. 1995; PDDH 1995b, p. 787). The authorities released those arrested on suspicion of belonging to Sombra Negra without explanation (PDDH 1995b, p. 788; EM, 22 July 1995). Tutela Legal, the Catholic Church's human rights office, found that this death squad's "logistical, intelligence and planning capacity" suggested that it had support from the state and private economic interests (PG, 17 May 1995).

The Human Rights Counsel's Investigation

The Office of the Human Rights Counsel (PDDH) began its investigation of Sombra Negra in response to a January 3, 1995 article published in *La Prensa Gráfica* (PDDH 1995b, p. 787). The PDDH found evidence suggesting that both political and economic leaders of the Department of San Miguel provided Sombra Negra with logistical and moral support. Human Rights Counsel Velásquez de Avilés was unable to prove that Sombra Negra was connected directly to the National Civilian Police (PNC). She did establish, however, that there was sufficient evidence to require further investigation of possible police links to this death squad. The PDDH also faulted the PNC and the courts for failing to protect the right to life through their inadequate investigations of these killings. Dr. Velásquez de Avilés called upon other state actors to continue investigating until they identified the intellectual authors of Sombra Negra's actions (PDDH 1995b, pp. 788–91).

The PDDH covered the murder of twenty-one individuals over a period of approximately four months in its report on Sombra Negra. Nevertheless, the agency issued a much shorter report than it had published on the murder of Adriano Vilanova—a single person. Furthermore, Dr. Velásquez de Avilés was unable to provide the same character of solid evidence to support her findings on Sombra Negra as she had in the Vilanova investigation (see Velásquez de Avilés 1996b). The superior results found in the Vilanova report can be explained in good measure by the fact that the PDDH was able to build upon an existing investigation carried out by journalist Violeta Rivera. A comparison of these two PDDH reports therefore underscores the invaluable contribution that the media can make by exercising their right to freedom of expression on human rights issues.

Dr. Velásquez de Avilés was not the only Salvadoran to call for further investigation of Sombra Negra. Legislative deputies from several parties complained that the lack of available information on Sombra Negra indicated that Public Security Minister Hugo Barrera was not interested in investigating the group (EM, 13 May 1995). FMLN leader Shafick Handal in particular complained that the executive branch was moving against Sombra Negra too slowly (EM, 10 May 1995). Archbishop Sáenz Lacalle called upon Salvadorans to reject the death squad and to demand police action against it (PG, 24 July 1995).

Police Action Against Sombra Negra Suspects

Salvadorans who denounced Sombra Negra and called for justice in these murders appeared to have a positive impact when the National Civilian Police (PNC) launched "Operation Ogre" in El Milagro de la Paz in the early hours of July 20, 1995—shortly before the PDDH released its report to the public. Three of the sixteen suspects arrested belonged to the PNC: Deputy Inspector Juan Diego Aguilar Flores, Corporal Ricardo Adalberto Rivas Alvarado and Agent José Umaña Rivera. The media indicated that most of the suspects had been the victims of serious crimes prior to the establishment of a PNC station in their section of San Miguel. The authorities accused merchant José Wilfredo Salgado of being one of the group's leaders and financial backers. He had organized neighborhood patrols armed with machetes before he helped to convince the government to create a new PNC delegation in the neighborhood (PG, 21 July 1995; PG 22 July 1995).

The authorities arrested PNC Deputy Commissioner César Vlademar Flores Murillo on July 26 and charged him with taking part in the Sombra Negra murders. Flores had been the head of the PNC in the department of San Miguel for almost two years. He had also served as an instructor at the National Academy of Public Security (CL, 27 July 1995).

The PDDH had named several of those arrested as possible suspects in its report. The media also indicated that the operation was based in part upon the Human Rights Counsel's investigation (PG, 24 July 1995; PG, 22 July 1995).

Past and Present Impunity for Sombra Negra Suspects

At least two of the suspects had ties to the structures that were responsible for some of the worst human rights violations during the war. Accused ringleader Salgado had been a sergeant in the Arce Battalion (DH 27, July 1995; PG, 22 July 1995).[2] Flores Murillo had worked on joint operations with the Third Infantry Brigade and the National Police, a hotbed of death squad activity (CL, 27 July 1995).

An unidentified National Civilian Police (PNC) source claimed that an informant told the police that Sombra Negra trained its members on a coffee farm in Berlín. Someone with many political connections in the far right reportedly owned the land. *CoLatino* pointed out that death squads used to train in this area (CL, 21 July 1995).

Both Salgado and Flores Murillo benefited from 1992 and 1993 amnesty laws, which protected them against any prosecution for crimes they may have committed during the war. The same laws would have protected anyone else who violated human rights during the conflict, such as the Berlín landowner rumored to have provided training grounds for the death squads. The charges against these figures therefore supported Human Rights Counsel Velásquez de Avilés's claim that the state's failure to fight impunity fostered social cleansing groups such as Sombra Negra (PG, 10 May 1995).

Once again, those who may have wished to express themselves in favor of human rights had to confront the barriers resulting from impunity. In sharp contrast to their coverage of the Vilanova case, the newspapers did not include any statements from the victims' relatives in the overwhelming majority of their articles on Sombra Negra. This difference must be understood in terms of the impact of class status on one's ability to confront human rights abusers who are confident that they enjoy impunity. As Elmer Mendoza Zamora, the president of the Committee of Family Members of Victims of Human Rights Violations in El Salvador (CODEFAM), explained, "[in] the well-known cases [such as] Vilanova, we're talking about people who have certain resources. But what about the poor people? [The Vilanovas] are in a condition to have their own [private] security if necessary, they have resources" (Mendoza Zamora 1999). Lower class Salvadorans, in contrast, would have had to rely upon the state to protect them if they spoke out. They certainly had reason to doubt the PNC's will to protect those who expressed themselves against Sombra Negra, given the fact that police agents had been implicated in the murders. The families of the victims therefore had to consider the possibility of police retribution against them if they challenged Sombra Negra.

Channel 12 News Director Mauricio Funes has explained how impunity has also impeded journalistic investigations of human rights cases such as this. "Here," he told me, "there are not [media] investigations that allow one to get to those who are or were behind the death squads or this extermination group 'Sombra Negra,' because the sources are afraid, the journalists censor themselves, [and] there are certain subjects that cannot be touched" (Funes 2000).

Witnesses in the case also had to confront the problems of impunity. The authorities revealed the identity of PNC Sergeant Vilma Mabel Quintanilla Vásquez after she gave information to the Division for the Investigation of Organized Crime (DICO) in July 1995. PNC Director Rodrígo Ávila and Deputy General Director for Operations Rolando García Herrera reprimanded her for mentioning the police. Quintanilla's superiors demoted her to the rank of corporal because of "immoral acts." She began receiving death threats the following month. García Herrera refused Quintanilla's request for security. Police agents followed her movements. The Human Rights Counsel reported that Quintanilla was held virtually incommunicado while at work. The PNC provided the witness with security by the Division for the Protection of Important Persons (PPI) on August 19, 1995. Instead of protecting her, however, the PPI agents actually took part in the efforts to intimidate Quintanilla. PPI Deputy Commissioner Miguel Angel Barquero Silva even blocked her attempts to report this abuse to the United Nations. The witness eventually fled the nation (Velásquez de Avilés 1996d, pp. 36–7; EM, 24 Apr. 1997; PG, 18 Apr. 1997).[3]

As in the previously discussed cases, public security officials made irresponsible statements which endangered the lives of those who spoke out against human rights abuses. Deputy Inspector Hernández Chávez, for example, argued that claims of PNC involvement in Sombra Negra were made by individuals and institutions that were out to destroy the police force (PG, 24 Jan. 1995). Amnesty International has pointed out that death threats against Human Rights Counsel Velásquez de Avilés coincided with the public statements from state officials criticizing her for her denunciations of death squad activity (Amnesty International 1996a).

Crime, the Media, and Support for Authoritarian Solutions

It is also important to consider the high level of anxiety regarding common and organized crime in Salvadoran society when discussing obstacles that hindered public expression against Sombra Negra. A survey by the University Institute of Public Opinion (IUDOP) in early 1995— the period in which Sombra Negra was carrying out summary executions—found that 45.3% of Salvadorans surveyed identified crime as the nation's main problem (IUDOP 1995a, p. 65). A poll conducted at the end of 1996 found that 41.2% of Salvadorans identified crime as the main problem (IUDOP-UCA 1996, p. 9).[4] According to the IUDOP, "almost 80 percent of those surveyed" in July 1998 "live with high levels of anxiety because of crime ... Salvadorans are terrified by the possibility of being affected by criminal violence" (IUDOP 1998a, p. 798).

It is therefore surprising to learn that the IUDOP has found that the number of Salvadorans who reported that either they themselves or close relatives had been recently victimized by criminals has actually declined since 1994. In an August 1994 survey, 35% of respondents indicated that a member of their family had been the victim of a crime within the previous four months. This figure fell to 25.7% in July 1998. Yet the majority of Salvadorans believed that the crime rate was actually increasing (Cruz 1996, p. 626; IUDOP 1998a, p. 792). Sixty-two percent of respondents indicated that they believed crime had increased in 1998. The IUDOP did not find any significant statistical relationship between this belief and whether or not the respondent had been the direct victim of crime in recent months (IUDOP 1998b, pp. 1072–3).

The media has been at least partially responsible for this contradiction between the crime rate and the perception of the severity of the crime. The IUDOP has found a statistically significant relationship between exposure to the media and identification of the main problem facing the nation (Cruz 1996, pp. 623–5). The IUDOP explained that the media have fostered the public's misperception about the crime rate through their "transmission of an extremely alarming and hostile image of the nation" (IUDOP 1998a, p. 800). Legal expert Margaret Popkin has also blamed the media for creating the false impression that juveniles have been responsible for the majority of crimes (Popkin 2000, p. 224). This is important, of course, because groups such as Sombra Negra have focused their violence against youths whom they identify as gang members.

Given that so many Salvadorans have been worried about crime, it is not surprising that many of them demonstrated hostility towards the rights of the accused. In 1995, for example, 61.2% of respondents agreed with the statement, "Human rights favor criminals and thus they [the criminals] cannot be done away with." The same survey revealed that 43.1% of Salvadorans agreed with the claim, "Human rights organizations in this nation only seek to protect criminals" (IUDOP 1995b, p. 353).

The public's attitude towards the rights of the accused must be understood in the context of policies of impunity. The government agreed to create the PNC in the peace accords in order to develop the investigative crime-solving capacity that had been severely lacking in the military security forces. The new force did not live up to these expectations, however. As the editors of *Estudios Centroamericanos* (*ECA*) have explained, "respect for due process and the laws appears to favor the criminal." "In reality," they continue, "the criminal is freed from jail because of lack of evidence and faulty procedures" (Editorial 1997a, p.

946–7). The Salvadoran government is responsible for these problems, in turn, through its policies of impunity, including the militarization of the PNC, inadequate police training, an insufficient public security budget, and the lack of systematic vetting of the police and the judicial system.

The Salvadoran media did not frame the state's failure to convict suspects as the result of the insufficient respect for due process. On the contrary, the media presented the problem of generalized impunity as a result of concern for human rights. Newspapers printed headlines and captions such as, "Law will benefit the criminals" and "Codes impose limits on the PNC" (DH, 16 Jan. 1996; PG, 5 May 1998). The press also framed the problem by quoting anti-rights statements from public officials without criticism or responses from pro-rights figures. *La Prensa Gráfica,* for example, quoted San Salvador Mayor Mario Valiente as saying that judicial reforms "gave more protection to the criminals than to their citizen victims" (PG, 22 Apr. 1995). It is therefore not difficult to understand why many Salvadorans have expressed their willingness to restrict human rights in exchange for greater security.

The Salvadoran public has also been receptive to draconian laws and authoritarian methods of dealing with crime. In 1995, almost 76% of respondents agreed with the claim, "El Salvador needs a strong and decisive leader who would bring order in the nation" (Coleman, Cruz, and Moore. 1996, p. 423). In a 1998 survey, 85.1% of respondents agreed with the statement, "What our nation needs instead of human rights is lots of law and order" (Cruz 1999, pp. 100–1).[5] Perceptions such as this confuse law with brute force, and thus undermine the rule of law by granting impunity to those responsible for enforcing the law.

Salvadorans have also shown support for vigilantism. In 1995, 53.1% of respondents agreed with the statement, "Given that the government cannot supply justice or security, the people have the right to seek justice through their own hands" (IUDOP 1995b, p. 353). Another 1995 survey found that 45% of Salvadorans agreed with Sombra Negra's actions (Cruz 1997, p. 981). 51.9% of respondents in a 1998 poll supported vigilante justice (IUDOP 1998a, p. 799).

The media were also frequently responsible for failing to point out the distinction between criminals and the *accused criminals* executed by Sombra Negra. *La Prensa Gráfica,* for example, did not offer any criticism of President Calderón Sol's reference to Sombra Negra as "the organization that has murdered several criminals" (PG, 22 Apr. 1995). The same newspaper failed to criticize Public Security Minister Barrera's description of Sombra Negra's victims as "dangerous evil-doers" (PG, 15 May 1995).

The media sometimes directly engaged in such misrepresentation.

In one article, for example, *La Prensa Gráfica* stated that Sombra Negra had killed "some twenty dangerous criminals" (PG, 22 July 1995). Even the opposition newspaper *CoLatino* described the paramilitary group's actions as "killing ... members of criminal organizations" (CL, 11 Apr. 1997). By making statements such as these, the media lent an air of legitimacy to the death squad's actions.

It should be acknowledged, however, that the media did make this distinction in *some* of their reports. In April 1995, for example, *El Diario de Hoy* referred to Sombra Negra's victims as "supposed criminals" (DH, 22 Apr. 1995). The media did not do so consistently, however.

The Sombra Negra Trial

The government brought only three of the individuals accused of taking part in the Sombra Negra executions to trial. The courts freed six defendants in November 1995 on the grounds of insufficient evidence (PG, 16 Nov. 1995). Other defendants benefited from a June 1996 ruling that the charges of illicit association they were facing violated international treaties. Some of the beneficiaries of this ruling had never actually been detained (PG, 10 June 1996; PG, 2 Mar. 1997).

The homicide trial against Jorge Alberto Castro, Carlos Ernesto Romero Suárez, and Jesús Romero Lazo Rosa took place in April 1997. Authorities moved the hearing from San Miguel to San Salvador in order to avoid possible disturbances (EM, 10 Mar. 1997). The prosecutors announced that they had received threats (DH, 24 Apr. 1997).

Reporter Jaime García observed a "'Cherokee' type vehicle ... continually circling around the Judicial Center, with some eight soldiers on board, with camouflage uniforms and assault rifles." He speculated that it might have been doing so as part of the security measures for the trial. The only other explanation he offered was that it could have been a coincidence (DH, 25 Apr. 1997).

Both of these explanations are problematic. Providing security under such circumstances should have been the exclusive responsibility of the National Civilian Police (PNC). Furthermore, even when the military has been sent into the streets to perform public security functions, its troops have always been placed under the command of civilian police. Yet García did not make any mention of PNC agents accompanying the soldiers. The fact that the vehicle was "continually circling" in the area undermines the possibility that it was there by chance.

The reporter left out one very important possibility, however: the military presence may have been intended as a message to the witnesses, the jurors, and others involved in the trial. Salvadoran military troops have made their presence known at previous trials for precisely this reason. This theory is also supported by the history of Cherokees being used by death squads during the war.

As in the Vilanova case, the key witness for the prosecution was a policewoman. Unlike Eva, however, Quintanilla was not present at the trial because she had fled the nation as the result of threats (EM, 24 Apr. 1997). This distinction can be explained by the fact that the prosecution used Eva as a surprise witness, whereas the media had identified Quintanilla long before the case came to trial. The prosecution therefore had to rely upon a one and a half hour videotape of Quintanilla's statements.

Quintanilla testified that she had secretly observed some of the executions. She reported hearing the killers identify each other by nicknames associated with the three defendants: "Alacrán," "Puma," and "Coyote." Quintanilla also claimed that the victims knew their killers because they called them by these nicknames. She further reported that she had spoken with one of the victims several days before his death. During this conversation, the soon-to-be victim told her that three men using these nicknames were going to kill him (PG, 17 Apr. 1997; EM, 6 Feb. 1997).

Quintanilla also claimed that four members of Sombra Negra had asked her to take part in the killings on February 4, 1995. They told her that Deputy Inspector Aguilar Flores and Deputy Commissioner Flores Murillo both knew about the group (EM, 24 Apr. 1997).

The policewoman had testified that several residents of San Miguel had told her that Aguilar Flores and González Magarín belonged to Sombra Negra. They also claimed that Flores Murillo knew about the agents' involvement. According to Quintanilla, Aguilar Flores admitted his connection with the death squad when she confronted him. She also maintained that his role was to verify that the targets were criminals, clear the areas where the executions took place, and monitor the events by radio. Finally, Quintanilla claimed that Aguilar Flores had told her that powerful economic and political figures in the department of San Miguel supported the death squad (PG, 18 Apr. 1997; EM, 24 Apr. 1997).

The defense attorneys countered that Quintanilla's testimony was unreliable because she had only heard the killers identify themselves by nicknames. They argued that she could not identify them physically because the executioners had worn hoods. They also claimed that the Division for the Investigation of Organized Crime (DICO) had planted evidence against their clients during Operation Ogre (DH, 14 Mar. 1997; DH, 24 Apr. 1997).

The jury took two and a half hours to reach a "not guilty" verdict. The jurors reported that there was insufficient evidence for a conviction (CL, 26 Apr. 1998). A superior court in San Miguel also cleared the three defendants of illicit association (PG, 29 Apr. 1997).

The Salvadoran justice system's many faults have left reasons for doubting the outcome of this trial. The Foundation for the Study of the Application of the Law (FESPAD) has argued that the investigation was carried out in such a manner as to guarantee failure in court (FESPAD 1998, p. 60). Office of the Human Rights Counsel (PDDH) investigator David Morales has also claimed that public security officials launched Operation Ogre prematurely in order to prevent the DICO from collecting solid evidence and building a case against those at the head of Sombra Negra. "The result," Morales stated, "is that in the course of the judicial process they all went free. After everything it is impossible to determine if they were guilty or innocent. The truth about Sombra Negra can no longer be established" (Morales 2000). Even before the trial was over, Human Rights Counsel Velásquez de Avilés had complained that the investigation had not been thorough enough (EM, 24 Apr. 1997). The perversion of an investigation such as this is consistent with the history of Salvadoran public officials protecting human rights violators.

The authorities were able to conduct a less than thorough investigation because of the relative lack of expression directed against the vigilante death squad. As Funes explained, "There was not very much citizen pressure to clear up this case and to investigate which police agents were inside Sombra Negra" (Funes 2000). This contrasts sharply with the Vilanova case, in which public pressure moved the investigation forward and ultimately contributed to the conviction of police agents for the crime.

The authorities closed the Sombra Negra case after the April 1997 trial. The prosecution stated that it would not make sense to continue the investigation because they believed that the jury had just acquitted the guilty parties. Public security officials did not take any further action against the possible intellectual authors behind Sombra Negra. Yet both the prosecution and the defense had argued that San Miguel Governor Mario Betagglio, high-ranking police officials, and eastern businessmen had directed the death squad's activities. Prosecutor Douglas Meléndez argued that he had charged some of these figures, only to have them released by the San Miguel courts (DH, 24 Apr. 1997; FESPAD 1998, p. 60).

More Death Squad Activity
Follows the Verdict

Vigilantes carried out several summary executions of accused criminals in little more than a week after the trial came to an end. Attorney General Manuel Córdova Castellanos argued that the social cleansing death squads had resurfaced because the "not guilty" verdict had set a precedent "that those who kill in this manner have impunity" (EM, 3 May 1997; EM, 8 May 1997). Indeed, I am unaware of anyone being prosecuted—much less convicted—for other cases of vigilante justice in postwar El Salvador.

There have been many other examples of social cleansing death squad activity since then. FESPAD reported a total of twenty-four summary executions in 1997. Most of these victims were in the age range for gang members; only three of them were over age twenty-five. National Civilian Police (PNC) Director Ávila reported that police had been offered money to commit these crimes (FESPAD 1998, p. 63). Corpses began appearing in the department of Santa Ana in 1998 as a new death squad, Good Boys (*Chicos Buenos*), announced its presence through flyers threatening alleged criminals (Amnesty International 1999a, p. 3; CL, 11 Sept. 1998). Unknown assailants carried out at least a dozen summary executions in the metropolitan area surrounding San Salvador in January 1999. The bodies were found partially nude with bound hands or feet (PG, 1 Feb. 1999). One vigilante group threatened legislative deputies who opposed legal changes that would weaken the rights of the accused (DH, 12 Feb. 1999). Incidents such as these support Attorney General Córdova Castellanos's conclusion that the acquittal in the Sombra Negra case has been interpreted as a green light for further vigilante killings.

Impunity remains a serious obstacle to those who express themselves against social cleansing. In 1999, for example, *La Prensa Gráfica* reported, "some bodies have been identified by relatives, who prefer to limit themselves to crying for their dead rather than cooperating in the investigation. The fear overwhelms them" (PG, Feb. 1 1999). In April 1999, unknown assailants abducted the president of the (nongovernmental) Human Rights Commission of El Salvador (CDHES), Miguel Montenegro—who had denounced death squad activity in February— by forcing him into his own vehicle. They blindfolded him and drove around for two hours while threatening him with death. They also warned him not to report the abduction because they had connections in the PNC (Amnesty International 1999b).

Vigilantism, Journalistic Ethics, and Impunity

The failure to identify and punish those responsible for these killings demonstrates the vast socioeconomic chasm that divides Salvadorans. While the Vilanovas and their supporters achieved at least partial justice for Adriano, the authorities have not convicted anyone for the twenty-one deaths blamed on Sombra Negra. The Vilanovas overcame tremendous obstacles in order to call for the punishment of the PNC agents who killed their son. The lower-class families of social cleansing victims have not been able to do so. As the PDDH has pointed out, "those least favored by society are those who suffer the most effects of human rights violations" (PDDH 1995a, p. 28). This is consistent with Shue's concept of basic rights; Sombra Negra's victims and their families have not been able to protect their rights to life and to integrity of the individual precisely because of they have not enjoyed full use of the right to freedom of expression.

Pro-rights forces in postwar El Salvador have encountered tremendous difficulties when they have attempted to use their right to freedom of expression to challenge human rights abuses directed at accused criminals. The media helped create this climate through their sensationalistic coverage of crime. This raises the difficult issue of how to balance the media's right to expression with the rights of the accused.

One place to look for answers is the ethics code of the Journalists' Association of El Salvador (APES). While this code was not published until 1999, it is nonetheless useful in terms of evaluating the media's past work according to professional norms. Article 9 states, "The morbid description of violence should be avoided" (APES 1999, p 5). In actual practice, however, the Salvadoran media has been obsessed with blood and gore (see Chapter Four). As discussed above, they have contributed to hostility toward the rights of others through this sensationalistic coverage. This violates Article 2 of the ethics code, which states, "journalists should always be at the service of truth, justice, human dignity, the democratic state, [and] the culture of tolerance" (APES 1999, p. 4).

The media would also have violated the APES code through their representation of Sombra Negra's victims as *criminals* rather than as *accused criminals*. Article 5 of the codes states, "The journalist should always observe a clear distinction between facts and opinions, avoiding a deliberate confusion or distortion of the two." This representation also violates Article 7, which establishes, "The journalist should publish only established information and avoid imprecise and unfounded information that could harm or devalue the dignity of individuals" (APES 1999, p. 5). The media violated these norms, however, when they presented quotes from public officials labeling the victims as criminals without any criticism or quotes from an opposing viewpoint. Article 23 states, "The journalist will not prejudge a case brought before a court, taking a side with regard to guilt or innocence" (APES 1999, p. 8). The media's representation of Sombra Negra's victims as criminals did not violate the letter of this article in the sense that the death squad was not a recognized court. It did, however, violate the spirit behind this article: the human right to due process and the presumption of innocence. The fact that Sombra Negra targeted individuals who had already been released by the courts makes this violation even graver.

The previous chapter on the Vilanova case has demonstrated how effective public exposure can be in combating clandestine structures. In contrast, the Sombra Negra case shows how difficult it can be to unearth these networks when they can protect themselves by attacking their opponents with impunity. This situation could have been avoided if the peace accords had dealt with the issue of death squads directly.

This case also has very dire implications for the development of the PNC. It demonstrates a lack of political will to correct deficiencies within the new police force. Authoritarian forces within the PNC sent out a warning to potential whistle-blowers through their persecution of Corporal Vilma Mabel Quintanilla. As the Attorney General pointed out, the "not guilty" verdict in the trial also established a dangerous precedent. Worst of all, clandestine groups have continued committing summary executions of accused criminals for years after the authorities arrested the suspected members of Sombra Negra.

The next chapter, the conclusion, examines the question of why democratic forces have successfully used freedom of expression to protect human rights in some cases, while their efforts have failed in others. This examination of the Sombra Negra case demonstrates that human rights advocates are unlikely to succeed when they are unable to overcome the restrictions on their freedom of expression.

10

Conclusion

The detailed cases and analyses presented in this study support the arguments that citizen participation promotes democratization and that accommodating authoritarian forces with impunity for past human rights violations undermines transitions to democracy. In a pattern that Alfred Stepan identified in his study of the Brazilian transition, the National Republican Alliance (ARENA) governments and their allies in El Salvador attempted to take back the significant concessions toward protecting human rights and eliminating impunity that the Cristiani Administration made in the peace accords (see Stepan 1988, p. 45). Furthermore, opposition forces had to engage in numerous denunciations of violations, criticisms of government deception, appeals to the international community, and other forms of expression in order to force the Salvadoran government to keep some—though far from all—of its promises in the peace accords. As we would expect, neither side achieved all of its goals during this dialectical struggle. It is therefore important to understand why opposition forces succeeded in some areas, as well as why they failed in others.

One of the main reasons why the democratic forces did not achieve more was precisely because they continued to face significant restrictions on their right to freedom of expression. This supports the argument that freedom of expression meets Henry Shue's criterion for a basic right, one that individuals must be able to exercise in order for other human rights to be genuinely secure. This chapter will therefore include a brief discussion of possible strategies for strengthening freedom of expression in democratizing nations, as suggested by the Salvadorans I interviewed. These include actions aimed at eliminating impunity, democratizing the media, and exercising human rights.

An Unprecedented Opportunity

In the decade following the signing of the peace accords in 1992, Salvadoran dissidents have enjoyed greater freedom of expression than ever before. As Chapter Two demonstrated, Salvadorans had never had true freedom of expression within their nation prior to the end of the civil war. Since then, the likelihood that outspoken opponents of the government will be attacked or killed has decreased substantially—especially after the Joint Group investigation of postwar death squads. While military forces had gunned down Salvadorans taking part in Archbishop Romero's funeral in 1980, tens of thousands of people took part in the events commemorating the twentieth anniversary of his death in 2000 without any serious problems. Farabundo Martí National Liberation Front (FMLN) members and supporters can proudly display their affiliation in public by wearing T-shirts, waving banners, and playing revolutionary music. Even the most antidemocratic media outlet during the war, *El Diario de Hoy*, made space for journalistic professionalism and investigations into human rights abuses.

The fact that there are fewer restrictions on the right to freedom of expression does not, however, mean that there are no longer any restrictions. Antidemocratic forces have continued to use violence, though in a more selective manner. Witnesses such as the police whistleblower "Eva" have been prime targets for attacks. Moreover, threats of violence have remained quite common and public officials have continued to react with great hostility when faced with criticism.

While there has been an important opening in the dominant media, most reporters have continued to censor themselves according to the political and economic interests of their employers and the advertisers, as happened when dominant media failed to cover a labor press conference directed against the powerful sponsor TACA. Government and private sponsors have also punished media organizations when they do not censor themselves, as demonstrated by the advertising boycott directed against Channel 12 and *CoLatino*. Alternative media outlets including *CoLatino* and Channel 12 have barely survived. Others, including *Tendencias* and *Primera Plana*, have closed. Furthermore, the major media organizations have remained in the hands of the same families who have always controlled them.

Journalists have also continued to violate professional ethics for political and economic gains. *El Diario de Hoy*, for example, libeled its own former reporter, Violeta Rivera, in an article clearly intended to discredit criticism of retired General Mauricio Vargas. The mainstream media have also engaged in crude sensationalism in an effort to attract audience members. As discussed in Chapter Nine, such news coverage has contributed to hostile attitudes toward due process and other human rights.

The Pivotal Role of the Dominant Media

In many of the cases examined in this project, the dominant media have played a pivotal role in either helping the democratic forces achieve conquests or supporting the Salvadoran government's attempts to take back important concessions. The major media organizations supported the government's false claims that retaining the corrupt and repressive military security forces would help prevent crime. They changed sides, however, when the military security forces facilitated the escape of the leader of a kidnapping ring which targeted wealthy businessmen and assaulted an armored car in broad daylight. These scandals clearly demonstrated that these institutions posed a threat to Salvadoran elites, including media owners and managers. Only then did the government fulfill its obligation to disband the National Guard, the Treasury Police, and the National Police. The dominant media have not, however, turned against the government's successful efforts to remilitarize the National Civilian Police (PNC) and its frequent use of military troops for public security duties. Indeed, the mainstream media's support for these actions is a large part of the reason why the government has been able to continue violating the public security provisions of the peace accords.

In other cases, the dominant media took sides according to the social status of the victims under consideration. *El Diario de Hoy*'s groundbreaking investigation into the murder of Adriano Vilanova served as the foundation for the successful prosecution of the PNC agents who beat the medical student to death. The media presented this victim as a friendly young man dressed in a tuxedo. In contrast, the dominant news organizations portrayed the Sombra Negra death squad's victims as criminals, thus clearly demonstrating their bias against the rights of the accused. This is especially problematic in a society such as postwar El Salvador, which has been ravaged by gang warfare and other violent crimes. In such a context, the media's sensationalism has encouraged Salvadorans to support authoritarian responses to criminal activity, including vigilantism. Therefore, it is not surprising that no one has ever been convicted for the executions carried out by this vigilante death squad.

The dominant media have also undermined the progress achieved in the peace process by simply ignoring information generated by bodies such as the United Nations, the Truth Commission, and the Joint Group. As discussed in Chapter Three, the Truth Commission clearly established the identities of those behind the Romero assassination, including ARENA founder Major Roberto D'Aubuisson. Yet even on the twentieth anniversary of the murder, *El Diario de Hoy* and *La Prensa Gráfica* continued to treat the case as if there were no leads. Indeed, the dominant media have largely ignored both the findings of the Truth Commission and the binding recommendations that body made with regard to ending impunity. It is therefore not surprising that most Salvadorans have very little knowledge of the Truth Commission Report. The only efforts to inform them of its findings have come through civil society organizations, which have published comic book versions of the report and developed programs to educate Salvadoran schoolteachers about the nation's history.

Those Who Have Impunity Want Even More Impunity

Authors such as Huntington and Nino have argued that it is necessary to grant human rights violators impunity for their past crimes in order to prevent them from destroying democracy and thus threatening the very foundation for human rights (Huntington 1993, pp. 220–1; Nino 1995, p. 418). In the case of postwar El Salvador, however, those human rights abusers who have enjoyed the protection of amnesty laws have taken advantage of their freedom and continuing power to undermine democracy by violating the rights of their opponents—including the right to freedom of expression. Indeed, the ARENA governments have had a good measure of success in taking back the Cristiani Administration's concessions toward democracy and human rights precisely because that party—with historical links to the death squads—continued to hold power. The implementation of the human rights provisions of the peace accords depended upon the will of Alfredo Cristiani, the very president who had participated in the cover-up of the Jesuit massacre by insisting that it was the work of the FMLN. Furthermore, he used his continuing power as president to help lock in his own impunity through the 1992 and 1993 amnesty laws.

Cristiani and his successors also helped expand impunity for human rights violators beyond the amnesties for their past crimes. Opposition forces attempted to condition the approval of the 1993 amnesty law, which covers those human rights violators identified by the Truth Commission, upon the complete implementation of the binding recommendations in the Truth Commission Report. By rushing the 1993 amnesty law through the Assembly, however, Cristiani and his allies in the Legislative Assembly undermined the opposition's main source of leverage on this issue. This is especially grave when we consider that the Truth Commission made these recommendations precisely for the purpose of reducing impunity through measures such as creating an independent judiciary and removing those officials whom it had identified as human rights violators from public and military service. The ARENA governments also violated the restrictions on assigning military figures to the new "civilian" police force. As a result, murderer Carlos Romero Alfaro was able to "investigate" (i.e., cover up) the murder of FMLN leader Francisco Velis, which he had helped plan and carry out. Furthermore, military figures including Romero Alfaro and Deputy Commissioner Mauricio Antonio Arriaza Chicas (who participated in the Vilanova investigation) took advantage of their impunity to intimidate and attempt to silence witnesses and journalists.

Obviously, democratic forces cannot use public expression to pressure the government to protect human rights if violators are able to silence them with impunity. In rare cases, Salvadorans such as the Vilanovas and policewoman "Eva" helped bring about justice by refusing to remain silent despite the risks. In many other cases, such as that of the Sombra Negra executions, even the victims' relatives have remained silent. As discussed in Chapter Nine, the relative lack of expression against that death squad was an important factor in the failure to resolve these murders. This, in turn, appears to have encouraged further vigilante killings.

Furthermore, human rights violators have not been content with the knowledge that they cannot be prosecuted for their wartime abuses. Authors such as Carlos Nino and Samuel Huntington have warned against provoking authoritarian forces by attempting to hold them accountable for prior widespread and systematic human rights abuses. Doing so, they argue, actually harms the prospects for human rights by risking the stability of the democratic regime (Huntington 1993, pp. 220–1; Nino 1995, p. 418). This implies that we should have expected the Salvadoran death squads to continue to threaten the opposition—as well as the stability of the transition—as long as they had reason to fear prosecution for their wartime atrocities. If the premise of this argument is correct, i.e., if those controlling the death squads were primarily motivated by fear of prosecution, then it would be irrational for them to commit further violations once the government passed the 1992 and 1993 amnesty laws. Doing so would only expose them to prosecution by creating criminal incidents which were not covered under the amnesties. Yet the death squads continued trying to destroy the peace process by killing FMLN leaders in the months after the government passed the 1993 amnesty. Indeed, they did not decrease their activity until the Joint Group began investigating them. As a result, those Salvadorans who called for the investigation actually helped promote stability by pressuring the government to take action to stop the killings.

Nino has also argued against criticizing governments during transitions to democracy, on the grounds that doing so undermines their legitimacy and thus strengthens the authoritarian forces (Nino 1995, p. 429). Yet the death squads were already undermining the Salvadoran government's legitimacy by demonstrating that it was unable to enforce the rule of law and protect the lives of its citizens. President Cristiani also helped undermine his own legitimacy through his inaction and his refusal to acknowledge even the possibility that right wing death squads were behind the attacks. As a result, human rights advocates had to force the president to take the necessary steps to protect his legitimacy by seriously investigating these murders.

The evidence in this study also demonstrates that impunity for human rights violations increases the dangers associated with organized crime. As discussed in Chapter Two, some elements of the Salvadoran military and the death squads took advantage of the general climate of impunity during the war to enrich themselves through activities such as kidnapping for ransom. The Joint Group clearly demonstrated that the Salvadoran death squads expanded their involvement in such activities in the postwar era. While they were obviously motivated by avarice, they also did so in part to finance further human rights violations. Some military officers continued to protect these groups, while others, such as National Police Colonel José Rafael Coreas Orellana, directly took part in such activity. Furthermore, organized crime groups regularly murder and threaten citizens in order to protect themselves from prosecution. In other words, they suppress freedom of expression.

Institutions Which Facilitate Expression

Given the long history of systematic human rights abuses in El Salvador, it would have been unrealistic to expect many Salvadorans to publicly denounce human rights violators and openly cooperate with investigations during the early years of the postwar transition. Indeed, we have seen that many Salvadorans are still afraid to testify as witnesses to current human rights abuses and other crimes. Human rights victims and their families especially needed protection during the early 1990s.

The government and the FMLN had agreed to establish two temporary bodies to gather information about wartime abuses from both public and confidential sources—the Ad Hoc Commission and the Truth Commission. The Cristiani Administration, the military leadership, and the dominant media later complained that both commissions had violated the rights of those they investigated by not identifying those making the accusations. Nonetheless, both bodies enjoyed widespread legitimacy in the international community. Furthermore, commissioners such as Thomas Buergenthal have explained the substantial steps these bodies took to verify the authenticity of the information they received. Without the protection of witnesses through guaranteed anonymity, neither the Ad Hoc Commission nor the Truth Commission would have been able to identify as many human rights abusers as they did (Buergenthal 1995, pp. 299, 301–3; Commission on the Truth for El Salvador 1995, p. 300).

It is certainly easy to identify the shortcomings related to the implementation of these provisions of the peace accords. President Cristiani delayed the removal of senior military officers whom the Ad Hoc Commission identified as human rights abusers. The government resisted implementing the Truth Commission's binding recommendations. The dominant media have supported the government's efforts to ignore the Truth Commission's findings.

Nonetheless, both commissions made unprecedented contributions to the Salvadoran transition. Aside from the two officers convicted of killing the Jesuits in 1989, no Salvadoran officer had ever been removed from service because of human rights violations. The Truth Commission Report reinforced important human rights provisions in the peace accords and brought additional pressure on the Cristiani Administration to remove the remaining officers whom the Ad Hoc Commission had identified as human rights violators. Only in response to such pressure did Cristiani remove Defense Minister General René Emilio Ponce and the remaining officers identified by the Ad Hoc Commission from active duty. Intergovernmental organizations have drawn upon the report in their rulings against the Salvadoran government's policies of impunity. The fact that the Salvadoran government has not complied with these rulings demonstrates one of the key weaknesses of international law: the inability of intergovernmental organizations to force sovereign states to comply with such rulings. This makes it even more important for domestic human rights advocates to pressure the Salvadoran government into complying with its legal obligation to protect the rights of its citizens.

The 1992 peace accords also created a permanent institution to respond to citizens' expression regarding human rights issues, the Office of the Human Rights Counsel (PDDH). During the war, there was little reason for citizens to report human rights abuses to the government because they knew that nothing would be done to punish those responsible or to protect the victims. In the postwar era, however, Salvadorans gained confidence in the PDDH under the leadership of Dr. Carlos Molina Fonseca and Dr. Victoria Velásquez de Avilés. The new institution responded to the citizens' complaints by launching thorough investigations. These investigations, in turn, gave other Salvadorans the opportunity to exercise their right to provide information. Furthermore, the PDDH brought pressure on violators by publicizing its findings and its recommendations for preventing further abuses. When the media informed the public of the PDDH's findings, this pressure forced the government to take important measures to protect human rights, such as dismantling the clandestine office which blocked the Vilanova investigation. The PDDH's support also helped Salvadorans such as the Vilanovas and journalist Violeta Rivera to bring human rights violators to justice.

Pressuring Opposition Elites

While the main focus of this study has been on how Salvadorans have used freedom of expression to create pressure on the Salvadoran government and its allies, it has also demonstrated the importance of maintaining pressure on opposition elites. In her study of the Argentine transition, McSherry found that pressure from below prevented civilian leaders from making further concessions to authoritarian forces (McSherry 1997, pp. 113, 270, 290). Some important FMLN leaders—including Popular Revolutionary Army (ERP) head Joaquín Villalobos—expressed their willingness to negotiate a pact with the authoritarian forces which would have allowed high-ranking officers identified as human rights violators by the Ad Hoc Commission to continue leading the Armed Forces. Democratic forces in society—especially human rights organizations, unions, universities, and other sectors from which the former guerrillas needed support—expressed themselves very strongly against such an arrangement. The leadership of the FMLN responded by categorically ruling out the possibility of compromising on this key element of the peace process.

Human rights advocates have not always been this successful. The FMLN leaders did make other pacts which they believed would move the peace process forward. The former guerrillas made some of their most significant concessions to the government and its allies in December 1992, when they agreed to support the Cristiani Administration's proposal to admit more National Police troops into the National Civilian Police (PNC) than had been agreed upon and to transfer the highly problematic Commission for the Investigation of Criminal Acts (CIHD) and the Executive Anti Narcotics Unit (UEA) into the new "civilian" force. In this case, the dominant media presented these violations of the peace accords as an effective response to the extremely high postwar crime rate. As a result, the leadership of the FMLN was reluctant to follow the lead of human rights advocates because opposing the government on these issues would make the party appear to be soft on crime. Ultimately, this pact between the government and the FMLN had an extremely negative impact on the peace process as the increasingly militarized PNC became the largest source of human rights violations.

Strategies for Increasing Freedom of Expression

One of the obvious lessons from this study is that human rights are more likely to be protected in new democracies and nations emerging from prolonged civil wars when democratic forces have greater opportunities to exercise their right to freedom of expression in support of human rights. This also means, of course, that authoritarian forces are more likely to continue committing human rights abuses and undermining the rule of law when they are able to silence their democratic opponents. It is therefore appropriate—and necessary—to offer some suggestions on what actions democratic forces can take to improve the status of this basic right—their ability to speak freely on human rights issues.

As we have seen, democratic forces in Salvadoran society have often failed in their attempts to pressure the government into complying with the peace accords and taking other measures to protect human rights because they have been unable to reach the public through the dominant media. It is therefore not surprising that many of the Salvadorans I interviewed mentioned changes within the media industry as their first response when I asked them how to protect and promote freedom of expression in their nation.

One way of doing so would involve challenging the oligopolistic ownership structure of the media. As we have seen, outsider media outlets such as Channel 12, Channel 33, and *CoLatino* have presented issues and opinions that were not available through Telecorporación Salvadoreña (TCS), *La Prensa Gráfica*, and *El Diario de Hoy*. According to Central American University (UCA) Rector José María Tojeira, these alternative institutions have also changed the dominant media themselves. He told me that he chooses to write op-ed pieces in *CoLatino*, for example, "not only because I can write more freely, but also [because] when these media publish things, the large media are forced to open themselves up a little in order to compete" (Tojeira 2000). As we have seen, however, supporting the existing alternative media and creating new ones has been very difficult. Channel 12 and *CoLatino,* for example, remain financially insecure, while promising new media organizations such as *Primera*

Plana and *Tendencias* have gone out of business. YSUCA Director Carlos Ayala Ramírez has suggested the creation of nonprofit media outlets such as community radio stations as one way of getting around this problem (Ayala Ramírez 2000). As discussed in Chapter Four, however, the neoliberal ARENA governments have been very willing to cooperate with the corporate media's efforts to block the development of the nonprofit sector. It is therefore unlikely that the community service media will be able to grow until there are significant political changes in the nation.

It is also important, however, to explore ways to improve the corporate media. Channel 12, for example, is not owned by a non-profit group. Like any other corporation, it seeks to bring in profits. Channel 12 is different, however, in that founder Jorge Zedan and News Director Mauricio Funes have not focused on profits as their only motivation, to the exclusion of other goals such as informing the public and contributing to development of democracy. Their willingness to sacrifice advertising revenue for honest journalism and independent reporting has allowed them to avoid the widespread self-censorship which exists in the dominant media. Many of the Salvadorans I interviewed emphasized the need for other media owners and directors to develop similar professional ethics. As the head of the Journalists' Association of El Salvador (APES), David Rivas, explained, "In democratic societies, a media organization is treated as a special business, which provides a service related to the public's consciousness, education, [and] culture. A media outlet cannot be run the same way as a factory that makes soap or shoes. They are not the same. [The media] are obligated to be more responsible, to take the side of public" (Rivas 2000). The efforts of APES and university journalism programs are expressly designed to teach reporters about professional ethics with the goal of eventually having an indirect impact on news directors.

Salvadorans would have greater freedom to express themselves if human rights violators were no longer able to silence them with impunity. It is important to understand, however, that the problem of impunity goes far beyond the 1992 and 1993 amnesty laws which protect wartime abusers from prosecution. As we have seen, the Salvadoran government has preserved institutions which continue to protect human rights violators. As discussed in Chapter Six, for example, the government incorporated the old military Commission for the Investigation of Criminal Acts (CIHD) into the new civilian police force and changed its name to the Criminal Investigation Division (DIC). This allowed corrupt agents within the DIC—such as those behind the murder of FMLN leader Francisco Velis (see Chapter Seven)—to threaten and attack witnesses and other Salvadorans who challenged their continuing impunity. As one human rights advocate explained, it is necessary for "the prosecution, the courts, and the police to carry out investigations in order to dismantle the death squads and any type of structure that could represent a threat for those who express a different opinion" (Flores 2000).

It is also necessary to create and strengthen institutions and procedures that protect vulnerable Salvadorans from reprisals when they express themselves against powerful institutions and individuals. As we saw in Chapter Nine, the main police unit responsible for protecting such individuals, the Division for the Protection of Important Persons (PPI), has actually helped silence witnesses such as Sergeant Vilma Mabel Quintanilla Vásquez. Without proper protection, victims' relatives such as the Vilanovas have had to hire their own bodyguards. Most Salvadorans, however, do not have the financial resources to do so. As a result, they have been faced with the choice of remaining silent or fleeing the nation after they have testified. As the mother of one human rights victim explained, "nobody here is going to testify, because people fear family members will be disappeared" (Giralt de García Prieto 2000).

Salvadorans have also used public expression to shine light on dark, clandestine structures and activities. As discussed in Chapter Eight, for example, the media's coverage of the parallel police office headed by Zacarías deprived that unofficial institution of the secrecy which it needed to continue functioning. This was an important step forward in terms of freedom of expression because Zacarías had used his position to threaten witnesses such as Eva and Nino Tinetti. Democratic forces must be able to obtain information on such dangerous organizations and practices in order to inform society about these problems. Salvadorans such as *Tendencias* Director Roberto Turcios have therefore emphasized the need to promote the right to information. "The citizenry's right to access to information is a fundamental point," he explained, because "it would help to reduce the practices of impunity among those with political power" (Turcios 2000). The government, however, has continued to ignore journalists who have repeatedly called for legislation modeled on the U.S. Freedom of Information Act. It is important to recall that the Office of the Human Rights Counsel (PDDH) helped provide the media with important information about problematic actions by other sectors of the state. It is not surprising, therefore, that journalists such as Fausto Valladares (of *El Noticiero*) have proposed restoring the credibility the PDDH lost during the tenure of Peñate Polanco as the head of that office as an important step toward promoting freedom of expression (Valladares 2000). This would enable the media and opposition groups to use information from the PDDH in their role as public watchdogs.

Many Salvadorans believe that the political system does not work in the interest of the majority of citizens. They therefore have very little reason to believe that denouncing their problems to state agencies will accomplish anything. As a result, many Salvadorans see no reason to exercise their right to express themselves to these institutions. It is therefore necessary to eliminate impunity so that government agencies such as the police and the court system can gain the population's trust. As the mother of a prominent human rights victim explained, "When the people see that justice is done, they will lose their fear" (Giralt de García Prieto 2000).

This project has demonstrated how citizens can use their right to freedom of expression to protect other fundamental human rights. It is also important to consider how they can further promote and protect freedom of expression by exercising it. When I asked Carlos Rafael Urquilla Bonilla of the Foundation for the Study of the Application of Law (FESPAD) about how to protect freedom of expression, he responded, "Exercise it. Perhaps that is the best way to protect it. Exercise it all the time" (Urquilla Bonilla 2000a). A journalist explained to me that Salvadorans have a saying, "custom becomes law." If Salvadorans become accustomed to exercising their right to expression, he suggested, "no one is going to be able to take away this right" (Arguda 2000).

Democratic forces can also use their right to expression to educate other citizens about their own right to freedom of expression. A lawyer at the PDDH explained that the population needs practical information on how to recognize human rights violations, where they should report them, and where they should turn if the authorities do not resolve their problems (Rivera 2000). A founder of the Committee of Mothers and Family Members of Prisoners, the Disappeared and the Politically Assassinated (COMADRES) suggested organizing conferences focusing on the relationship between human rights and the media (de García 1999).

Citizens can also protect their right to freedom of expression by exercising their right to freedom of association. According to APES president David Rivas, his organization "denounces an act of aggression" against journalists "and that same day we are invited to a meeting in the Presidential House." "Problems have been resolved very quickly," he continued, "when we have met with the president" because public officials "are aware that APES is a strong institution" (Rivas 2000). While some journalists do not believe APES has provided them with enough support, they nonetheless suggest organizing the members of their profession as a means toward greater freedom of expression.[6] On a less formal level, Channel 12 News Director Mauricio Funes has suggested that journalists join forces to investigate certain topics because it is more difficult for human rights violators to retaliate against a large group of reporters than against a few of them (Funes 2000).

Citizen Participation and the Fight for Democracy

While the Salvadoran government and the FMLN included some very important human rights provisions in the 1992 peace accords, these two contending forces did not give secured and fully developed democracy and human rights to the citizens of El Salvador. The three ARENA administrations have all attempted to take back key concessions that the Cristiani Administration made in the peace accords, such as the removal of human rights violators from the Armed Forces and the demilitarization of public security. As it gradually dissolved its military structure, the FMLN lost its ability to hold the Salvadoran government to its word. Indeed, it became apparent that some FMLN leaders were willing to allow the government to take back some of its most important concessions. Instead, democratic forces within El Salvador have had to pressure the government into implementing the human rights provisions of the peace accords. They have also had to remain vigilant and respond to serious human rights abuses in the postwar era. Despite the serious obstacles that continue to restrict freedom of expression in El Salvador, they have used this right to push the transition to democracy forward.

Naturally, they have not always been successful. Quite often, the dominant media did not support their efforts to hold human rights violators accountable and to dismantle or thoroughly reform the institutions that have facilitated impunity during the postwar era. When the large media organizations have taken the side of democratic forces, however, the government has taken positive actions, such as demobilizing the National Police and punishing the PNC agents who killed Adriano Vilanova. On the other hand, democratic forces have been unsuccessful when Salvadorans have been (understandably) afraid to express themselves against human rights abusers. It is important to recognize, however, that changes such as the creation of the Office of the Counsel for the Protection of Human Rights (PDDH) have made a great difference by facilitating freedom of expression.

The Salvadoran case material presented here has demonstrated that freedom of expression and the rule of law are not won without struggle. This study has also shown that Salvadorans' achievements in these areas remain precarious. This means that democratic forces in El Salvador have to continue pressing for greater freedom of expression and an end to impunity. We should also remember, however, that it would be unwise for the citizens of any nation—including our own—to take freedom of expression and the rule of law for granted. Following the September 11, 2001, terrorist attacks in New York and Washington, DC, some U.S. citizens have become increasingly intolerant of anyone who expresses disagreement with the George W. Bush Administration's counter terrorism strategy. This is especially troubling because some of the government's plans—including military tribunals and reduced congressional oversight—undermine the rule of law as established in the United States Constitution. We can therefore learn something from those groups and individuals struggling to increase freedom of expression and to end impunity in other nations.

Appendix I: Acronyms and Abbreviations

AIFLD	American Institute for Free Labor Development
ANSP	National Public Security Academy (PNC)
ANTEL	National Administration of Telecommunications
APES	Journalists' Association of El Salvador
ARENA	National Republican Alliance
ARPAS	Association of Participatory Radio and Programs of El Salvador
ASC	Salvadoran Civic Association
AVIOLESAL	Association of Victims of Human Rights Violations of El Salvador
CDHES	(nongovernmental) Human Rights Commission of El Salvador
CEB	Christian Base Community
CEPAZ	Peace Center
CIHD	Commission for the Investigation of Criminal Acts (National Police)
CISPES	Committee In Solidarity with the People of El Salvador
CODEFAM	Committee of Family Members of Victims of Human Rights Violations in El Salvador

COMADRES	The Monseñor Romero Committee of Mothers and Family Members of Prisoners, the Disappeared and the Politically Assassinated
COPAZ	National Commission for Consolidation of Peace
CPDH-ML	Madeleine Lagadec Pro Human Rights Commission
CPDN	Permanent Committee for the National Debate
CPJ	Committee to Protect Journalists
CSJ	Supreme Court of Justice
DAN	Anti-Narcotics Division (PNC)
DIC	Criminal Investigation Division (PNC)
DICO	Division for the Investigation of Organized Crime (PNC)
DNI	National Intelligence Department (Armed Forces)
ECA	Central American Studies (*Estudios Centroamericanos*, an UCA journal)
ERP	Popular Revolutionary Army (FMLN faction)
FAN	Broad National Front
FEASIES	Federation of Associations and Independent Unions of El Salvador
FENASTRAS	National Union Federation of Salvadoran Workers
FESPAD	Foundation for the Study of the Application of Law
FGR	Office of the Attorney General of the Republic
FMLN	Farabundo Martí National Liberation Front
FPL	Popular Forces of Liberation (FMLN faction)
IACHR	Inter-American Commission on Human Rights
IDHUCA	Human Rights Institute of the Central American University
IUDOP	University Public Opinion Institute (UCA)
NGO	Nongovernmental Organization
OIE	State Intelligence Organization
ONUSAL	United Nations Observer Mission in El Salvador
ORDEN	Nationalist Democratic Organization

PDDH	Office of the Human Rights Counsel
PNC	National Civilian Police
PPI	Division for the Protection of Important Persons
SINPESS	Union of Journalists and Related Fields in El Salvador
TCS	Telecorporación Salvadoreña
UCA	Central American University (Jesuit)
UEA	Executive Anti Narcotics Unit (National Police)
UNTS	National Unity of Salvadoran Workers
USAID	United States Agency for International Development

Appendix II: Salvadoran Newspapers Consulted

CoLatino (CL), 1992–2000

El Diario de Hoy (DH), 1992–2003

El Mundo (EM), 1992–2000

La Prensa Gráfica (PG), 1992–2003

Primera Plana (PP), 1994–1995

Notes

Acknowledgments

1. Professor Adamantia Pollis created this award in memory of her mother. Recipients are chosen by the Awards Committee, not by its donor.

Chapter 2

1. There are no hard records of exactly how many campesinos the military killed. Montgomery uses the figure of thirty thousand Stanley cites various sources who place the number of victims between eight thousand and twenty-five thousand (Stanley 1996a, p. 42).

2. See Thomas P. Anderson's *Matanza: El Salvador's Communist Revolt of 1932* for a thorough account of these events (Anderson 1971).

3. The quote is from p. 29.

4. Observers had been using the figure of 75,000 for several years before the war ended. Some people therefore claim that this figure should be higher. Assistant Human Rights Counsel Dr. Marcos Alfredo Valladares Melgar, for example, estimated the real number to be somewhere between 80,000 and 100,000 (Valladares Melgar 1999).

5. The Truth Commission was not able to assign blame for about 10% of the human rights violations.

6. See Pedelty 1995 for more information on the limitations of the U.S. media.

7. The quote is from Americas Watch.

8. Ponce did not become Defense Minister until after the massacre.

9. The quote from Moakley appears on p. 106.

10. The accords signed in Mexico on January 16, 1992 refer to earlier agreements reached in Mexico, Geneva and New York. (For more information on the Truth Commission's mandate, see Commission on the Truth for El Salvador 1995, pp.386–8).

Chapter 3

1. See Chapter Five for an explanation of why the Ad Hoc Commission was unable to remove all human rights abusers from the military.

2. I believe that the charges against Valencia were eventually dismissed.

3. The quote is from p. 158.

4. Katya's father was a captain in the Presidential Guard at the time of her death. He was originally charged with failing to care for his daughter. His father, a famous lawyer, was charged with the murder itself. The investigation was handled very poorly, however, and the charges were eventually dropped (PG, 14 Nov. 2000).

5. While some Salvadorans work at the CIS's office, it is led mostly by U.S. expatriates.

6. The *New York Times* has published an excellent article on the revival of the national security doctrine throughout Central America following September 11th, as well as the possible consequences that this has for human rights and democracy in the region (González 2001).

Chapter 4

1. Florentín Meléndez was serving as the head of the San Salvador office of the UN High Commission on Human Rights at the time of this interview. He did not, however, speak to me on behalf of his office. The reader should not take the views expressed during this interview as official UN positions.

2. Between seventy and ninety percent of Salvadorans watch television news. In contrast, only seven percent of Salvadorans get their news from the papers. The third potential source of news, radio, is relatively unimportant (Cruz 1996, pp. 619, 622; Janus 1998, p. 12).

3. It is important to remember that the typical copy of a Salvadoran newspaper usually passes through the hands of several readers.

4. *CoLatino* was previously known as *El Diario Latino*.

5. The fact that I did not get to do so was not due to lack of trying. I had an interview scheduled with Lafitte Fernández of *El Diario de Hoy*. This turned into a meeting with one of the paper's reporters. The management at *La Prensa Gráfica* would not even speak to me on the phone. The fact that I interviewed news directors from YSUCA, Channel 12, Channel 33, and ARPAS was partially due to the fact that they were more open and interested in talking to me. I also interviewed the director of *El Mundo*, a smaller paper which is firmly associated with the political right.

6. Given that this section of the chapter involves journalists making strong criticisms of their employers, it would not be appropriate for me to identify reporters or other non-management respondents.

7. The quote is from p. 23.

8. The ten principles of the Declaration of Chapultepec are published at the end of Richard R. Cole's conclusion to *Communication in Latin America*. The quote is taken from principle 7 (Cole 1996, p. 251). This statement on

freedom of expression written at the 1994 Hemisphere Conference on Free Speech should not be confused with the 1992 peace accords between the Salvadoran government and the FMLN, which are sometimes referred to as the Chapultepec Agreements.

9. A converso was Spanish Jew who converted to Christianity. The Catholic Church sought to uproot those *conversos* who continued to practice Judaism in secret.

10. The quote is from p. 10.

11. I am quoting the article's paraphrasing of Martínez Varela's comments. This is not a direct quote from the Defense Minister.

12. Once again, it would not be appropriate to identify reporters criticizing their bosses. I will, however, identify managers.

Chapter 5

1. The quote is from Boutros-Ghali.

2. Both articles refer to the demonstrators as a mob.

3. The quote is from p. 135.

4. The parentheses around "military" appear in the article as quoted.

5. The quote is from page 16 of Ball 2000.

6. The quote is from p. 303.

7. The quote is from p. 302.

8. The quote is from p. 372.

9. 14.1% did not answer (IUDOP 1993, p. 719).

10. The quote is from Popkin.

11. (See PDDH 1995a, p. 74; Annan 1997, 18 for more information on the PDDH budget shortfalls.) The PDDH has also relied on international assistance.

12. El Salvador del Mundo, a tall statue of Christ standing on top of the globe, is one of the most recognizable landmarks in San Salvador. It is located in the Plaza of the Americas, an important symbolic space that is used for electoral rallies and outdoor masses.

13. Popkin, for example, has argued that the FMLN "virtually abandoned the issue" (Popkin 2000, p. 158).

Chapter 6

1. I presented an earlier version of this chapter at the 56th Annual New York State Political Science Association Conference at Niagara University on April 19, 2002.

2. The quote is from Government of El Salvador and FMLN 1995.

3. The quote is from p. 15.

4. Cruz and González 1997, p. 956.

5. As discussed in Chapter Two, 1980–3 and 1989 were the bloodiest years of the war. As a result, the homicide rate was much higher than 130 per 100,000 during these years, and less during the limited opening of the mid 1980s.

6. (See also IDHUCA 1994a, p. 824; Joint Group for the Investigation of

Politically Motivated Illegal Armed Groups in El Salvador 1994, p. 25; Stanley 1996b, p. 10)

7. The quote is from p. ii.

8. Twelve percent of the leaders came from the FMLN. Only thirty six percent came from the civilian population—the category that was supposed to be predominant (Costa 1999, p. 258).

9. The report indicated that Cornejo Quiños was motivated by a personal dispute with the victims' family (PDDH 1995a, p. 453).

10. The quote is from p. 455.

11. Another 26.3% of respondents classified the PNC as the same as the National Police, while 18% indicated that the new force was actually worse than its predecessor (IDHUCA 1997b, p. 12).

12. The quote is from paragraph 76.

13. See Chapter Two for information on Moakley's investigation of the massacre.

14. See Chapter Nine for more information on Sombra Negra.

Chapter 7

1. These are indirect quotes. I am quoting Boutros-Ghali, who is paraphrasing Sánchez Cerén's statements.

2. This does not mean, however, that the crowd's actions were justifiable. Indeed, they violated due process and undermined the rule of law.

3. See, for example, Inter-American Commission on Human Rights 1996.

4. I believe this refers to the office headed by Benjamín Cestoni. This office had become discredited through its inability to do anything about human rights violations during the war. It eventually withered away as the PDDH assumed its functions.

5. As discussed above, the media did criticize the CIHD's role in the Velis murder in 1998.

6. As discussed in Chapter Four, *La Prensa Gráfica* became more open and politically independent after the paper replaced most of its leadership in 1993. This change was gradually reversed, however, as the former leaders regained power.

7. The quote is from paragraph 20.

8. The quote is from p. 27.

9. The quote is from p. 87.

10. Human Rights Counsel Molina Fonseca had direct knowledge of the report's contents, of course, because he helped write it as a member of the Joint Group.

11. The investigation and eventual trial of the Velis case will be discussed below.

12. See Chapters Three and Nine for more information on postwar death squad activities.

13. The National Action Party emerged from the former civil patrol mem-

bers who have staged violent protests to demand material benefits in recognition of their service during the war.

14. I have decided not to identify this respondent because the benefits of doing so are outweighed by the harm to his reputation and that of his NGO that could result from such identification. My reasoning is consistent with the ethics guidelines of the Institutional Review Board at CUNY Graduate Center.

15. The government and the media have identified Martín Martínez as a former FMLN urban commando, implying that the FMLN was responsible for the murder. The media itself later reported that the suspect had served as an informant for the National Police, demonstrating that he was far from a loyal FMLN member (PG, 4 Oct. 1998). This fact explains why Martín Martínez had been at the CIHD.

Chapter 8

1. I presented an earlier version of this chapter at the Latin American Studies Association (LASA) Congress in Washington, DC, on September 6, 2001.

2. There is a typographical error in this article. It refers to "Saturday September 2," "Sunday September 3" and "Monday September 3." I have therefore checked a calendar and corrected this to be "Monday September 4."

3. The quote is from p. 36.

4. The quote is from p. 19.

5. The quote is from p. 22.

6. The newspaper coverage of this case refers to "Hugo Orlando Perlera Saravia." While the PDDH report identifies the agent as "Corporal Hugo Orlando Saravia Perlera" on page 38, it refers to him simply as "Corporal Perlera" on pages 9 and 15. If the person in question had the surnames (*apellidos*) "Saravia Perlera," he would be referred to as "Corporal Saravia" rather than "Corporal Perlera." This indicates that the PDDH mistakenly switched the order of the surnames. As a result, this is the same PNC agent identified in the newspaper coverage.

7. The quote is from p. 1.

8. As discussed in Chapter Three, Salvadoran law does not explicitly recognize the right of journalists to protect the confidentiality of their sources.

9. The quote is from DH.

10. I have been asked why Mrs. de D'Aubuisson would have wanted Vilanova to stop seeing her daughter. The media coverage of the trial did not provide an explanation, so I prefer not to speculate on this point.

11. See the PDDH report on the Valle Nuevo massacre for more information on this case (PDDH 1999b).

12. I am not citing specific interviews out of concern for the safety of my sources. Some of them specifically told me that they did not want to be quoted on this.

13. See above.

Chapter 9

1. I presented an earlier version of this chapter at the New England Council of Latin American Studies (NECLAS) Annual Conference in November 2001. A version of this chapter has also been published in the *Southwestern Journal of Law and Trade in the Americas* (Ladutke 2002).

2. See Americas Watch 1991, pp. 59–60, 99, 102 for information on abuses committed by this unit.

3. The quote is DH, 14 July 1997.

4. Both surveys had a margin of error of +/-4%.

5. The quote from p. 101.

6. I believe it is best not to identify particular respondents here because doing so may create friction between them and their professional association.

References

ADES. 1992. Demanda acción inmediata en caso de fuga de secuestrador (paid ad). *La Prensa Gráfica*, 24 April.

Al Dia. 1992a. San Salvador, El Salvador. Television. 19 May.

_____. 1992b. San Salvador, El Salvador. Television. 19 May.

_____. 1992c. San Salvador, El Salvador. Television. 4 November.

_____. 1992d. San Salvador, El Salvador. Television. 7 April.

_____. 1992e. San Salvador, El Salvador. Television. 14 July.

_____. 1993a. San Salvador, El Salvador. Television. 25 October.

_____. 1993b. San Salvador, El Salvador. Television. 31 October.

_____. 1993c. San Salvador, El Salvador. Television. 24 March.

_____. 1993d. San Salvador, El Salvador. Television. 15 March.

_____. 1994. San Salvador, El Salvador. 28 July.

Alder, Daniel. 1993. *Cristiani defends delay of military purge*. United Press International, 6 January [cited 18 November, 2001]. Available from Lexis-Nexis.

Almendáriz Rivas, José Antonio. 2000. Interview by author in Spanish. San Salvador, El Salvador, 28 March.

Altamirano, Fabricio. 1996. Los "luchadores" de la libertad". *Tendencias*, January, 13.

Americas Watch. 1991. *El Salvador's decade of terror*. New Haven: Yale University Press.

Amnesty International. 1996a. *Defensores de los derechos humanos en primera línea: América Central y México (actualización)* [web page]. Amnesty International, December 10, 1996 [cited July 13, 2001]. Available from http://web.amnesty.org/library/engindex

_____. 1996b. *El Salvador: The spectre of death squads* [web page]. Amnesty International [cited July 13, 2001]. Available from http://web.amnesty.org/library/engindex

_____. 1999a. *Anual report 1999* [annual report]. Amnesty International [cited July 13, 2001]. Available from http://www.amnesty.org/ailib/aireport/

_____. 1999b. *Special appeals on behalf of human rights defenders in Latin America* [web page]. Amnesty International [cited July 13, 2001]. Available from http://web.amnesty.org/library/engindex

_____. 2001a. *AI Report 2000: El Salvador* [cited 13 July, 2001]. Available from http://www.web.amnesty.org/web/ar2000web.nsf/

_____. 2001b. *AI report 2001: El Salvador* [cited 13 July, 2001]. Available from http://www.web.amnesty.org/web/ar2001.nsf/

243

_____. 2001c. *Peace can only be achieved with justice* [cited 13 July, 2001]. Available from http://web.amnesty.org/library/engindex

Anderson, Thomas P. 1971. *Matanza*. Lincoln: University of Nebraska Press.

Annan, Kofi. 1997. Assessment of the peace process in El Salvador: Report of the Secretary-General. UN doc. A/51/917.

AP. 2000. *El Salvador's president doesn't believe new general killed French nurse*. Associated Press [cited 11 December, 2001]. Available from Lexis Nexis.

APES. 1999. *Código de ética de al prensa de El Salvador*. San Salvador, El Salvador: Imprenta Universitaria de la Universidad de El Salvador.

_____. 2002. *Estado de la prensa en E.S.* APES [cited 23 May, 2003]. Available from http://www.apes.org.sv/index.php

Araujo Cárdenas, Vincente. 1992. Una inquietud sobre la "Comisión Ad-Hoc". *El Diario de Hoy*, 21 May.

ARENA. 1993. A la conciencia nacional e internacional. *ECA* 48(534–5):491.

Arguda, Ulises. 2000. Interview by author in Spanish. San Salvador, El Salvador, 21 February.

Arnson, Cynthia J. 2000. Window on the past: A declassified history of death squads in El Salvador. In *Death squads in global perspective*, edited by Bruce Campbell and Arthur D. Brenner. New York: St. Martin's Press.

ARPAS leader. 2000. Interview by author in Spanish. San Salvador, El Salvador, 17 March.

Asamblea Legislativa de El Salvador, La. 1992. Decreto No. 147. *ECA* 47(519–20): 184–5.

Ayala, Edgardo. 1995. La PNC: un vigilante a quien nadie vigila. *Primera Plana*, 9 June.

Ayala Ramírez, Carlos. 1997a. Democratización de las comunicaciones en un contexto de transición política. In *Comunicación alternativa y sociedad civil*, edited by Carlos Ayala Ramírez. San Salvador, El Salvador: Talleres Gráficos UCA.

_____. 1997b. La comunicación alternativa. In *Comunicación alternativa y sociedad civil*, edited by Carlos Ayala Ramírez. San Salvador, El Salvador: Talleres Gráficos UCA.

_____. 1999. Consideraciones en torno al código de ética de la prensa de El Salvador. *ECA* 54(612):927–35.

_____. 2000. Interview by author in Spanish. Antiguo Cuscatlán, El Salvador, 1 February.

Ball, Patrick. 1996. *Who did what to whom? : planning and implementing a large scale human rights data project*. American Association for the Advancement of Science (AAAS) Science and Human Rights Program [cited 30 November, 2001]. Available from http://shr.aaas.org/www/contents.html

_____. 2000. The Salvadoran Human Rights Commission: Data processing, data representation, and generating analytical reports. In *Making the case*, edited by Patrick Ball, Herbert F. Spirer and Louise Spirer. Washington, DC: American Association for the Advancement of Science.

Belejack, Barbara. 1998. Latin American journalists under the gun. *NACLA* 32(1): 6–10.

Berger, Peter L. 1991. *The capitalist revolution*. New York: Basic Books.

Berrios, Wilfredo, Wilmer Erroa, Carlos Miranda, and Jorge Portillo. 1999. Interview by author in Spanish. San Salvador, El Salvador, 13 December.

Binford, Leigh. 1996. *The El Mozote massacre*. Tucson: The University of Arizona Press.

Bollerslev, Anne. 1996. La batalla de las radios ilegales. *Tendencias*, January, 15–6.

Boutros-Ghali, Boutros. 1995a. Introduction *The United Nations and El Salvador: 1990–1995*. New York: Department of Public Information, United Nations.

_____. 1995b. Letter dated 2 April 1993 from the Secretary-General to the President of the Security Council concerning the purification of the armed forces. In *The

United Nations and El Salvador: 1990–1995. Vol. 4, *The United Nations blue book series.* New York: Department of Public Information, United Nations.

_____. 1995c. Letter dated 7 January 1993 from the Secretary-General to the President of the Security Council concerning the implementation of the provisions of the peace agreements relating to the purification of the armed forces. In *The United Nations and El Salvador: 1990–1995.* Vol. 4, *The United Nations blue books series.* New York: Department of Public Information, United Nations.

_____. 1995d. Letter dated 7 July 1993 from the Secretary-General to the President of the Security Council concerning the purification of the armed forces. In *The United Nations and El Salvador: 1990–1995.* Vol. 4, *The United Nations blue book series.* New York: Department of Public Information, United Nations.

_____. 1995e. Report of the Secretary-General concerning illegal arms deposits. In *The United Nations and El Salvador: 1990–1995.* Vol. 4, *The United Nations blue books series.* New York: Department of Public Information, United Nations.

_____. 1995f. Report of the Secretary-General containing an analysis of the recommendations of the Commission on the Truth. In *The United Nations and El Salvador: 1990–1995.* Vol. 4, *The United Nations blue books series.* New York: Department of Public Information, United Nations.

_____. 1995g. Report of the Secretary-General on all aspects of ONUSAL's activities from 21 November 1993 to 30 April 1994. In *The United Nations and El Salvador: 1990–1995.* Vol. 4, *The United Nations blue books series.* New York: Department of Public Information, United Nations.

_____. 1995h. Report of the Secretary-General on all aspects of ONUSAL's activities from 22 May to 20 November 1993. In *The United Nations and El Salvador: 1990–1995.* Vol. 4, *The United Nations blue books series.* New York: Department of Public Information, United Nations.

_____. 1995i. Report of the Secretary-General on all aspects of ONUSAL's operations. In *The United Nations and El Salvador: 1990–1995.* Vol. 4, *The United Nations Blue Book Series.* New York: Department of Public Information, United Nations.

_____. 1995j. Report of the Secretary-General on developments concerning the identification and destruction of clandestine arms deposits belonging to the FMLN. In *The United Nations and El Salvador: 1990–1995.* Vol. 4, *The United Nations blue books series.* New York: Department of Public Information, United Nations.

_____. 1995k. Report of the Secretary-General on ONUSAL's Activities. In *The United Nations and El Salvador: 1990–1995.* Vol. 4, *The United Nations blue books series.* New York: Department of Public Information, United Nations.

_____. 1995l. Report of the Secretary-General on the activities of ONUSAL. In *The United Nations and El Salvador: 1990–1995.* Vol. 4, *The United Nations blue book series.* New York: Department of Public Information, United Nations.

_____. 1995m. Report of the Secretary-General on the activities of ONUSAL since the cease-fire (1 February 1992) between the Government of El Salvador and the FMLN. In *The United Nations and El Salvador: 1990–1995.* Vol. 4, *The United Nations blue books series.* New York: Department of Public Information, United Nations.

_____. 1995n. Report of the Secretary-General on the implementation of the recommendations of the Commission on the Truth. In *The United Nations and El Salvador: 1990–1995.* Vol. 4, *The United Nations blue books series.* New York: Department of Public Information, United Nations.

Brackley, Dean. 2000. Yanquis return to El Salvador. *NACLA* 34(3):20–1.

Buenos Días. 1992a. San Salvador, El Salvador: Canal 12. Television. 13 August.

_____. 1992b. San Salvador, El Salvador: Canal 12. Television. 24 September.

Buergenthal, Thomas. 1995. The United Nations Truth Commission for El Salva-dor. In *Transitional justice: How emerging democracies reckon with former regimes,* edited by Neil J. Kritz. Vol. 1. Washington, DC: United States Institute of Peace Press.

Burgerman, Susan. 2001. *Moral victories.* Ithaca, NY: Cornell University Press.

Cáceres Hernández, Joaquín Antonio. 1993. Petition to Supreme Court of Justice challenging Ley de Aministía General Para la Paz. Available at CIDAI, UCA José Simeón Cañas.

Calderón de Buitrago, Anita. 2000. Interview by author in Spanish. San Salvador, El Salvador, 22 March.

Calderón Sol, Armando. 1997. Discurso del Presidente de la República, Dr. Armando Calderón Sol, en el quincaugésimo segundo período ordinario de sesiones de la Asamblea General de las Naciones Unidas. *ECA* 52(587):928–9.

Cantarero, Mario Alfredo. 1998. Periodismo en El Salvador: Construcción limitada de la realidad social. *CoLatino*, 21 August.

Cantón, Santiago A. 2001. Interview by author. Washington, DC, 15, February.

Cardenal, Rodolfo. 1992. Las crisis del proceso de pacificación. *ECA* 47(529–30):963–81.

_____. 2000. Interview by author in Spanish. Antiguo Cuscatlán, El Salvador, 2 February.

Cassel, Douglass W. 1995. International truth commissions and justice. In *Transitional justice: How emerging democracies reckon with former regimes*, edited by Neil J. Kritz. Vol. 1. Washington, DC: United States Institute of Peace Press.

Castillo, Fabio. 2000a. Interview by author in Spanish. San Salvador, El Salvador, 9 February.

Castillo, Narciso. 2000b. Interview by author in Spanish. San Salvador, El Salvador, 16 February.

CDHES. 1992. El supuesto escape del Mayor Jiménez confirma la vigenica de la impunidad en El Salvador (paid ad). *La Prensa Gráfica*, 28 April.

_____. 1995. La voz special edition: Report on the human rights situation in El Salvador. San Salvador, El Salvador: CDHES.

CDHES, Departamento de Derechos Humanos del Sínodo Luterano Salvadoreño, CESPAD, Socorro Jurídico Cristiano, and IDHUCA. 1992. Lo injustificable de la Ley de reconciliación nacional. *ECA* 47(521):303–4.

CESPAD, SJC, IDHUCA, CDHES, and DDH. 1993. La depuración de la Fuerza Armada. *ECA* 48(531–2):135–6.

CIDAI. 1999. El Salvador en 1998. *ECA* 54(603):69–94.

CODEFAM. 2000. Urgente urgente urgente [E-mail]. CODEFAM, 10 November [cited 10 November, 2000].

Cole, Richard R. 1996. Conclusions. In *Communication in Latin America*, edited by Richard R. Cole. Wilmington: Scholarly Resources, Inc.

Coleman, Kenneth M., José Miguel Cruz, and Peter J. Moore. 1996. Retos para consolidar la democracia en El Salvador. *ECA* 51(571–2):415–40.

Comisión de la Verdad para El Salvador, La. 1993. Analisis de la prensa. Annex Vol. 1, no. 3 of the annexes of *Informe de la Comisión de la Verdad para El Salvador*. San Salvador and New York: The United Nations.

Commission on the Truth for El Salvador. 1995. Madness to hope. In *The United Nations and El Salvador: 1990–1995*. Vol. 4, *The United Nations blue books series*. New York: Department of Public Information, United Nations.

Consalvi, Carlos Henríquez. 2000. Interview by author in Spanish. San Salvador, El Salvador, 28 January.

Constitución de la República de El Salvador de 1983 1998. Sistema Internet de la Asamblea Legislativa [cited 30 April, 2002]. Available from http://www. asamblea.gob. sv/constitucion/1983.htm

Corado Figueroa, Humberto. 1997. Las Fuerzas Armadas y el acuerdo de paz: Una transformación necesaria. Commentary to *Las Fuerzas Armadas y el acuerdo de paz: La transformación necesaria del ejército salvadoreño* by Walter Knut. San Salvador, El Salvador: Imprenta Ricaldone.

Costa, Gino. 1999. *La Policia Nacional Civil de El Salvador (1990–1997)*. San Salvador, El Salvador: UCA Editores.

Coto de Cuéllar, Marta Lilian. 2000. Interview by author in Spanish. San Salvador, El Salvador, 17 March.

CPJ. 2000. *El Salvador 1999 country report.* CPJ [cited 27 June, 2001]. Available from http://www.cpj.org/CPJespanol/paises/elsalvad.htm

_____. 2001. *El Salvador 2000 country report.* CPJ [cited 27 June, 2001]. Available from http://www.cpj.org/attacks00/americas00/El_Salvador.html

_____. 2002. *Americas 2001: Guatemala.* The Committee to Protect Journalists [cited 13 June, 2002]. Available from http://www.cpj.org/attacks01/americas01/guatemala.html

Cristiani, A. 1995. Letter dated 30 March 1993 from President Cristiani to the Secretary-General concerning the report of the Commission on the Truth. In *In The United Nations and El Salvador: 1990–1995.* Vol. 4. New York: Department of Public Information, United Nations.

Cristiani, Alfredo. 1992. Alfredo Cristiani, Presidente de El Salvador. *ECA* 47(519–20):165–7.

_____. 1993. Mensaje dirigido a la nación, 18 de marzo de 1993. *ECA* 48(534–5): 483–4.

Cruz, José Miguel. 1996. El papel de la prensa y la opinión pública. *ECA* 51(573–4): 615–30.

_____. 1997. Los factores posibilitadores y las expresiones de la violencia en los noventa. *ECA* 52(585):977–91.

_____. 1999. El autoritarismo en la posguerra. *ECA* 54(603):95–106.

Cruz, José Miguel, and Luis Armando González. 1997. Magnitud de la violencia en El Salvador. *ECA* 52(588):953–6.

Cruz, Pedro. 2000. Interview by author in Spanish. Antiguo Cuscatlán, El Salvador, 14 March.

Cuéllar, Benjamín. 1997. La procuradora le toma el pulso al país. *ECA* 52(579–80):142–9.

_____. 2000. Interview by author in Spanish. Antiguo Cuscatlán, El Salvador, 10 March.

Currlin, Sarah. 1999. Tan firmes como su verdad. *Vértice (Weekly Magazine in El Diario de Hoy)*, 18 April, 1–4.

_____. 2000. Interview by author. San Salvador, El Salvador, 23 February.

de García, Alicia Emelina. 1999. Interview by author in Spanish. San Salvador, El Salvador, 15 December.

Diskin, Martin, and Kenneth E. Sharpe. 1986. El Salvador. In *Confronting revolution: Security through diplomacy in Central America*, edited by Morris J. Blachman, William M. LeoGrande and Kenneth E. Sharpe. New York: Pantheon Books.

Driotes, Juan Carlos. 2000. Interview by author in Spanish. San Salvador, El Salvador, 3 February.

Editorial. 1993. Los "escuadrones de la muerte". *ECA* 48(540):941–9.

_____. 1994. Violencia institucionalizada. *ECA* 49(549):615–28.

_____. 1995. Una economía excluyente exige represión. *ECA* 50(565–6): 1071–80.

_____. 1997a. La cultura de la violencia. *ECA* 52(588):937–49.

_____. 1997b. Reflexiones sobre la reconciliación nacional. *ECA* 52(579–80): 3–23.

_____. 1999. Cien días perdidos. *ECA* 54(611):699–712.

El caso Velis (I) 2001. Proceso [cited 20 November, 2001]. Available from http://www.uca.edu.sv/publica/proceso/procind.html

El caso Velis (II) 2001. Proceso [cited 20 November, 2001]. Available from http://www.uca.edu.sv/publica/proceso/procind.html

El Noticiero. 1993a. San Salvador, El Salvador: TCS. Television. 25 October.

_____. 1993b. San Salvador, El Salvador: TCS. Television. 6 January.

_____. 1993c. San Salvador, El Salvador: TCS. Television. 15 March.

_____. 1993d. San Salvador, El Salvador: TCS. Television. 1 April.

_____. 1993e. San Salvador, El Salvador: TCS. Television. 3 March.

Ellacuría, Ignacio. 1990. Historización de los derechos humanos desde los pueblos oprimidos y las mayorías populares. *ECA* 45(402):589–96.

Ensalaco, Mark. 1994. Truth commissions for Chile and El Salvador: A report and assessment. *Human Rights Quarterly* 16(4):656–75.

Escobar Galindo, David. 2000. Interview by author in Spanish. Ciudad Merliot, 2 March.

Farah, Douglas. 1992. Civilian commission may seek to purge El Salvador's military. *The Washington Post*, 20 September.

Female CPDH-ML leader. 2000. Interview by author in Spanish. Mejicanos, 31 January.

Female reporter from Canal 33. 2000. Interview by author. San Salvador, El Salvador, 18 February.

FESPAD. 1998. Informe seguridad pública y derechos humanos 1997. San Salvador, El Salvador: FESPAD.

Flores Allende, Jorge. 2000. Interview by author in Spanish. San Salvador, El Salvador, 31 January.

Flores, Danillo. 2000. Interview by author in Spanish. San Salvador, El Salvador, 30 March.

Flores, Victor. 1995. El caso Lagadec reabre las heridas de la guerra. *Primera Plana*, 5 May.

FPL. 1993. Fuerzas Populares de Liberacíon (FPL) 'Farabundo Martí', ante el asesinato de Francisco Velis. *ECA* 48(540):1067–8.

Friedman, Milton. 1982. *Capitalism and freedom*. Chicago: The University of Chicago Press.

Fromson, Murray. 1996. Mexico's struggle for a free press. In *Communication in Latin America: Journalism, mass media, and society*, edited by Richard R. Cole. Wilmington: Scholarly Resources, Inc.

Fundación Friedrich Ebert Stiftung. 1994. *Informe laboral: 1993*. San Salvador, El Salvador: Fundación Friedrich Ebert Stiftung.

Funes, Mauricio. 1995. Medios y transición democrática en El Salvador. *Tendencias*, May, 20–2.

_____. 1996. Modernización a medias. *Tendencias*, October, 20.

_____. 2000. Interview by author in Spanish. San Salvador, El Salvador, 9, 24 February.

Gamson, William A. 1989. News as framing: Comments on Graber. *American Behavioral Scientist* 33(2):157–61.

García, Gilberto. 2000. Interview by author in Spanish. San Salvador, El Salvador, 22 February.

García, José. 1992. The tanda system and institutional autonomy of the military. In *Is there a transition to democracy in El Salvador?*, edited by Joseph S. Tulchin and Gary Bland. Boulder: Lynne Rienner Publishers.

Gibb, Tom. 1992. Elections and the road to peace. In *Is there a transition to democracy in El Salvador?*, edited by Joseph S. Tulchin and Garry Bland. Boulder: Lynne Rienner Publishers.

Giralt de García Prieto, Gloria. 2000. Interview by author in Spanish. San Salvador, El Salvador, 30 March.

González, David. 2001. Central America reminded of its own era of conflict. *The New York Times*, 20 October.

González, Eduardo R. 1993. Basta ya de ofensas a la dignidad nacional. *El Diario de Hoy*, 16 March.

Government of El Salvador, the, and FMLN. 1995a. Mexico agreements. In *The United Nations and El Salvador: 1990–1995*. Vol. 4, *The United Nations blue books series*. New York: Department of Public Information, United Nations.

Government of El Salvador, the, and the FMLN. 1995b. Agreement on human rights. In *The United Nations and El Salvador: 1990–1995*. Vol. 4, *The United Nations blue books series*. New York: Department of Public Information, United Nations.

_____. 1995c. Peace agreement. In *The United Nations and El Salvador: 1990–1995*. Vol. 4, *The United Nations blue books series*. New York: Department of Public Information, United Nations.

Guzmán, Gloria. 2000. Interview by author in Spanish. San Salvador, El Salvador, 3 February.

Hammond, John L. 1998. *Fighting to learn*. New Brunswick: Rutgers University Press.

Handal, Schafick. 1997. Discurso en el quinto aniversario de los acuerdos de paz. *ECA* 52(579–80):167–70.

Hayner, Priscilla B. 2001. *Unspeakable truths*. New York: Routledge.

Herman, Edward S., and Noam Chomsky. 1988. *Manufacturing consent*. New York: Pantheon Books.

Hernán Gutiérrez, Roger. 1999. Interview by author in Spanish. San Salvador, El Salvador, 15 December.

Herrera Palacios, Antonio. 1998. *Un breve recorrido por la televisión en El Salvador* [journal article]. Revista Latina de Comunicación Social [cited October 28, 2000]. Available from www.ull.es/publicaciones/latina/a/02 nherrera.htm.

Herzog, Geoff. 1999. Interview by author. San Salvador, El Salvador, 9 December.

Holiday, David. 1995. Pérdida de legitimidad de los acuerdos y la fragilidad de los proceso de pacificación y democratización, acciones y mecanismos en materia de lucha contra la impunidad. In *La impunidad en Centroamérica: Causas y efectos*. San José, Costa Rica: CODEHUCA.

Holiday, David, and William Stanley. 1997. En la mejor de las circunstancias. *ECA* 52(584):549–72.

_____. 2000. Under the best of circumstances. In *Peacemaking and democratization in the western hemisphere*, edited by Tommie Sue Montgomery. Miami: North-South Center Press.

Human Rights Watch/Americas. 1992a. The massacre At El Mozote: The need to remember. *Human Rights Watch/Americas Report* 4(2).

_____. 1992b. Peace and human rights: Successes and shortcomings of the United Nations Observer Mission in El Salvador (ONUSAL). *Human Rights Watch/Americas Report* 4(8).

_____. 1993. Accountability and human rights: The report of the United Nations Commission on the Truth for El Salvador. *Human Rights Watch/ Americas Report* 5(7).

_____. 1994. Darkening Horizons: Human Rights on the Eve of the March 1994 Elections. *Human Rights Watch/Americas Report* 6(4).

Huntington, Samuel P. 1993. *The third wave*. Norman, OK: University of Oklahoma Press.

IAPA. 2000. *Freedom of the press report 2000: El Salvador*. IAPA [cited 11 January, 2001]. Available from http://www.sipiapa.com/default.cfm

_____. 2001. *Freedom of the press report 2001: El Salvador*. IAPA [cited 27 January, 2001]. Available from http://www.sipiapa.com/default.cfm

IDHUCA. 1992. Los derechos humanos en los acuerdos de paz. *ECA* 47(519–20):55–68.

_____. 1993. *Los derechos humanos en El Salvador en 1992*. San Salvador, El Salvador: IDHUCA.

_____. 1994a. Derechos Humanos: los primeros cien días de Calderón. *ECA* 49(550):822–9.

_____. 1994b. *Los derechos humanos en El Salvador en 1993*. San Salvador, El Salvador: IDHUCA.

_____. 1996. *Los derechos humanos en El Salvador en 1995*. San Salvador, El Salvador: IDHUCA.

_____. 1997a. Buscando entre las cenizas. *ECA* 52(589–90):1115–56.

_____. 1997b. *Los derechos humanos en El Salvador 1996*. San Salvador, El Salvador: IDHUCA.

_____. 1998a. *Los derechos humanos en El Salvador 1997*. San Salvador, El Salvador: IDHUCA.

_____. 1998b. Nuestra Policía Nacional: ¿Civil? *ECA* 53(601–2):1081–103.

Inter-American Commission on Human Rights. 1995. *Annual report 1994*. Inter-American Commission on Human Rights [cited 30 January, 2001]. Available from http://www.cidh.oas.org/

_____. 1996. *Comadres v. El Salvador, Case 10.948, Report No. 13/96*. Inter-Am.C.H.R. [cited 30 January, 2001]. Available from http://www1.umn.edu/humanrts/

_____. 1999a. *Laws on contempt, compulsory membership in a professional association, and murder of journalists*. Inter-American Commission on Human Rights [cited 30 January, 2001]. Available from http://www.cidh.oas.org/

_____. 1999b. *The public's right to know: Principles on freedom of information legislation*. Inter-American Commission on Human Rights [cited 30 January, 2001]. Available from http://www.cidh.oas.org/

_____. 1999c. *Report n° 1/99 Case 10.480 Lucio Parada Cea, Héctor Joaquín Miranda Marroquín, Fausto García Funes, Andrés Hernández Carpio, Jose Catalino Meléndez and Carlos Antonio Martínez*. Inter-American Commission on Human Rights [cited 30 January, 2001]. Available from http://www.cidh.oas.org/

_____. 1999d. *Report N° 136/99 case 0.488 Ignacio Ellacuria, S.J.; Segundo Montes, S.J.; Armando López, S.J.; Ignacio Martin-Baró, S.J.; Joaquin Lopez y López, S.J.; Juan Ramón Moreno, S.J.; Julia Elba Ramos; and Celina Mariceth Ramos*. Inter-American Commission on Human Rights [cited 30 January, 2001]. Available from http://www.cidh.oas.org/

_____. 2000. *Report N° 37/00 Case 11.481 Monsignor Oscar Arnulfo Romero y Galdámez*. Inter-American Commission on Human Rights [cited 2 February, 2001]. Available from http://www.cidh.oas.org/annualrep/99eng/Merits/ElSalvador11.481.htm

International Commission of Jurists. 1992. *A Breach of impunity*. New York: Fordham University Press.

IUDOP. 1993. La comisión de la verdad y el proceso electoral en la opinión pública salvadoreña. *ECA* 48(537–8):711–34.

_____. 1995a. Discurso oficial versus discurso popular: La opinión de los salvadoreños sobre las medidas económicas y la situación política del país. *ECA* 50(555–6):51–71.

_____. 1995b. Los derechos humanos en la opinión pública salvadoreña. *ECA* 50(558):351–66.

_____. 1996. La violencia en El Salvador. *ECA* 51(569):240–9.

_____. 1998a. Delincuencia y opinión pública. *ECA* 53(599):785–802.

_____. 1998b. Economía, política y violencia. *ECA* 53(601–2):1067–80.

IUDOP-UCA. 1996. Encuesta de evaluación política de 1996: Consulta de opinión pública de noviembre—diciembre de 1996. San Salvador, El Salvador: Universidad Centroamericana "José Simeón Cañas".

Janus, Noreen. 1998. Latin American Journalism Project: El Salvador. Washington, DC: USAID.

Johnstone, Ian. 1995. *Rights and reconciliation*. Boulder: Lynne Rienner Publishers.

Joint Group for the Investigation of Politically Motivated Illegal Armed Groups in El Salvador. 1994. Report of the Joint Group for the Investigation of Politically Motivated Illegal Armed Groups in El Salvador. UN doc. S/1994/989.

Jonas, Susanne. 1997. The peace accords. *NACLA* 30(6):6–10.

Jones, Bruce B. 1992. La frágil línea defensiva de El Salvador. *El Diario de Hoy*, 9 December.

La periodista que mordió el anzuelo. 2000. *Vértice (Weekly magazine section of El Diario de Hoy)*, 23 January, 4–5.

Ladutke, Lawrence Michael. 2002. Expression for and against the vigilante death squad Sombra Negra. *Southwestern Journal of Law and Trade in the Americas* 8(2):283–309.

LaFeber, Walter. 1984. *Inevitable revolutions.* New York: W.W. Norton & Company.

Larose, Stephen. 2001. Interview by author. Washington, DC, 14 February.

Las organizaciones no gubernamentales de derechos humanos ante comunicado oficial del Ministerio de la Defensa Nacional.1992. *ECA* 47(527):816–7.

Lazo de Quiñónez, Cristela. 1992. Población indefensa. *La Prensa Gráfica*, 7 April.

Lentner, Howard H. 1993. *State formation in Central America:.* Westpor, Connecticut: Greenwood Press.

Linz, Juan J., and Alfred Stepan. 1996. *Problems of democratic transition and consolidation.* Baltimore: The Johns Hopkins University Press.

López-Geissmann, Roberto. 1993. La verdad de la Comisión. *El Diario de Hoy*, 15 March.

Los GAIMOP (Grupos armados ilegales con motivaciones políticas) amenazan el proceso electoral. 1994. *Tendencias*, January, V.

Löwy, Michael. 1996. *The war of gods.* New York: Verso.

Luers, Richard Paolo. 1995. El escuadrón de la muerte Sombra Negra. *Primera Plana*, 19 May.

_____. 2000. Interview by author. San Salvador, El Salvador, 10 February.

Malamud-Goti, Jaime. 1996. *Game without end.* Norman, OK: University of Oklahoma Press.

Male CPDH-ML leader. 2000. Interview by author in Spanish. Mejicanos, 31 January.

McGovern, James. 2001. Interview by author. Washington, DC, 14 February.

McSherry, J. Patrice. 1997. *Incomplete transition.* New York: St. Martin's Press.

Megavisión. 1993a. San Salvador, El Salvador: Canales 19 y 21. Television. 25 October.

_____. 1993b. San Salvador, El Salvador: Canales 19 y 21. Television. 9 November.

_____. 1993c. San Salvador, El Salvador: Canales 19 y 21. Television. 25 March.

_____. 1993d. San Salvador, El Salvador: Canales 19 y 21. Television. 19 March.

_____. 1993e. San Salvador, El Salvador. 14 March.

Mejia, Guillermo. 1994. ¿Apostando a la guerra sucia? *Tendencias*, January, 5–8.

_____. 2000. Interview by author in Spanish. San Salvador, El Salvador, 14 March.

Meléndez, Florentin. 2000. Interview by author in Spanish. San Salvador, El Salvador, 28 March.

Melgar Henríquez, José Manuel. 2000. Interview by author in Spanish. San Salvador, El Salvador, 24 March.

Mendoza Zamora, Elmer. 1999. Interview by author in Spanish. San Salvador, El Salvador, 9 December.

Military Source. 2000. Interview by author in Spanish. San Salvador, El Salvador, 21 March.

Moakley, Joe. 1994a. Discurso al aceptar el doctorado honoris causa. *ECA* 49(545–6): 351–4.

Moakley, John Joseph. 1994b. Letter to Secretary of State Warren Christopher, 21 April.

_____. 2001. Interview by author. Washington, DC, 14 February.

Molina Fonseca, Carlos Mauricio. 2000. Interview by author in Spanish. San Salvador, El Salvador, 13 March.

Molina Olivares, Eduardo. 2000. Interview by author in Spanish. San Salvador, El Salvador, 18 February.

Montalvo, Atilio. 1993. *Los acuerdos de paz un año después.* San Salvador, El Salvador: CINAS.

References

Montenegro, Miguel. 2000. Interview by author in Spanish. San Salvador, El Salvador, 10 February.

Montgomery, Tommie Sue. 1984. El Salvador: The Roots of Revolution. In *Central America*, edited by S. Ropp and J. Morris. Albuquerque: University of New Mexico Press.

_____. 1995. *Revolution in El Salvador.* 2nd ed. Boulder: Westview Press.

Montonya, Aquiles. 1997. ¡Qué viva la democracia! *ECA* 52(588):1015–7.

Morales, David. 2000. Interview by author in Spanish. San Salvador, El Salvador, 9 March.

Newfarmer, Richard S. 1986. The economics of strife. In *Confronting revolution: Security through diplomacy in Central America*, edited by William M. LeoGrande and Kenneth E Sharpe. New York: Pantheon Books.

Nikken, Pedro. 1993. Informe del Experto independiente sobre El Salvador, Sr. Pedro Nikken, designado por el Secretario General de conformidad con la resolución 1992/62, de 3 de marzo de 1992, de la Comisión de Derechos Humanos. UN doc. E/CN.4/1993/11.

_____. 1994. Report of the Independent Expert, Mr. Pedro Nikken, on developments in the human rights situation in El Salvador. UN doc. ECN.4/ 1994/11.

_____. 1995. Report of the Independent Expert, Mr. Pedro Nikken, on developments in the human rights situation in El Salvador, prepared pursuant to Commission on Human Rights resolution 1994/62. UN doc. E/CN.4/1995/ 88.

Nino, Carlos S. 1995. Response: The duty to punish past abuses of human rights put into context. In *Transitional justice: How emerging democracies reckon with former regimes*, edited by Neil J. Kritz. Vol. 1. Washington, DC: United States Institute of Peace Press.

No se conocían. 1999. *Vértice (Weekley magazine section of El Diario de Hoy)*, 18 April, 3.

ONUSAL Human Rights Division. 1992. Report of the ONUSAL Human Rights Division for the period from 1 January to 30 April 1992. UN doc. A/46/935-S/ 24375.

_____. 1993a. Report of the Director of the Human Rights Division of the United Nations Observer Mission in El Salvador up to 30 April 1993. UN doc. A/47/968-S/26033.

_____. 1993b. Report of the Director of the Human Rights Division of the United Nations Observer Mission in El Salvador up to 31 January 1993. UN doc. A/47/912-S/25521.

_____. 1993c. Report of the Director of the Human Rights Division of the United Nations Observer Mission in El Salvador up to 31 July 1993. UN doc. A/47/1012-S26416.

_____. 1994a. Eleventh report of the Director of the Human Rights Division of the United Nations Observer Mission in El Salvador. UN doc. A/49/281-S/1994/886.

_____. 1994b. Report of the ONUSAL Human Rights Division for the period from 1 August to 21 October 1993. UN doc. A/49/59-S/1994/47.

_____. 1994c. Tenth report of the Director of the Human Rights Division of the United Nations Observer Mission in El Salvador. UN doc. A/49/116-S/1994/385.

_____. 1995. Thirteenth report of the Director of the Human Rights Division of the United Nations Observer Mission in El Salvador (ONUSAL). UN doc. A/49/888-S/1995/281.

Palmieri, Gustavo Federico. 1998. Reflexiones y perspectivas a partir de la reforma policial en El Salvador. *Pena y Estado* 3(3):314–40.

PDDH. 1994. Cuarto informe sobre la situación de derechos humanos. San Salvador, El Salvador: PDDH.

_____. 1995a. *Informe 94–95.* San Salvador, El Salvador: Libros de Centroamérica, S.A. de C.V.

_____. 1995b. Resolución en torno al caso del accionar del grupo clandestino autodenominado "Sombra negra" en el departamento de San Miguel. *ECA* 50(561–2):787–91.

_____. 1999a. *Expediente SS-0871-99, violación al derecho humano a la libertad personal* CDC. PDDH [cited 29 May, 2001]. Available from http://www.pddh.gob.sv/

_____. 1999b. *SS-0388-97 Violación al Derecho a la Vida, por muerte arbitraria consumada, en perjuicio de la señora Ermelinda Gaytán y de dieciséis personas más* [cited 21 May, 2001]. Available from http://www.pddh.gob.sv/

_____. 1999c. *SS-2331-98 04-06-1999 Violación a los Derechos Humanos a la Seguridad y Privacidad Personal y a la Libertad de Expresión, por coacción e intimidación, allanamiento de morada, investigaciones policiales injustificadas y censura de prensa, en perjuicio de Violeta Evelyn Rivera Castillo* [web page]. PDDH [cited 23 January, 2001]. Available from http://www.pddh.gob.sv/

_____. 2000. *Violación al derecho humano a la integridad personal ISSS*. PDDH [cited 29 May, 2001]. Available from http://www.pddh.gob.sv/

Pearce, Jenny. 1986. *Promised land*. London: Latin America Bureau (Research and Action).

Pedelty, Mark. 1995. *War stories*. New York: Routledge.

Pérez, Oscar, and Carlos Ayala Ramírez. 1997. La radio comunitaria en El Salvador. In *Comunicación alternativa y sociedad civil*, edited by Carlos Ayala Ramírez. San Salvador, El Salvador: Talleres Gráficos UCA.

Pérez, Renato Antonio. 2000. Interview by author in Spanish. San Salvador, El Salvador, 30 March.

Perla de Anaya, Mirna. 1995. Las violaciones de los derechos humanos en El Salvador en el contexto de la negociación, cambio o renovación de poderes, relacionados con los aspectos operativos de la impunidad. In *La impunidad en Centroamérica: Causas y efectos*. San José, Costa Rica: CODEHUCA.

Peterson, Ana L. 1997. *Martyrdom and the politics of religion*. Albany: State University of New York Press.

Pike, Paulita. 2000. Interview by author in English and Spanish. San Salvador, El Salvador, 27 March.

Piñeda, Milagro Emely. 2000. Interview by author in Spanish. San Salvador, El Salvador, 4 February.

Pinheiro, Paulo Sérgio. 1996. Democracies without citizenship. *NACLA* 30(2):17–30.

Popkin, Margaret. 1993. *Justice impugned*. Cambridge, MA: Hemisphere Initiative, Inc.

_____. 2000. *Peace without justice*. University Park: Pennsylvania State University Press.

Popkin, Margaret, Jack Spence, and George Vickers. 1994. *Justice delayed*. Cambridge, MA: Hemisphere Initiative, Inc.

Proclamation of the Armed Forces of the Republic of El Salvador, 15 October 1979. 1996. Annex *The protection racket state: Elite politics, military extortion and civil war in El Salvador*. Philadelphia: Temple University Press.

Przeworski, Adam. 1991. *Democracy and the market*. Cambridge: Cambridge University Press.

Radio Farabundo Martí. 1993. Radio Farabundo Martí. Radio. 3 March.

Rank, Julio. 2000. Interview by author in Spanish. San Salvador, El Salvador, 28 January.

Rivas, David. 2000. Interview by author in Spanish. San Salvador, El Salvador, 20 January.

Rivera, Joaquín. 2000. Interview by author in Spanish. San Salvador, El Salvador, 8 February.

Rockwell, Rick, and Noreen Janus. 1999. Vertical integration and media oligarchy in Central America. Paper read at The International Mass Communications Symposium.

Rodríguez Cuadros, Manuel (ed.). 1997. *Manual para la calificación de violaciones de los derechos humanos*. San Salvador, El Salvador: Imprenta Criterio.

Roehrig, Terence. 2002. *The prosecution of former military leaders in newly democratic nations*. Jefferson, NC: McFarland & Company, Inc.

Ruballo, Thirza. 1999. La nueva misión del ejército. *Tendencias*, December, 14–9.

Salgado M., Kirio Waldo. 1993. Un proyecto de guerra psicológica de la izquierda. *El Diario de Hoy*, 7 January.

SAPRIN, CODEFAM, Fundación Olof Palme, Asociación "Mujeres por la Dignidad y la Vida", AMD, ADEMUSA, CPDH "Madeleine Lagadec", MSM, IMU, CONAMUS, COM, PROCOMES, FESPAD, Asociación Cooperativa de Producción Agropecuaria "La Muralla" de R.L., CODHES, FUNDE, IDHUCA, and CDC. 1999. Petición de destitución de Antonio Eduardo Peñate Polanco de su cargo de Procurador para la Defensa de los Derechos Humanos. *ECA* 54(603):141–7.

Shue, Henry. 1980. *Basic rights*. Princeton: Princeton University Press.

Silva, Hector. 2000. Interview by author. San Salvador, El Salvador, 22 March.

Sims, Beth. 1992. *Workers of the world undermined*. Boston: South End Press.

Smeets, Marylene. 2000a. Interview by author. New York, 6 September.

———. 2000b. *Speaking Out: Postwar Journalism in Guatemala and El Salvador*. CPJ [cited 20 July, 2000]. Available from http://www.cpj.org/

Spence, Jack, David R. Dye, Mike Lanchin, Geoff Thale, and George Vickers. 1997. *Chapúltepec: Five Years Later, El Salvador's Political Reality and Uncertain Future*. Cambridge, MA: Hemisphere Initiative, Inc.

Spence, Jack, David R. Dye, George Vickers, Garth David Cheff, Carol Lynne D'Arcangelis, Pablo Galarce, and Ken Ward. 1994. *El Salvador: Elections of the Century*. Cambridge, MA: Hemisphere Initiative, Inc.

Spence, Jack, David R. Dye, Paula Worby, Carmen Rosa Leon-Escribano, George Vickers, and Mike Lanchin. 1998. *Promise and reality*. Cambridge: Hemisphere Initiatives, Inc.

Spence, Jack, Mike Lanchin, and Geoff Thale. 2001. *From elections to earthquakes*. Cambridge, MA: Hemisphere Initiatives.

Spence, Jack, and George Vickers. 1994. *Toward a level playing field? A report on the post-war Salvadoran electoral process*. Cambridge, MA: Hemisphere Initiative, Inc.

Spence, Jack, George Vickers, and David R. Dye. 1995. *The Salvadoran Peace Accords and Democratization*. Cambridge, MA: Hemisphere Initiative, Inc.

Spence, Jack, George Vickers, David Holiday, Margaret Popkin, William Stanley, and Philip Williams. 1992. *Endgame*. Cambridge, MA: Hemisphere Initiative, Inc.

Spence, Jack, George Vickers, Margaret Popkin, Philip Williams, and Kevin Murray. 1994. *A Negotiated Revolution? A Two Year Progress Report on the Salvadoran Peace Accords*. Cambridge, MA: Hemisphere Initiative, Inc.

Stanley, William. 1993. *Risking Failure*. Cambridge, MA: Hemisphere Initiative, Inc.

———. 1996a. *The protection racket state*. Philadelphia: Temple University Press.

———. 1996b. Protectors or Perpetrators? The Institutional Crisis of the Salvadoran Civilian Police. Washington, DC: WOLA.

Stanley, William, and Robert Loosle. 1998. *El Salvador: The civilian police component of peace operations*. Institute for National Strategic Studies [cited 11 April, 2002]. Available from http://www.ndu.edu/inss/books/policing/chapter4.html

Stepan, Alfred. 1988. *Rethinking military politics*. Princeton: Princeton University Press.

TCS Noticias. 1992. San Salvador, El Salvador: TCS. Television. 24 March.

———. 1993. San Salvador, El Salvador: TCS. Television. 17 March.

Teleprensa. 1992. San Salvador, El Salvador: Teleprensa. Television. 24 March.

———. 1993. San Salvador, El Salvador: Teleprensa. Television. 25 October.

Tojeira, José María. 2000. Interview by author in Spanish. Antiguo Cuscatlán, El Salvador, 11 February.

Tula, María Teresa. 1994. *Hear my testimony*. Translated by Lynn Stephen. Edited by Lynn Stephen. Boston: South End Press.

Turcios, Roberto. 1998. Lucha de Tendencias. *Tendencias*, December, 9.

———. 2000. Interview by author in Spanish. San Salvador, El Salvador, 1 February.

Two TCS reporters. 2000. Interview by author in Spanish. San Salvador, El Salvador, 24 February.

Two U.S. Government Sources. 2001. Interview by author. Washington, DC, 15 February.

UCA. 1992a. El Acuerdo de paz: expectativas y riesgos (paid ad). *La Prensa Gráfica*, 6 February.

_____. 1992b. Es hora de cumplir con el pueblo salvadoreño. *ECA* 47(528): 827–33.

_____. 1992c. Pronunciamiento del Consejo Superior Universitario. *ECA* 47(529–30):pp. 955–61.

UES. 1993. El fin de la impunidad. *ECA* 48(531–2):133–4.

United States Department of State. 1994. *El Salvador human rights practices, 1993*. U.S. Department of State [cited 12 July, 2001]. Available from http://www.state.gov/www/global/human_rights/hrp_reports_mainhp.html

_____. 1996. *El Salvador Human Rights Practices, 1995* [gopher document]. U.S. Department of State [cited 12 July, 2001]. Available from http://www.state.gov/www/global/human_rights/hrp_reports_mainhp.html

_____. 1997. *El Salvador country report on human rights practices for 1996*. U.S. Department of State [cited 12 July, 2001]. Available from http://www.state. gov/www/global/human_rights/hrp_reports_mainhp.html

_____. 1998. *El Salvador Country Report on Human Rights Practices for 1997* [web page]. U.S. Department of State [cited 12 July, 2001]. Available from http://www. state.gov/www/global/human_rights/hrp_reports_mainhp.html

_____. 2000. *1999 Country Reports on Human Rights Practices* [web page]. U.S. Department of State [cited 12 July, 2001]. Available from http://www.state.gov/www/global/human_rights/hrp_reports_mainhp.html

_____. 2001. *El Salvador: Country reports on human rights practices -2000: El Salvador.* United States Department of State [cited 12 July, 2001]. Available from http://www.state.gov/www/global/human_rights/hrp_reports_mainhp.html

_____. 2002. *El Salvador: Country reports on human rights practices* [cited 5 March, 2002]. Available from http://www.state.gov/www/global/human_rights/hrp_reports_mainhp.html

United States Embassy labor source. 2000. Interview by author. Antiguo Cuscatlán, El Salvador, 2 February.

United States Embassy press source. 2000. Interview by author. Antiguo Cuscatlán, El Salvador, 2 March.

Urquilla Bonilla, Carlos Rafael. 2000a. Interview by author in Spanish. San Salvador, El Salvador, 23 February.

_____. 2000b. *La prescripción procesal penal de los casos amnistiados: ¿La supervivencia de la Ley de Amnistia General para la Consolidación de la Paz?* [Sent to author via email] [cited 25 October, 2000].

_____. 2000c. *Ley de Amnistia General para la Consolidación de la Paz en El Salvador ¿Requiescant in peace?* [Sent to author via email] [cited 25 October, 2000].

Valencia, Francisco Elias. 2000. Interview by author in Spanish. San Salvador, El Salvador, February 4.

Valenzuela, J. Samuel. 1992. Democratic consolidation in post-transitional settings. In *Issues in democratic consolidation,* edited by Scott Mainwaring, Guillermo O'Donnell and J. Samuel Valenzuela. Notre Dame: University of Notre Dame Press.

Valladares, Fausto. 2000. Interview by author in Spanish. San Salvador, El Salvador, 10 February.

Valladares Melgar, Marcos Alfredo. 1999. Interview by author in Spanish. San Salvador, El Salvador, 14 December.

Vaquerano, Omar Arturo. 1995. Efectos de la terminación del conflicto este-oeste con la seguridad nacional salvadoreña. In *El nuevo concepto de la seguridad nacional salvadoreña*. San Salvador, El Salvador: CEDEM.

Velásquez de Avilés, Victoria Marina. 1996a. *Derecho a la libertad de expresión, caso: Radios comunitarias*. San Salvador, El Salvador: Impresos 3Hs.

_____. 1996b. *El derecho a la vida, caso: Manuel Adriano Vilanova Velver*. San Salvador, El Salvador: Graficolor S.A.

_____. 1996c. *El derecho a la vida, caso: Ramón Mauricio García-Prieto Giralt*. San Salvador, El Salvador: Graficolor S.A.

_____. 1996d. *Informe sobre la evolución de los derechos humanos en El Salvador: 1995*. San Salvador, El Salvador: Libros de Centroamérica, S.A. de C.V.

_____. 1997a. *Evolución de los derechos humanos en El Salvador: 1996*. San Salvador, El Salvador: Algiers Impresores.

_____. 1997b. *Protección de los derechos humanos: Casos investigados y concluidos con Resolución 1996*. Vol. 1, *Delegaciones departamentales*. San Salvador, El Salvador: Graficolor S.A.

_____. 2000. Interview by author in Spanish. San Salvador, El Salvador, 8 March.

Velver de Vilanova, Lidya Rosa. 2000. Interview by author in Spanish. San Salvador, El Salvador, 30 March.

Villacorta, Flavio. 1998. Agua bendita para el periodismo. *Tendencias*, May, 20–4.

Villacorta Zuluaga, Carmen Elena. 1998. La desafortunada elección del Procurador. *ECA* 53(597–8):675–8.

Walter, Knut. 1997. *Las Fuerzas Armadas y el acuerdo de paz*. San Salvador, El Salvador: Imprenta Ricaldone.

William. 2000. Interview by author in Spanish. San Salvador, El Salvador, 1 February.

Williams, Philip J., and Knut Walter. 1997. *Militarization and demilitarization in El Salvador's transition to democracy*. Pittsburgh: University of Pittsburgh Press.

WOLA. 1994. El Salvador peace plan update #3: Recent setbacks in the police transition. Washington, DC: WOLA.

YSU. 1992a. San Salvador, El Salvador: YSU. Radio. 11 August.

_____. 1992b. San Salvador, El Salvador. Radio. 24 September.

_____. 1993a. San Salvador, El Salvador: YSU. Radio. 25 October.

_____. 1993b. San Salvador, El Salvador. Radio. 16 March.

_____. 1994. YSU. Radio. 16 August.

Zalaquett, José. 1995. Balancing ethical imperatives and political constraints: The dilemma of new democracies confronting past human rights violations. In *Transitional justice*, edited by Neil J. Kritz. Vol. 1. Washington, DC: United States Institute of Peace Press.

Zamora, Rubén. 2001. Interview by author in Spanish. Washington, DC, 6 September.

Zeldón, Rubén. 1993. Violaciones que quizás no conoció la Comisión de la Verdad. *El Diario de Hoy*, 15 March.

Index

257